A-Z
E-COMMERCE

A-Z
E-COMMERCE

Sumit Sethi

CENTRUM PRESS
NEW DELHI-110002 (INDIA)

CENTRUM PRESS
H.O.: 4360/4, Ansari Road, Daryaganj,
New Delhi-110 002 (India)
Ph.: 23278000, 23261597
B.O.: No. 1015, Ist Main Road, BSK IIIrd Stage
IIIrd Phase, IIIrd Block,
Bangalore - 560 085 (India)
Tel.: 080-41723429
Visit us at: www.centrumpress.com

A-Z E-commerce

First Edition, 2009
ISBN 978-93-80106-15-1

PRINTED IN INDIA

Printed at Salasar Imaging Systems, Delhi-110035 (India)

Contents

Preface

This Encyclopaedia relies on extensive analysis of academic and managerial research, along with a review of company successes and failures during the foundation and short history of e-commerce. It provides industry and company cases and specific recommendations for actions that managers can take to improve e-commerce success. It provides a framework for measuring the benefits and costs of potential e-commerce investments that can aid in deciding how much to invest and how to achieve the greatest potential payoffs. It places e-commerce in a value creation frame, so that corporate and business unit managers can more effectively evaluate the possibilities and trade-offs.

With the growth of the Internet, corporations have struggled with the determination of the appropriate level of investment in the new technology. CEOs faced the quandary of whether to fully commit or wait and watch. Academics devoted effort to determining ways to formulate e-commerce strategies. But, little research has focused on how to choose among alternative strategies or how to execute an e-commerce strategy. The author hopes that lessons learned can guide managers to effectively formulate, evaluate, and implement an e-commerce strategy. The lessons we learn from prior successes and failures and the frameworks presented here to better develop, evaluate, and implement e-commerce strategies. IT managers should be aided to better analyze the value creation potential of investing additional resources in e-commerce initiatives.

Author

Chapter 1

Introduction to Internet

In 1969, the Internet was just a demonstration project linking up four university campuses in the USA, but it now boasts in excess of 300 million users across the world. It was supported by the US Department of Defense's Advanced Research Project Agency (ARPA). The Internet was based on an original concept developed by the Rand Corporation in the early 1960s, and added to by bodies such as the UK's National Physical Laboratory (NPL).

The objective of the research was to provide the USA with a communications network that would survive in the event of a nuclear conflagration. The project was codified into a set of protocols (eventually called TCP/IP) by Vinton Cerf during the mid-1970s, and deployed across all the interlinked networks in 1983. Growth between 1980 and 1987 shows numbers of hosts in the tens of thousands.

Before we explore the legal and commercial realities of e-commerce it is first necessary to consider the nature of the Internet. We must do this in order to be able to apply the law to it. Common misconceptions can arise merely from the description of *the* Internet. Use of 'the' implies that it is some constant 'thing' which has definable edges and a shape and even a legal presence. Actually the Internet is a communications infrastructure, nothing more.

It is made up of countless thousands of computers that are connected together by means of telecommunications systems. Not all these computers will be connected at any one time and hence it is impossible to define its size and presence. When one user's computer is in communication with another user's computer, the information that is sent and received by each will travel in different and unpredictable routes and will pass through many computers on its journey. All the computers and communications services providers that are not either the original sender or the final recipient of the information are intermediaries or 'conduits'.

Internet connectivity is commonly established by using an Internet Service Provider (ISP). ISP's are organisations that have a permanent presence on the Internet and provide a fixed line or dial-up service. Some ISP's make a charge for this service, but many do not.

However, most businesses will require a website, and hence web space on the ISP's server, and this is normally a chargeable service. Businesses wishing to establish a web presence for the first time are advised to consult the trade press (business Internet magazines such as *The Industry Standard*) for information on ISP's.

THE NATURE OF E-COMMERCE

Before looking at the legal detail and common pitfalls of e-commerce, we will initially consider the nature of e-commerce — what exactly is it? We will also look at some terminology that is frequently used by e-commerce lawyers and business people, always bearing in mind that what we are dealing with here is not the technology, but rather the way the law applies to the transactions that are undertaken using the technology.

E-commerce (or electronic commerce) is the term used to denote a commercial (usually contractual) transaction that takes place between two or more people using the communications infrastructure known as the Internet. The first thing to note is that there is a range of e-commerce transactions, the following of which are examples:

- The purchase by an individual of a book from a commercial website such as that run by Amazon.com
- The ordering by Company A of office stationery from Company B's website
- The exchange of e-mails between two persons

whereby it is agreed that a certain service will be carried out by one party in exchange for a fee from the other.

We do not usually think of the latter type of transaction as falling within the category of e-commerce, but it is just as much an electronically formed contract as the other two examples: an exchange of e-mails can result in a legally binding contract. For example, if anyone send you an e-mail offering to sell you one dozen doughnuts, and you respond accepting my offer, this is just as much an e-commerce transaction as one taking place using the colourful pages and flash technology of the World Wide Web.

Initially it will be important for an e-commerce business to identify whether its e-commerce transactions will be classified as B2B (business-to-business) or B2C (business-to-consumer).This is because the law applies in a different way to each. Of course, it may be that the e-commerce business anticipates engaging in both types of transaction. The differences between these two types of transaction will be referred to throughout this Report.Other terms commonly referred to throughout this Report are as follows:

- World Wide Web – that part of the Internet which uses the Hyper Text Transfer Protocol (HTTP) to display so-called web pages and to allow links between such pages anywhere on the Internet.
- ISP (Internet Service Provider) a provider of Internet connectivity.
- ASP (Applications Service Provider) — an online provider of computer applications, such as software.

THE LAW OF COMMERCE

The law does not currently recognise an e-commerce transaction as being inherently different from a non e-commerce transaction. However, due to the online nature of e-commerce, particular aspects of the law apply differently where a transaction takes place online. This section will briefly consider those aspects of the law that apply to *both* online and offline transactions.

This will be followed by an introduction to those areas of the law that have particular application in the case of e-commerce. None of the topics listed below – aspects of law that apply to commercial transactions generally – will be looked at in any detail in this Report, but it is important to put the e-commerce transaction in the context of its commercial and legal setting.

TRADING VEHICLE

In the case of an existing business wishing to move online, the legal infrastructure will already be in place. For start-ups it is important to consider the way that trading is to be carried out. It may be that the business will be a partnership. Alternatively it might be a registered limited company. E-commerce start-ups should usually be advised to use a company for trading purposes. The advantages are many, the two main ones being that it is easier to attract investment capital, and that the owners of the company (its shareholders) will benefit from limited liability.

Shares and Responsibilities

This is an issue for start-ups. If a company is chosen as the appropriate trading vehicle then there will be a number of issues that must be agreed upon by the participants:What are the appropriate proportions for share ownership? Who are the directors going to be? Who will be Company Secretary? Will a shareholder agreement be needed? Appropriate legal advice should be sought on these issues.

Taxation

Once again the normal considerations will apply to both offline and online transactions. The position is slightly complicated in an e-commerce transaction due to the greater likelihood that such a transaction will involve parties who are not located in the same country.

Intellectual Property Rights

The subject of intellectual property is relevant to all

businesses but may be particularly important to e-commerce as the business model may involve a greater use of intellectual property.

Terms and Conditions of Trade

Again, this is relevant to all businesses. The terms on which a business obtains its supplies, and upon which it trades with its customers, are of fundamental importance. Incorporation of a business's terms into its contracts is not usually a problem with offline transactions but significant issues commonly arise with an e-commerce business. Choice of law and jurisdiction will be an issue in some contractual arrangements, both on and offline.

THE LAW OF E-COMMERCE

Of greater significance, and the subject of this Report, are those areas of the law that apply specifically to e-commerce. This may be due to the fact that 'old' law applies in an unusual way to e-commerce due to the unpredictable (at the time that law was made) nature of the transaction.

Or it may be due to the presence of 'new'law, which, though it may not have been formulated to deal with e-commerce exclusively, clearly has it in contemplation as the main target of its intended regulation. The list that appears below contains those areas of law that are of particular (and in some cases exclusive) interest to e-commerce businesses:

FORMATION OF CONTRACT

How does the law of offer and acceptance apply to an online transaction? In other words, how will a contract be formed in the virtual world? Will a web page that displays a product for sale be an offer or an invitation to treat? This issue has yet to be decided by the courts.

INTELLECTUAL PROPERTY RIGHTS

Much of the value in an *idea* for an e-commerce website can be tied up in the Intellectual Property Rights (IPR's).It is essential, particularly when trying to attract seed money from venture capitalists, that these IPR's are delineated and transferred to the trading vehicle. They may be owned by a number of different people and so IPR assignments will need to be executed at an early stage.

In any event the value of IPR's is notoriously underestimated by businessmen. Appropriate steps must be taken to protect this value and to take steps to safeguard any brand name and associated goodwill.

COPYRIGHT

Copyright is of course comprised in IPR's, but there are some specific considerations in relation to copyright that need to be looked at. We know that the law of copyright protects literary and artistic works and that these are the sorts of works that comprise a web page. So far so good. But what about links from one web page to another?

Could they constitute breach of copyright? Of course in most instances, there would be no complaint because a link from one website to another would generate increased traffic and this surely is the objective of websites. But in one case a newspaper's website contained a link to the news section of another newspaper's website.

It was held in an interim application to the court that this could constitute copyright infringement. The reason for the case was that the link bypassed the front (or home) page of the other website and so the users did not get to see the advertising messages on that home page — this technique is known as deep-linking. Sites that undertake deep-linking should be aware of the potential legal challenges that could arise.

DOMAIN NAMES AND CYBERSQUATTING

The fact that every website must have a unique Internet address means that many commercial enterprises will be disappointed in their desire for a specific domain name. This is the problem that is inherent in a first-come-first-served system of domain name registrations.

Difficulties can arise when one business feels it should be

entitled to use a domain name that has already been registered by someone else. Domain names are considered in detail together with the practice known as 'cybersquatting'and the possible methods for acquiring a domain name that has already been registered by someone else.

DATA PROTECTION

This area of the law governs what may and what may not be done with individuals' personal information. In many cases much of the value in an e-commerce business is in its customer database, which may consist of a variety of information including name, address, e-mail address, date of birth, shopping habits, annual household income, etc.

The law establishes a code of conduct (known as the Eight Data Protection Principles) for the processing of such data as well as a right for every individual to see a copy of such data if they request it.

DISTANCE SELLING REGULATIONS

Towards the end of 2000, and in response to European Union legislation, the UK passed the Consumer Protection (Distance Selling) Regulations. These regulations require all UK businesses that enter contracts with consumers 'at a distance' (clearly this includes, but is not exclusive to, Internet transactions) to do two main things that they were not legally obliged to do before.

The first is to provide certain specific information to the consumer and the second is to allow consumers a 'cooling-off' period of seven working days from receipt of goods to return the goods for a full refund.

IT Requi rements

There will be a number of legal considerations which arise from the infrastructure and services which are required for an e-commerce business. Hence there may be purchase or rental of hardware and software, rental of server space if required and a website hosting and development agreement where the hosting is to be outsourced.

These topics are considered where relevant throughout this Report.

Law and Jurisdiction

One of the difficulties with an Internet transaction is that the buyer and seller may be in different parts of the world. The question then arises as to which legal system will govern the contract in the absence of any binding express provision. A related question but one which is more complex and somewhat political is which court system will have jurisdiction to hear any relevant litigation?

E-MANAGEMENT E-MAIL

Before proceeding to look at the law of e-commerce, it is useful to consider some particular aspects of e-business management. There is no doubt that, for the managers of any commercial enterprise, the Internet presents the most significant universal challenge that has yet been presented in the history of commerce.

It is tempting to think of the Internet as merely an electronic expression of what has gone before: e-mails replace typed letters, websites replace glossy brochures and electronic invoices replace their paper equivalents. But the Internet is not merely a more efficient replacement for existing systems. Its significance lies in its ability to be not merely a communications device, but a market, an information system and a manufacturing tool.

It allows managers to do not only what they have done before communicating with suppliers, advertising products and services, collecting customer data and obtaining payment more efficiently, cheaply and comprehensively, but also opens up significant new possibilities for the core operations of every business.

Of course it is the potential to increase productivity and cut costs that is a most attractive feature of the Internet, and this must not be overlooked. Suppose, for example, you are a car manufacturer. Traditionally you have obtained orders for new cars from a network of showrooms that have in turn obtained orders from their customers. Where outsourcing has been required, you have placed orders with your suppliers.

Assembly takes place, the car is customised to the customer's requirements and is shipped to the dealer. With the Internet comes the possibility of the customer placing their order online. They can choose their accessories and colour scheme and create a virtual image of how the car will look on-screen before proceeding with their order. Direct electronic communication of the order eradicates possible mis-communication in, and later arguments over, choice of specification.

The delivery date can be electronically calculated and arrangements for payment can be finalised. The manufacturer's automated system will communicate electronically with suppliers so that the alloy wheels, or whatever has been selected, can be delivered precisely when needed for fitting to the vehicle. The finished product can be delivered via an intermediary dealer or direct to the customer.

E-MAIL

The spread of electronic communication brings transparency and openness to the management process. The ease with which an e-mail can be forwarded to hundreds or thousands of people changes the nature of communication — one must now assume that not just the recipient will read an e-mail that is sent to him. It is no longer possible to hide behind mountains of paperwork or to 'lose' a letter to which it is currently not desirable to respond.

It is common knowledge that the ability to send and forward e-mails causes two main concerns for employers. The first is that time will be wasted — some employees spend several hours each week in sending e-mails to friends. The second is that the employer will incur some liability as a result of the content of such e-mails. Both these concerns can be met by an 'e-mail policy', which should be clear and comprehensive.

It should set out the employer's attitude to e-mail and explain that employees'e-mails will be monitored (if this is desired) to ensure quality of service and appropriateness of communication. The presence of such a policy should have the effect of employees exercising some caution when sending and forwarding e-mails.

It should also mean that embarrassing incidents such as the Norton Rose 'blow job' e-mail debacle can be avoided. It should be noted that the monitoring of employee e-mails has data protection and privacy implications that are beyond the scope of this Report.

A related issue is that of pornography. Pornographic images are popular with employees but cause great concern for employers. Not only do they waste employee time, they cause offence and clog vital server space. They could also lead to liability for the employer. To avoid the sort of situation experienced by Orange when it dismissed 30 employees for downloading and distributing pornographic images, a clear statement should be made to employees of the employer's attitude to this activity.

To stem the flow closer to its source, the business should consider installing software capable of screening-out unwanted material.E-businesses should remember that an e-mail is a business document in the same way as is a letter or a fax. E-mails must therefore comply with the requirements of the Companies Act 1985, namely that the following information must appear:

- The full name of the company;
- The registered number of the company;
- The address of the registered office; and
- The country of registration of the company.

Human Resources

Given the current climate of short-term working practices and the need to have efficient and productive staff, e-businesses need to focus on staff attraction and retention. E-businesses, generally speaking, need fewer but better staff. This may require a review of working conditions, working practices, pay structures and benefits. The e-business revolution has, significantly, created new jobs that did not exist in the offline economy — examples include website designers, knowledge management officers and e-business managers.

Workers in e-business are increasingly flexible, many working from home or onthe-road. Rather than being feared, such practices should be embraced by businesses.

Not only do they lead to a lowering of overheads (heat, light and a desk in the office are not required for mobile workers) but they can create greater satisfaction and loyalty amongst staff. Appropriate communication infrastructures should be employed so that staff are kept fully informed of events 'back at the office'and are able to communicate with other staff members, as well as customers and suppliers. Where sales teams spend much of their time out of the office, they too should be kept fully informed and accountable.

The lack of office presence of individual employees and the globalisation of businesses mean that the 'drink after work' and the 'training weekend' become increasingly difficult. Many businesses are developing corporate portals for their business to employee (B2E) communications. Such portals can prove invaluable in providing information and training to employees.

Larger companies can additionally use the portals as an online job market and to provide maps of buildings and photographs and locations of staff. Some companies motivate employees to log on to the portal on a daily basis by posting the share prices of the company or by displaying a list of employee birthdays for the relevant week. A section of the portal can be used for selling the company's products to the employees.

The Internet can be used for recruiting staff. Potential job applicants can be given up-to-date information on vacancies, be taken on a virtual tour of the business and be invited to apply online. Communications between the HR department and job applicant can be undertaken by e-mail. The expense of using a recruitment agent can be saved.

CUSTOMERS

The Internet gives rise to the possibility of a wider marketplace. Customers may now be located anywhere on the planet but have equal access to the marketing material of the business. Systems should be set up to deal with this new global presence.

Better information on customers is available from the monitoring of their activities whilst visiting the website. Using cookies it is possible to 'personalise' the content of the site for each particular customer. Knowing that a customer lives in Oxford, for example, it is possible to display a banner advertisement for an Oxford-based pizza restaurant on your homepage.

Were a different customer to visit the homepage, the advertisement would be of a different kind. Location-specific and targeted advertising have data protection implications and detailed proposals should be submitted to a data protection lawyer before procedures are implemented.

As the technology grows, so do customers' expectations. Customers will expect to be kept informed of the process of their order and will want more information than would have previously been available. Electronic order tracking systems should be available to customers online to provide them with this information. DHL, for example, has a system which enables a customer to see the location of their package at each stage of its journey and to know the precise moment that it is 'signed-for' by the recipient.

DOMAIN NAMES

THE NATURE OF DOMAIN NAMES

One of the first things that an e-business must do is to choose a domain name. A domain name is essentially an 'e-commerce logo' which provides companies with their 'e-identity'. It is in fact a user-friendly alphanumeric alias for an Internet Protocol (IP) address.

An IP address is a unique number that identifies a particular computer that is attached to the Internet. A user wishing to connect with a particular website will type in the domain name relating to that site. Computers searching for the site will then convert this name back to the IP address so as to connect to the relevant server. It is important that the domain name chosen is memorable. Many companies choose a domain name that is associated with their product, brand or company name.

The process of domain name registration is easy and cheap and for this reason, as well as other legal reasons, the business would be wise to maximise the protection of its goodwill by registering alternate versions of its domain name.

To see how the law applies to domain names and to understand the difficulties that can arise it is important to understand the difference between the constituent parts of a domain name. The section to the furthest right of the domain name is known as the Top Level Domain (TLD). TLD's are split into 'generic'top-level domain names (gTLD's) and 'country-code specific' top-level domain names (ccTLD's).

There are only three gTLD's that are generally available on a first-come-first-served basis to anyone in the world:

For generic top-level domains there is no need to prove anything to the registering authority before registration can be effected. In other words, despite its name, a person wishing to register a.com domain name, is not required to prove that the website will be used for a commercial organisation — they could for example intend to use the site to display photographs of their cats. Traditionally however.com,.org and.net have been used by commercial enterprises, not-for-profit organisations and Internet infrastructure companies respectively.

Many ccTLD's are generally available to anyone on a first-come-first-served basis worldwide. *The Economist* for example recently registered economist.tv for its new venture, web broadcasting in video format of topical news stories. However, some countries restrict the use of their ccTLD — for example the Australian authority, which regulates the.au ccTLD, requires the applicant to show some connection with Australia.

In Norway (.no) would-be registrants are required to provide an 'enterprise number', obtainable only by Norwegian companies. Some ccTLD's include more than one TLD so that they can be used for a specific type of organisation, e.g..co.uk,.ac.uk and.org.uk to denote a commercial body, academic institution and not-for-profit organisation respectively. The remaining.uk domains are. ltd. uk,. plc. uk,. net. uk, and.sch.uk. The next part of the domain name is the Second Level Domain (sometimes called sub-domain). For example in the case of the law firm Charles Russell, the SLD is cr-law. The combination of the TLD and the SLD is the part of a domain name that it is possible to register (e.g. cr-law.co.uk).

All commercial enterprises should put in place a strategy for registering the new gTLD's when they go live. A 'sunrise' period of registration restriction will mean that only those applicants that own registered trade marks will be successful during the first few weeks of the new system.

MANAGEMENT OF DOMAIN NAMES

No serious commercial enterprise is without a domain name. Indeed the number of domain names that have been registered during the past five years could be graphically represented by an exponential curve. By 1995 approximately 100,000 domain names had been registered. At the beginning of 2000 this number had increased to 6 million. At the time of writing the number of domain names registered stood at more than 40 million.

Commonly there are no pre-conditions for registering a domain name and no restriction on the number of domain names that can be registered. In the case of start-ups or new ventures for existing businesses, it is important to register the chosen domain name as soon as possible, and certainly before any publicity about the business is released to the public.

There have been several cases in the past few years where a company has sent out a press release concerning a new business venture, including the proposed business name without having secured the domain name. The same day a member of the public who has seen the publicity surrounding the venture has registered the proposed business name as a domain name. Mediation with Nominet or dispute resolution with ICANN can produce a satisfactory resolution but will inevitably be expensive and time-consuming.

E-commerce businesses are advised to register all ccTLD

variations of the domain name that relate to those countries where the client expects to do business as well as all gTLD's that are available. This prevents someone from registering the same SLD as the business, albeit with a different TLD.Businesses should also register all variations of the name, for example using hyphens where the SLD consists of more than one word or even common misspellings.

This prevents anyone from taking unfair advantage of the goodwill in the business by engaging in the activity known as cybersquatting. An appropriate and sensible commercial strategy for domain name registrations, coupled with relevant trade mark registrations, can reduce the risks posed by cybersquatters.

It should also be remembered that a domain name is not a property right as such. Rather, a domain name registration allows the registrant the exclusive use of that domain name for the period of registration. Registration periods are commonly either one or two years. It is vital that renewal is made otherwise use of the domain name will be lost.

Trade Marks and Branding

For the protection of a business or its product or service, the registration of a trade mark or service mark should be considered. An infringement action can then be brought against anyone using the same or similar mark in respect of a similar business in the jurisdiction of registration.

Where brand protection is not available by use of a registered trade mark (due to, for example, the business being unable to comply with the strict requirements of the registration process) some protection may be available from that branch of the law known as 'passing off'. This section considers the law of trade marks and passing off specifically in the context of protection of domain names.

Trade Marks

The fundamental difference between a trade mark and a domain name is that there can be several identical trade marks registered in different parts of the world, or even in the same jurisdiction, by different people. Each identical trade mark can relate to a different type of goods without any possibility of the trade mark use constituting an infringement.

By contrast there can only ever be one of each domain name, as such names are necessarily unique. Whilst use of an identical domain name to one registered by an e-business is therefore impossible, registration and use of a similar domain name by a third party is not unlikely. For example, although we may register the domain name, pwcarey.com, this does not stop someone else registering the domain name p-w-carey.com or pcarey.com.

In other words, the domain name registration system offers no protection against the registration of similar names. An action for trade mark infringement on the other hand can be brought against not only those persons who use an identical mark in relation to similar goods or services, but also against those who use a similar mark in relation to similar goods or services. E-businesses should therefore aim to support the protection of their brands by registering a trade mark for their domain names in each of their principal trading territories. Trade mark registrations can be undertaken by law firms or trade mark agents.

It is possible that use of a domain name by one person may constitute the infringement of a registered trade mark of another. The claimant must show, under s10 TMA 1994, that there has been use of an identical mark in relation to identical goods/services or use of a similar mark in relation to identical/similar goods/services where there is likelihood of confusion.

PASSING OFF

Where goodwill in a business is being used by another for their own benefit but that other is not using an identical or similar registered trade mark, the business may be able to bring an action for 'passing-off'. An action by one business against another or against an individual in the tort of passing off usually requires a misrepresentation in the course of trade, which leads to financial loss.

An exception to the rule that to succeed in a passing off

action the claimant must show that the defendant was using the same or similar mark in the course of trade was established in the context of domain names in the case of *BT and Others v. One in a Million Ltd* (1999) FSR.

In the case, brought by BT, Virgin, Sainsburys and others, the court held that the 'mere creation of an instrument of fraud' could amount to passing off. One in a Million Ltd was forced to give up its interest in certain domain names that it had registered such as sainsbury.com, virgin.com and bt.org. It had registered these domains in the hope of selling them to the relevant companies for a profit.

Some would argue that the companies should have had the foresight to resister these domain names themselves and should not expect the law to rescue them from their lack of commercial awareness. Nevertheless the court showed a willingness to adapt the common law to the changing commercial environment.

The laws of both trade mark infringement and passing off are difficult to prove and in any event litigation takes a good deal of time and money. For these reasons businesses that have found that others have registered domain names that they feel should in fact belong to themselves have chosen to engage in dispute resolution as an alternative to a court action.

CYBER SQUATTING AND DISPUTE RESOLUTION

Cyber squatting is the activity that involves the bad faith registration of trade marks as domain names. Where an e-business finds itself to be the victim of a cyber squatter there are a number of potential courses of action. In appropriate circumstances the cyber squatter can be sued in a court of law for infringement of a registered trade mark or in the tort of passing off. An alternative, and often cheaper and faster procedure is to enter into domain name dispute resolution.

Dispute resolution is a useful alternative to litigation for those cases where a claimant feels that they should be entitled to use a domain name that has been registered by someone else. Such a situation commonly arises under the existing procedure for domain name registrations, which is essentially a 'first-come-first-served'system. In most cases anyone can purchase the exclusive right to use a domain name, provided that no one has registered it beforehand. The *One in a Million Case* showed that it is possible to obtain a court order for the transfer of a domain name, but litigation is inevitably costly and time consuming.

The Internet Corporation for Assigned Names and Numbers (ICANN) set up a dispute resolution system for the top-level generic domain names (.com,.net and.org) in December 1999.That system, known as the Uniform Dispute Resolution Policy (UDRP), has proved very popular and successful.

It is administered by four bodies (the best known of which is the World Intellectual Property Organisation) and frequently results in a domain name being transferred to the claimant. This section considers the dispute resolution procedures of ICANN and Nominet (which administers all.uk domain names).

ICANN DISPUTE RESOLUTION PROCEDURE

The important thing to bear in mind is that domain names are not property as such. The registrant's rights to use a domain name derives from the contract that it enters into with the registration authority. As far as gTLD's are concerned, the registration authority is ICANN (Internet Corporation for Assigned Names and Numbers). ICANN set up a Uniform Dispute Resolution Policy (UDRP), which became operational on 1 December 1999. The UDRP applies only to those domains administered by ICANN i.e. the three gTLD's.com,.net and.org. ICANN has subcontracted out the job of hearing and adjudicating on the disputes to four bodies (listed in Appendix five), the best known of which is the World Intellectual Property Organisation (WIPO). The UDRP relates only to an 'abusive registration'. This means that applicants will only be successful where they are able to show that:

- The disputed domain name is identical or confusingly similar to a trade mark or service mark in which the applicant has rights
- The registrant has no rights or legitimate interests in the domain name

- The domain name has been registered and is being used in bad faith.

Unfortunately the UDRP does not provide any guidance on how 'confusing similarity' is to be assessed. A 'legitimate interest' can be demonstrated by the registrant by showing some use or preparatory steps to use the domain name dating from prior to any notice by the applicant; evidence that the registrant is commonly known by the domain name or evidence that the registrant has engaged in a legitimate non-commercial use of the domain name.

'Bad faith', the most important element of the UDRP, can be shown where the registrant's main purpose in registering the domain name was to sell it to the applicant; where it was designed to prevent the applicant using its trade mark as a domain name or where there was an intention to attract users to the registrant's website by creating a likelihood of confusion with the applicant's mark.

It should be noted that bad faith can be shown not only by a demand for money, but also by a request for services. In a case involving the domain name uwyoming.com the respondent wanted free tuition for his daughter at the University of Wyoming, and in the gearmagazine.com case the respondent demanded the contract to build the complainant's website. In both cases the complainants were successful in getting the domain names transferred to themselves.

If the applicant is successful at the arbitration hearing (which is by written submission, no live witnesses) then ICANN will immediately transfer the domain name to the applicant. By way of example, Julia Roberts was able to obtain reregistration of the domain name juliaroberts.com in her own name by using the UDRP.

By contrast Bruce Springsteen failed in a similar application for brucespringsteen.com, largely because the registrant was able to show legitimate use (for a Bruce Springsteen fan club website).

DISPUTE RESOLUTION FOR.UK DOMAIN NAMES

Nominet, the UK domain name registry, has announced

its intention to radically update its dispute resolution procedure for applications by claimants against cybersquatters.

The principal criticism of the Nominet system to date has been that it does not allow transfers of the disputed domain name into the name of the claimant. Under the new system, to operate from Autumn 2001, Nominet will be able to remove the existing name from the register and replace it with that of the claimant.

The new system proposed by Nominet for all.uk domains is modelled on the UDRP but has some interesting differences.

At present the dispute resolution system available from Nominet, the second largest of the country code specific domain name registries, is a mediation service. It is free of charge and is undertaken by written submissions by the parties. Of the 1,200 mediations dealt with by Nominet since it began the service in 1997, approximately one third have been successfully resolved. Of the two thirds of claims that are not amicably resolved by the parties, the remaining alternative is litigation. Nominet will currently withdraw or suspend a domain name (but not transfer it) in the following circumstances:

- If the name is administered in a way that is likely to endanger the operation of the domain name system.
- If the basis on which the domain name was registered has changed.
- If Nominet finds that the name is being used in a manner likely to cause confusion to Internet users.
- Where Nominet UK has been informed that legal action has been commenced regarding use of the name.
- Where Nominet UK is of the opinion that one of the above is likely to occur.

The need for a new dispute resolution system arises out of increased public awareness in the activity known as 'cybersquatting' and the desire for a quick and effective procedure for the transfer of a.uk domain name which has been registered by a third party. There is also, according to Nominet, a perception that cybersquatting threatens the principles of a first-come-first-served registration system, and that self-regulation is preferable to an enforced solution.Under the proposals Nominet will continue to offer a mediation service for disputed domain names but the mediation will 'time-out' if it has been unsuccessful after ten working days.

The application will then be automatically referred to an independent expert who will be appointed in a 'cab-rank' fashion from a list held by Nominet (under the UDRP applicants can choose particular experts — there may be up to three experts deciding each case).

A fee — likely to be in the region of £500 to £1,000 — will be payable to Nominet for use of the service and all decisions of the experts will be published.In order to succeed in its application for domain name transfer, a claimant will be expected to show that the registration is 'abusive'.There is to be a two-stage test for abusive registrations. The claimant must show that:

- They have rights in respect of a name or mark which is identical or similar to a domain name.
- The registrant has and/or is using the domain name in bad faith.

This test is similar to that under the UDRP, except under the latter, the claimant must additionally show that the registrant has no rights or legitimate interest in the domain name. Under the UDRP where the mark of the claimant is not identical to the domain name, the claimant must show that it is 'confusingly similar', as opposed to merely 'similar', to the domain name.

The central requirement for both the UDRP and the Nominet proposal is that the domain name be registered (or used) in bad faith. However, although the burden of proof under both schemes is on the claimant, the standard of proof is different. Under the Nominet proposal, the claimant will be expected to prove, *beyond a reasonable doubt,* the bad faith of the registrant.

Bad faith is commonly shown by a clear motive to siphon business goodwill away from the claimant or an attempt by the registrant to sell the domain name to the claimant at a grossly inflated price. It is unclear how the higher standard of proof will affect claims for the transfer of.uk domains.

E-COMMERCE CONTRACTS

Virtually all commercial transactions are undertaken in the setting of a legally binding contract. Indeed, without the presence of such a contract the parties would generally be unwilling to perform their obligations (such as the delivery of goods, the performance of a service or the payment of money) under the transaction.

Contracts provide certainty as to the obligations of each party and, more importantly, a guarantee of the right to sue the non-performing party for breach.The law of contract dates back centuries, and has equal application to an ecommerce transaction as an offline contract. But the nature of an e-commerce transaction gives rise to some special problems that do not arise offline:

- Formation of the contract — for each party to have confidence that the performance of its obligations will have legal effect, it is of vital importance that the contract has actually been formed at the time of that performance. In the offline world the existence of a contract can be evidenced in many ways — such as a signature on a printed order form or a note of a conversation — that are not available in the online world.
- Incorporation of contractual terms — commercial transactions take place under a set of contractual rules. Usually these rules are set out in written form and will apply to the contract by virtue of being 'incorporated' within it.

  In the offline world terms are included in a contract by agreement. There is a considerable body of caselaw that describes how and why such terms will be incorporated. That caselaw may not, and indeed in some cases cannot, apply to online transactions.
- Non face-to-face transactions — e-commerce transactions, by their definition, take place

electronically. The advantage of this is that the parties do not need to be in each other's presence at the time of formation of the contract.

One disadvantage of this is that the law treats differently those contracts that are entered into between a business and a consumer 'at a distance' — the e-business must comply with a set of rules that do not generally apply to its offline competitors.

Formation of a Contract

It is generally well-known that a legally binding contract will arise where there is an offer to do something that is met by an unconditional acceptance of that offer. By way of example, where X offers to pay £250 for the delivery of a case of champagne to her home and Y agrees to perform that task for that sum of money, a contract is formed. To complicate matters, the law distinguishes an *offer* from an 'invitation to treat'. An *invitation to treat* is something that might appear to be an offer, but in fact is not.

An example is the display of goods in a shop window or on the shelf of a supermarket. It has long been decided that such displays are not offers and that therefore they cannot be 'accepted'.This is the rule that prevents a customer from being able to force a shopkeeper to sell goods to him at the displayed price, even where that price is clearly erroneous.

Whilst in the offline world it is easy to determine when a particular communication is an offer or an invitation to treat, such a distinction is unclear in a virtual transaction. Argos recently felt the effect of this when it mistakenly advertised televisions on its website with a price tag of £2.99 instead of £299.When several people placed orders for the televisions Argos realised its mistake and refused to supply the televisions at the price advertised.

One 'purchaser' sued the company for failure to deliver on the contract that she said had been created. The case was settled before it reached trial so we do not know what the judge would have decided. Although we can speculate that, in English law at least, a website is probably an invitation to treat as opposed to an offer, it would be wise for e-businesses to make clear the status of pricing and other information on their sites.

Incorporation of Terms

Of central importance to the e-commerce transaction are the terms and conditions on which the contract is based and by which it is governed. An e-business will always wish to trade on those terms that are favourable to it. For example, the business may wish to state that it is not to be held liable for late delivery of goods, or that its total liability for defective goods is to be limited to a certain monetary figure.

In most cases this will be done by the insertion of terms and conditions on the website and by making some reference to them during the contracting process. By completing the transaction the customers will effectively be binding themselves to those terms and conditions.

For the reasons mentioned above it is important for the terms and conditions of trade to form part of the contract. Without them we must rely on the 'default position' provided by the law and this is rarely ideal for a seller. The difficulty with e-commerce transactions is incorporating the terms into the contract is rarely a straightforward matter. There are various techniques, such as those listed below:

- Click-through with acceptance — here the customer is required to click on a button which says,'I accept' or similar. This is the best position for the e-commerce business because the acceptance by the customer is clear and traceable. However, there is a perception that customers may be 'put off' by the need for this formality.
- Click-through without acceptance — the customer is required to scroll through the conditions but there is no acceptance button. Here there will be, at the very least, implied acceptance by the customer if they continue with the transaction after having scrolled through the terms and conditions.
- Reference with link—here the customer is referred

to terms and conditions of trade but not forced to scroll through them. However, there is a link that will take the customer to the terms should they wish to see them. This is not ideal but may amount to 'incorporation by reference' under English law — this has not yet been tested by the courts in the context of online transactions.

- Reference without link—there is a reference to terms and conditions of trade but they do not appear on the site. Again this is an attempt at incorporation by reference. It is the least satisfactory method and is unlikely to have the desired effect in an e-commerce transaction as there is no reason why the terms and conditions could not appear somewhere on the website.

The legal formalities for online trading are expected to grow. The European Union, for example, has recently proposed several new laws which will govern e-commerce in the future. With this in mind, businesses would be wise to adopt a policy of requiring those persons they contract with online to click an 'acceptance button' to demonstrate their assent to the terms and conditions displayed on the website.

UNFAIR TERMS

E-businesses must be aware that since 1999 certain terms in their contracts with consumers will be void, i.e. unenforceable and of no legal effect. The Unfair Terms in Consumer Contracts Regulations 1999 apply, by definition, only to B2C contracts.For the purpose of the Regulations a 'consumer' is a person acting privately and not in the course of business. In contracts with such persons any unfair term is void. An 'unfair' term is one which,'contrary to the requirements of good faith, causes a significant imbalance in the consumer's rights under the contract, to the detriment of the consumer'.Examples of terms that would be regarded as unfair under the Regulations include:

- Allowing the business to change the characteristics of goods or services offered without recourse to the consumer; and

- Allowing the business to terminate the contract without reasonable notice of such termination being given to the consumer.

THE DISTANCE SELLING REGULATIONS

A consumer who purchases goods or services from an e-commerce business is protected to a greater degree than a business purchaser is. It is important therefore, at an early stage, to determine whether the e-business will engage in B2B or B2C transactions.

In many cases of course the e-business will wish to trade with both businesses and individual customers. Where the e-business anticipates that part of its customer base will be individual consumers, the so-called 'Distance Selling Regulations' become relevant.

The Consumer Protection (Distance Selling) Regulations 2000 (reproduced in Appendix three) came into force on 31 October 2000.

They apply to contracts between a business and a consumer that are not 'face-to-face' e.g. contracts concluded by way of coupons in newspapers,'teleshopping', and of course the Internet. The Regulations impose two main obligations on suppliers of goods or services.

The first is to provide certain information to the consumer. The second is to furnish the consumer with a 'cooling off' period of seven working days during which the consumer is able to return the goods to the e-business for a full refund.

It is interesting to note that a recent survey of all 235 UK websites listed on Yahoo!, offering goods in the publishing, music and computer hardware sectors, found that 92% of the sites gave incomplete or incorrect advice on the right to withdraw. About half contained key contractual information that was not clear or prominent.

Most of those companies would be shocked to be informed that after each online sale has taken place the customer could contact the business at any time within three months and request the business to collect the goods from them.

The e-business would then be required to refund the purchase price to the customer, whether or not it decided to collect the goods.

The Information Requirements

In most cases the 'information requirements' in the Distance Selling Regulations can be satisfied by posting the appropriate information online. Consumers must be provided with the information shown in the box below in a clear and comprehensible manner.

The consumer must also be informed of any intention by the supplier to provide substitute goods if the goods ordered are not available, and of the fact that the supplier will meet costs of return of such substitute goods by the consumer to the supplier in the event of cancellation.

THE COOLING-OFF PERIOD

The requirement of a 'cooling-off' period for distance contracts puts e-commerce businesses at a disadvantage when compared with their offline competitors. For a consumer to be legally entitled to return goods purchased in the offline world (for example in a shop) for a full refund, they must prove that there is some defect in the goods or that the goods are not of satisfactory quality.

The Regulations however allow an online purchaser to return goods within seven working days for a full refund, without obliging the purchaser to furnish any reason for doing so.

As far as the cooling off period is concerned, consumers must be given a period of seven working days, from the day after *receipt* of the goods, in which to change their mind. During that period the consumer has the right to return the goods to the e-commerce business for a full refund.

Crucially, if consumers are not informed of their right to cancel in this way, then the time period during which they have the right to cancel increases automatically to three months plus seven working days. Businesses should therefore be aware that their failure to inform consumers of the cooling-off period will effectively extend their potential liability to refund the purchase price by three months.

Excluded Contracts

The requirement to provide consumers with the above information, and to give a cooling-off period, does not apply to the following contracts:

- For the sale or other disposition of an interest in land except for a rental agreement
- For the construction of a building
- For financial services
- Contracts concluded by means of an automated vending machine
- Contracts concluded with a telecommunications operator by use of a public payphone
- Contracts concluded at an auction.

It should be remembered that the Distance Selling Regulations apply to contracts with consumers, but not to contracts with corporate and business customers. The information above must be stated clearly and concisely on the website — this may mean some changes to existing sites. Additionally, the cooling-off period does not apply to bespoke or tailor-made products. Any attempt to exclude the operation of the Regulations will have no legal effect.

WEBSITE LINKING AGREEMENTS

To date operators of websites have provided links from their own sites to those of third parties with little thought for the legal consequences. Several legal actions in recent months have shown that this carefree attitude to linking is not good business practice. In one case, involving the website of a Scottish newspaper, an e-business was sued for providing a link to a page within the site of the newspaper.

This practice, known as deep linking, was challenged on the basis that it allowed users access to the site without being required to travel via the homepage — it was the homepage on which revenue-generating advertising appeared. In a case by Stepstone, the recruitment site, an injunction was obtained in early 2001 that forced OFiR, a Danish media company, to remove links to Stepstone's site.Recently a view has emerged that a link from one website to another could infringe the database right in the linked-to site.

In any event, it seems that there is an emerging right for e-commerce businesses to control how users experience their sites, and a growing willingness by the courts to recognise such a right.E-commerce businesses should therefore consider, in appropriate circumstances, putting in place a written contract that sets out the obligations of the parties to a linking agreement. The contract should deal with the following issues:

- The link — consideration should be given as to how the link should be constructed, any technical requirements and where on the relevant web page the link should appear.
  If deep linking is to be allowed then the requirements and specifications for this should be set out. The contract should set out those circumstances in which the parties are able to sever the link.
- Intellectual property — even where a copy of part of the site is not made when the link is used (this would raise copyright issues), there may be use of the linked site's trade mark on the link itself. A licence to use all relevant Intellectual Property Rights should appear in the contract.
- Commission — sometimes the motivation for providing a link will be in receiving revenue as a result of users travelling to a third party site via the link.
  The commission arrangements should be clear in their terms — will commission be paid for example merely upon the site visit by a user or must the user first purchase goods from the site?
  There should be appropriate provisions for monitoring traffic such that commission can be verified and charged.
- Data protection — if there is to be a sharing of customer information between the linked sites then it must be clear that each site is to obtain the data

protection consent of its customers for that transfer to be able to take place
- Database right — the contract should make it clear that the links envisaged by the agreement will not constitute infringement of the database right. investment.

This book provides the objectives, drivers, and measures of e-commerce success.

From a perspective that we didn't have a few years ago, we can now analyse why certain approaches to e-commerce were destined to fail. The twelve industry cases provide an opportunity to examine both successes and failures and identify specific lessons learned. The guidelines set out here characterize the most successful actions of established e-commerce leaders, providing pertinent advice to senior managers in all segments, industries, and stages of e-commerce.

The dynamic model centered on these guidelines focuses on the key factors for corporate success in e-commerce integration. It includes the critical inputs and processes that lead to success in e-commerce (outputs), as measured by its contribution to overall corporate profitability (outcome). We see how a company that lacks significant e-commerce operations can become a company that uses e-commerce operations to significantly enhance its profitability.

A company's existing strategy, structure, and systems represent important inputs to the model, leading to processes through which a strong leader can transform all three to achieve e-commerce success. This book is grounded both in the latest academic and managerial research and in extensive research on company activities and experiences.

This book is written for the many large corporations that are reexamining the formulation and the implementation of e-commerce strategies and their level of investment in e-commerce. Its target is the large manufacturing, distribution, and service firms that would like to improve their return on e-commerce investments.

The processes begin with leadership in the formulation and implementation of a successful e-commerce initiative.

Leadership starts with a commitment by the CEO and other senior managers to consider a significant role for e-commerce in the organization. The CEO should initiate a dialogue within the company on the changes necessary for a full-scale e-commerce effort. The CEO, along with other key executives, must examine the emerging role of e-commerce within the company's industry, ascertain its current position with respect to its competitors, and determine an appropriate level of investment.

Next, proven guidelines for e-commerce strategies permit the company to build on its position and quickly increase its online business activities. Though these strategies do represent some different options, successful e-commerce operations will likely incorporate all of them into its activities.

Senior managers must decide how to organize, finance, manage, and provide IT solutions for e-commerce. We encourage a perspective that looks at the various alternatives and generally propose a structure that leads to full integration of e-commerce throughout the fabric of the organization. The company should avoid the temptation of small benefits in one company segment in favor of the larger benefits of total or near-total integration.

Appropriate systems must also be implemented to ensure the successful integration of e-commerce. Corporate culture, performance and operational measures, and compensation systems must all be considered unique challenges. Customer data management and demand and supply chain management are vital to maximizing the value of e-commerce. The introduction of changes to these systems may not have any deleterious effect on traditional commerce, but systems designed for traditional commerce may fail to provide proper management control for e-commerce.

LEADERSHIP

To move forward with e-commerce, the CEO and other senior managers must pursue several initial activities. Leadership comprises words and deeds, explicit and implicit behaviour, control of purse-strings, and leadership by example. Successful e-commerce leadership has four main characteristics, which can be implemented as follows.

- *Commitment at the Top: The CEO and Other Senior Managers Must Embrace E-Commerce.* Implementing an e-commerce plan requires strong leadership at the top of the organization. The CEO and other senior managers must understand the issues surrounding e-commerce well enough to evaluate the organization's strengths and weaknesses and make appropriate decisions on strategy, structure, and systems.

  The CEO must view IT and its applications as a vital component of the company's strategy and publicly demonstrate this belief through words and actions. The CEO must also adopt the attitude that e-commerce is not optional. The company may decide to have a larger or smaller role for e-commerce and may develop that role quickly or slowly, and it may sell directly to customers or limit its major initiative to the back-end systems, but it cannot ignore e-commerce entirely.

  — Commitment at the top
  — Thorough competitive analysis
  — Significant financial investment
  — Cultural transformation

Many CEOs have become e-commerce believers by discussing the topic with more experienced executives at other companies. For example, a conversation with Michael Dell of Dell Computer led Jack Welch at GE to hasten his company's movement into large scale e-commerce activities.

Others, such as Howard Lester at Williams-Sonoma, have been convinced by believers within their own firm through some positive pilot e-commerce projects. In any case, the CEO should begin an earnest dialogue with people who understand e-commerce to learn about its successes and failures in relevant industries.

Other leadership roles are also important. The CIO must be a proactive member of the senior management team who communicates well with the CEO about the usefulness of IT applications. Rather than serving strictly as a technologist, the CIO must also be a strategist. The CIO should serve in a leadership role in cross-functional teams that combine business units, IT, and e-commerce.

The CFO needs to understand the strategic role of IT in the business and consider its ramifications in funding decisions. Other members of the senior management team should have an active role in e-commerce, in a direct advisory role when it relates to specific relevant areas of responsibility and in a support role for other areas of the company. If possible, senior management should include persons who have prior e-commerce experience.

- *Thorough Competitive Analysis: Determine Company's E-Commerce Position.* In crafting an appropriate e-commerce strategy, it is vital for the company first to understand its e-commerce position relative to competitors. At this point, there are few industries where there has not been a first mover in the use of e-commerce. Even in industries where traditional companies have been laggards, pure-play companies have stepped into the void with varying levels of success. In fact, in most industries, a pure-play of some type was the first mover.

This existence of a first-mover competitor does not mean that other companies in an industry cannot gain competitive advantage over their traditional competitors by making significant e-commerce investments and efforts. CEOs who find themselves in an early-mover position should continue to invest and innovate to maintain their advantage. Charles Schwab built a significant advantage over competitor Merrill Lynch, despite having been preceded online by pure-play competitors such as E*Trade.

If a company is a late mover into e-commerce, it can still desire to be the first to provide a particular service, combination of services, or other unique value proposition. Catching up, however, often requires a very high level of investment and a willingness to explore new business models and processes. Regardless of position, a CEO must adopt a broader mode of thinking about competitors because in e-commerce, industry boundaries are more blurred and competition can come from unlikely sources.

- *Significant Financial Investment: Determine Appropriate Role of E-Commerce.* Once the CEO has evaluated the company's e-commerce position relative to other industry members and specific competitors, a decision must be made as to the appropriate role of e-commerce within the company. Given the increased usage of the Internet by leading companies in most industries, the senior managers will typically need to move forward with expanding or at least maintaining the company's current e-commerce position relative to its competitors.

The relevant decisions include whether the company is going to sell online and, if so, how its offerings will compare with its traditional offerings. It should also consider the geographic scope of its e-commerce sales, since the Internet permits unlimited worldwide access, which can introduce a myriad of complications and challenges. The extent to which e-commerce will be utilized in procurement and distribution must also be considered, as well as internal functions such as human resources, accounting, and marketing.

Of primary importance is that the company determine appropriate levels of IT activities and provide for appropriate levels of IT funding. This approach requires taking all necessary steps, including acquisitions or strategic alliances, to ensure that the company's IT capabilities are sufficient for a successful e-commerce venture.

The CEO must then work with other executives to ascertain the amount of investment necessary to fully implement the chosen e-commerce strategy. Investment decisions should be primarily strategic, and returns should be viewed, including the measurement of both short-term and long-term value creation, with a broad view of potential impacts.

- *Cultural Transformation: Determine Implementation Needs.* Since structure and systems can be used to implement strategy, most systems decisions are made after an e-commerce strategy has been formulated. But at an attitudinal level, cultural transformation will usually begin even earlier.

Senior managers have a responsibility to establish a minimum level of IT acceptance and competence throughout the company by demonstrating and communicating commitment and creating appropriate training programs. Some companies will be better prepared for this transition than others; senior managers must carefully consider the required preparation and the implications for implementation speed.

To rapidly implement an e-commerce strategy, IT and e-commerce basics and the purpose of e-commerce must be understood. Communicating purpose is one of the most important actions of a CEO. Employees must realise that e-commerce represents an important challenge and opportunity rather than a threat.

Whether the e-commerce strategy is to be implemented within a month or a year, a sense of urgency is required. The CEO must present e-commerce as having the power to transform the organization in a positive way. Equivocation at every level, from the CFO's hesitation to fund technology to the salesperson's fear that e-commerce will decrease personal commissions, must be avoided. That does not mean reckless risk-taking to move forward, but it does mean a committed acceptance of e-commerce throughout the organization.

STRATEGY

In designing an e-commerce strategy, it is critical to recognize what the Internet changes. Not every value proposition in traditional commerce can attract customers in e-commerce, and not every traditional strategy is a viable source of increased profitability. The best strategies do not ignore the fundamental properties of the Internet and the behaviour of its users.

The organization must develop strategies for e-commerce

operations that are consistent with overall corporate strategy. (Since this is a dynamic model, the order of appearance of these elements may be different. Strategy may precede leadership and resource commitments and structure and systems already in place may constrain the strategy decision.) The goals should include an increase in customer acquisition, enhanced channel optimization, improved customer loyalty and retention, and capturing value for the organization.

- Well-positioned online brand
- Online-friendly offerings
- Reliable customer service
- Cross-channel coordination

Four strategic moves are:

- *Well-Positioned Online Brand: Acquiring Customers and Building Trust.* The simplest way for companies to initiate e-commerce operations is to transfer the brand name to the Internet, using the company's name as the domain name so that existing customers and potential new customers can easily find the company's Web site.

  The company can then advertise the Web site in various physical locations and in all print publicity materials. All letterheads, business cards, other types of business publications, and traditional advertising media should include the Web site address.

  In-store signage, kiosks, advertising on bags, and other materials have also been successful in drawing customers to the online channel. Large online marketing campaigns are likely to produce click-throughs and hits, but not customers, and have typically proved to have poor payoffs.

A brand name will draw customers to the company's site and can help assure customers about the quality of the offerings, the accuracy of the information, and the security of the Web transactions on that site. The brand name can also promote customer loyalty.

The company must continue to provide the level of service and security that the brand name implies, or it will fail to attract repeat online customers and may even damage the traditional brand.

If the company's traditional brand is centered on price competition, it must reevaluate this strategy for e-commerce. Price competition is rarely a viable source of profitability in e-commerce. Search costs for comparing prices are negligible online, and price wars have typically led to prices decreasing to just at or above cost.

The Internet also offers easy access to stores that offer price differentials, because customers do not need to travel any physical distance to get to any given store. Only in limited contexts should companies expect to achieve long-term competitive advantage based on price.

- *Online-Friendly Offerings: Product Selection and Differentiation.* The company must decide what products to offer on the Web site. Companies such as Office Depot have found that they are able to provide more total products to customers through Web sites. Physical store space limits the number of inventory items available in stores, while the Web enables the company to provide a larger product offering.

  Even when integrating their offline and online brand management, a company should not feel compelled to offer precisely the same products online as in its physical stores. The ability to offer a large quantity of products, especially in retail industries, is a major inducement to acquiring an online channel.

Further, it is fully appropriate for a company to eliminate online offerings that are simply unprofitable or otherwise inappropriate. General retailers such as Wal-Mart and grocers have used price minimums, margin requirements, and category restrictions to limit their online offerings. Some companies also require a minimum total purchase on their Web site.

Companies should also consider peripheral offerings in addition to those provided by the company's physical facilities. Such additions are especially appropriate for companies in service industries and companies with large business-to-business (B2B) components. For example, Office Depot's business services offerings are a strong complement to its office supplies business.

Another differentiator is offering customers the ability to obtain unique or uniquely tailored products or information. Customization can be a powerful differentiator because it allows customers to control the product or service choices, and loyalty can be built partly due to high switching costs. Personalization gives customers their very own version of the site that can include information and recommendations based on the customers' prior purchases and demographics.

- *Reliable Customer Service: Inspiring Loyalty among Customers.* Building trust online requires more than a strong brand; it requires strong customer service practices that emphasize the convenience of the online channel. The customer must trust the company and its Web site.

  Trust can be built through assurances of privacy and transaction security and by providing accurate information. Trust in the transaction's completion is built through prompt and accurate fulfillment of orders. Many people purchase at Amazon rather than other Web sites because of its consistently highly rated fulfillment and customer service operations.

Web site design also contributes to satisfying customers. Basic characteristics of the site, such as simplicity, legibility, clarity, and a professional look, are necessities for all Web sites. Strong search engines are especially important for companies with a large number of product offerings. Information about physical stores, customer service, and delivery and return policies should be easily accessible from the home page.

Technology should be a facilitator and not an end in itself, however, and the company should not invest too heavily in design features without being confident of their appeal. Neiman Marcus found that its customers were not interested in viewing luxury products on a high-technology platform. Barnes and Noble discovered that they could not create interest in online parallels to their in-store coffee bars and author visits. The site should also provide a number of services for customers who need information about the site, the offerings, or products they have purchased. These include comprehensive FAQ (frequently asked questions) sections, easily accessible information on delivery and returns, and rapid email response and technical support, where appropriate.

Numerous delivery options should be available to the customer to allow for both speed and low-cost preferences. Companies such as Nordstrom's, which offers products that need to be examined in person before the sale is complete, have provided particularly generous return policies to overcome the hesitation to purchase online inherent in their product line.

Physical stores can also be used for pick-up of items that are needed immediately in industries such as pharmacies. Customers should also be offered convenient opportunities to return defective or unsatisfactory products, including returning such products to the physical stores.

- *Cross-Channel Coordination: Convenience and Revenue Stimulation.* The Web site and physical stores should not be seen as two separate entities that happen to share a brand name. Cross-marketing is an important component, but ultimately, the online and traditional stores must have complementary roles in the overall corporate strategy. Exploiting the advantages of integration means more than drawing customers to the Web site through promotion in the physical store.

Allowing online customers to pick up and return orders to physical stores provides customers with choices and convenience, bringing more traffic to the physical stores. Initially many traditional companies did not allow online customers to return purchased products to their stores. Today, virtually everyone allows customers to return undesired items to physical store locations.

Numerous studies have shown the propensity of customers to make additional purchases when drawn to the store by online-generated functions. Therefore, the Web site should include an easily accessible store locator function that includes a map to the location, a phone number, and store hours. The physical store and online operations can each be used to stimulate sales in the other channel.

Some products that require high levels of interaction with the product can be introduced to the online customer but sold in the physical locations. Kiosks that provide a computerized access to the online site, on the other hand, have been a successful mechanism in physical stores to stimulate online traffic. Many retailers have encouraged the use of kiosks to order online products not available in the physical store or when delivery of the products is more convenient.

Kiosks are also effective in overcoming concerns about online shopping for less computer literate customers. The Web site can also provide more convenience for customers who wish to purchase specific items immediately rather than wait for delivery.

For example, Office Depot can now direct customers to local stores that currently have the product in inventory. Customers need not call all the local stores and tolerate taped messages and long waits to find a product. Even Internet pure-play companies like Amazon, through its alliance with Borders, for which it provides Web site operations, can direct customers to the nearest Borders store that has a desired product. Customers need only provide a zip code.

Integration of physical stores and online operations can also lead to greater efficiencies. Supply chain advantages that lead to more effective purchasing, inventory control, and logistics management may enhance the company's overall cost structure and result in greater profitability.

STRUCTURE

After formulating an e-commerce strategy, senior managers must develop a plan for implementation. The company's organizational structure may at times conflict with the goals of e-commerce, and senior managers must anticipate these conflicts and act accordingly, whether by changing the structure of the traditional organization or by creating new structures specific to e-commerce. These considerations span the areas of financing, management teams, and operations. A final consideration is the use of strategic alliances.

- *Internal Investment: Maintain Full-Equity Interest in E-Commerce.* The company faces a decision about equity for the e-commerce venture, whether to retain complete ownership in the e-commerce venture or to spin it off as an independent company.

  The lessons are clear. Many high-profile failures occurred in traditional companies that tried to imitate the pure-play model by spinning off. Investment in the venture should be made from within the firm, and reliance on outside capital typically seems like an indicator of trepidation about e-commerce on the part of senior management.

Spinning off e-commerce was popular in the early period of e-commerce, and the results have generally been disastrous. Building up large market capitalizations through IPOs was a popular trend, but it has become less desirable in a weaker and more skeptical stock market. The vast majority of these companies, including Wal-Mart, Kmart, Barnes and Noble, and Staples, have bought back the stock from equity partners and folded the e-commerce spin-offs back into the company.

- Internal investment
- Integrated management teams
- IT know-how from within
- Strategic partnerships

The other main justification for spinning off was that the company lacked the experience needed to pursue e-commerce or that additional investment capital was necessary. While it may be true that stand-alone firms sometimes find it easier to quickly develop e-commerce expertise, integrated e-commerce ventures in large organizations can also do this. Since e-commerce capabilities are becoming an increasingly important core competency, companies should develop the expertise and control the e-commerce operation inside the company through a full integration into business units and functions.

- *Integrated Management Teams: Innovate without*

Spinning Off. From the distribution side, e-commerce should often be seen as simply another sales channel and thus changes in the management structure are kept to a minimum. In industries that already have multiple channels such as banks (i.e., physical branches, ATM) and catalog businesses (e.g., Nordstrom), an integrated structure is particularly relevant. With full integration, business functions such as marketing are easy to coordinate and organizational territorial conflicts are reduced.

A less ideal but still viable alternative is to create a separate business unit for e-commerce. Many companies that began with spin-offs and then brought e-commerce back within the company chose to adopt separate strategic business units (SBUs).

Many companies have started their e-commerce operations with entirely separate management teams, often proposed to increase the focus on innovation and e-commerce, under the premise that e-commerce will not be given enough attention or independence by senior management at the parent organization. These management teams have often been established far from company headquarters, have had loose organizational cultures, and have been led by independent leadership often drawn from pure-play or other entrepreneurial companies.

Certainly innovation, flexibility, and creativity are needed to drive a successful e-commerce operation. But we have seen that this can occur successfully within traditional organizational boundaries. A formal set of management control structures and systems is necessary to balance the desired empowerment. When separate business units are established, they should function primarily to coordinate the full integration of e-commerce throughout the business units.

As with other organizational functions, it is sometimes desirable initially to establish a central organization both to drive and to coordinate these new activities. But, as the function matures, it should generally be more fully integrated into the business units. The separate functional units and the integrated functions within the business units may need unique structures and systems including unique performance measures and compensation and reward systems, but this customization of the organizational structure can be accomplished within existing organizational boundaries. There is no need to spin off core capabilities and detach valuable corporate assets.

- *IT Know-How from Within: Building Future Capabilities.* Not every company, especially those late to e-commerce, will have invested well enough in IT to develop e-commerce independently. Many e-commerce companies, even those with strong IT departments, have chosen to outsource e-commerce because of the necessity of speed. Speed is indeed a powerful motivation for outsourcing, but outsourcing should be used to catch up, not to give up.

  Although outsourcing may be used initially to create e-commerce solutions, the company can reassume control over e-commerce and IT and eventually can use the e-commerce systems for traditional commerce as well. Staples followed this approach in attempting to catch its IT-leader rival, Office Depot. Staples invested heavily in IT to build technology close to its core capabilities, but also created a sole-sourcing partnership to avoid delays in more peripheral areas of the business.

Another alternative is to acquire IT capabilities by purchasing a small IT firm and integrating the firm while the e-commerce solution is being implemented. UPS has followed this approach several times in its attempt to hold its IT leadership position over rival Federal Express, and UPS has been able to continually roll out new services while integrating its acquisitions.

Other companies, however, have made the mistake of selling equity to venture capitalists and then relied on these partners for all of their IT needs. Barnes and Noble made this mistake and then was hamstrung further when Amazon sued them for a patent violation related to their Web platform.

Borders and Toys 'R' Us have taken the dramatic approach of having a competitor, Amazon, run their Web site for them. Companies must learn from these mistakes and not place themselves in such a precarious position with respect to IT.

- *Strategic Alliances: Moving beyond Core Competencies.* Although companies are advised to maintain equity interest, management control, and IT integration, traditional businesses can benefit from alliances with online companies in other ways. These relationships are most beneficial when the arrangement gives the traditional company access to supply-chain management, peripheral offerings, and customer bases.

Supply-chain management is a particularly useful area for partnership when the company cannot simply supply online customers from the same distribution channels as physical stores. Wal-Mart, Kmart, and Target have all made such arrangements to deal with their general merchandising businesses. CVS also simplified its procurement process for its Web site by entering into a partnership with Merck.com.

To provide peripheral offerings that will be available only online, alliances have also proven to be a successful approach. Neiman Marcus partnered with several luxury retailers to create a limited-scope "luxury portal" of high-end goods within its Web site. CVS partnered with WebMD to provide medical advice to complement pharmacy services.

Finally, traditional companies can gain access to large online customer bases by making strategic alliances with portal and ISP companies. Wal-Mart and Kmart entered agreements with AOL and Yahoo respectively to co-brand Internet service packages that would bring their customers online and to their site in particular.

Traditional companies may also profit from providing a physical presence to online companies that are realizing the inevitable trend toward integrated channels. Target has agreed to house E*Trade kiosks and customer representatives in its stores, in what has been a beneficial relationship for both parties. For E*Trade, the Target deal was just one aspect of a bricks-and-clicks strategy that culminated with the building of a New York super-centre.

SYSTEMS

Senior managers must finally ensure that organizational processes are capable of implementing the e-commerce strategy. Information practices, human resources, performance measures, and customer management are all areas in which traditional systems may require adaptation to implement an e-commerce strategy.

- *Modernized Internal Processes: Using Information Effectively.* The cultural transformation described earlier may be enough to make e-commerce possible, but more must be done to maximize its benefits. Information practices must be adapted to promote transparency and availability. Changes must ensure that information flows freely throughout the company and is not hampered by artificial organizational boundaries or personal ambitions.
  - Modernized internal processes
  - Incentive-laden HR practices
  - Aligned performance measures
  - Improved customer management

In addition to information sharing, the decision-making processes of the company should be reconsidered. Cross-functional teams and remotely located teams should be assembled with greater frequency, with less emphasis on hierarchical reporting. Decision makers should also have greater self-governance and flexibility.

An important internal process is value chain management. Every company should identify ways to leverage the Internet in each part of the value chain, from procurement to distribution to delivery. In fact, failure to adopt e-commerce-specific cost savings will likely put a company at a serious competitive disadvantage.

Strong supply chain management is often the basis for providing superior service. In the area of procurement, a company can reduce the cost of goods sold by obtaining products through the Internet. Distribution strategies must not only cut costs but also provide the fastest and most convenient customer service. Delivery strategies should maximize convenience and speed for customers, using both the Internet and the company's existing infrastructure to provide these benefits. The best supply-chain practices, however, depend on the type of offering.

- *Incentive-Laden HR Practices: Bringing Your People on Board.* Compensation systems must be aligned with strategy and structure for the e-commerce venture to be a success. The CIO must be compensated as a member of the senior management team to signal the importance and respect shown for the IT function and the centrality and commitment to improved IT and e-commerce.

  At lower organizational levels, compensation systems have additional consequences on alignment. By compensating e-commerce managers the same as managers in traditional commerce, the company sometimes fails to create the necessary incentives for e-commerce success. Though parallel compensation systems can often work, both market forces and the need for speed, creativity, flexibility, innovation, and extra diligence often requires additional incentives and rewards.

Differential compensation, often through stock options, can create an incentive to cannibalize from the company's traditional channels. Such practices can cause conflicts with traditional business units but are often necessary to optimize the use of each channel, especially during the formative years of the e-commerce initiative.

Typically, e-commerce compensation should be tied to the overall success of the venture rather than rewarding individual units or channels for performance. This is particularly relevant when the company is seeking full integration, because it helps ensure cooperation and seamlessness between departments.

The Internet also provides opportunities to improve the hiring process. Cisco is just one company that has found great benefits from hiring online, including lowered costs, faster filling of positions, and higher competence. Companies may also want to consider specialized HR practices for their IT departments.

- *Aligned Performance Measures: Planning for the Long-Term.* Strong measurement practices are among the cornerstones of all good systems. Performance measures for e-commerce must overcome the uncertainty and unique dynamics associated with the Internet, and they may be more frequently adjusted in response to real-time information.

  With these considerations, it is clear that no company should simply extend its existing performance measures to the e-commerce venture without extensive customization.

  Still, long-term cost differentials, balanced with a variety of financial, nonfinancial, and leading and lagging indicators, are particularly useful for successful e-commerce implementations.

Some skeptical companies have made unreasonable demands with respect to e-commerce performance. Because they misconceived e-commerce risks and rewards, they had unrealistic expectations of immediate growth and ROI that would not be demanded of any traditional long-term investment. Worse yet, they tied further investment to achievement of these goals, dooming e-commerce before it even could get off the ground.

In most companies, new projects and ventures require short-term ROI, and revenue projections, many of which an e-commerce venture and its related projects may not meet. If the company decides to enter or expand e-commerce, it cannot hamstring the venture by insisting on such short-term requirements throughout.

E-commerce has also led many companies to create performance measures other than revenue, ROI, and traditional financial indicators. Some of the new, poorly designed performance measures have had a disastrous effect on strategy implementation. For example, indiscriminate customer acquisition and attempting to maximize revenue through online advertising often have negative implications for long-term profitability. Single-purchase customers and advertising revenue independent of the company's value proposition are not sustainable strategies.

Worse still are nonfinancial measures such as Web page hits and registered users, which may not even be tied to a short-term revenue stream. In addition to measuring the performance of the business, e-commerce brings added importance to measuring the value and functionality of operations. Most e-commerce strategies will have a strong operational component, including cost savings from value chain management and cuts in labour costs for the online channel. Operational measures should be tracked by some dedicated resource and balanced between financial and nonfinancial assessments of operational performance.

Moreover, companies must create a value capture process to evaluate the success of IT projects associated with the e-commerce venture. Looking at nonfinancial performance measures, the value capture process can help convince skeptical employees of the importance of IT. Even with the value capture process, however, the full benefits of IT investment are often underestimated.

- *Improved Customer Management: Better Service and Better Data.* Companies must also reconsider the internal processes required to provide the high levels of customer service necessary in e-commerce. Online customers need access to some level of customer service at all times. There is a trade-off between service that entails a high level of human input and service that is automated and more cost-efficient. Finding the proper balance is a function of the company's offerings, its customer base, and customer feedback.

Customer data is a significant benefit in e-commerce, because of the vast amount that can be learned about customers during a Web site visit in contrast to an in-store visit. Many Web sites, however, have mistakenly focused only on counting hits and visits, while ignoring the more valuable information that can be gathered. Tracking of customers' interaction with the Web site can be used to identify customers' price sensitivity and information preferences and to gauge satisfaction with the Web site design and accessibility.

Gathering and using customer information is important to refine the value proposition and better allocate internal resources. Marketing strategies for the Web site can also be continually refined, using real-time information gathered from customers during their visits, a practice that Staples has used well.

CHARACTERISTICS OF E-COMMERCE SUCCESS

These guidelines provide a general outline of our prescriptions for an e-commerce venture.

Characteristics of Successful E-Commerce Implementations

LEADERSHIP	STRATEGY
1. Commitment at the top	1. Well-positioned online brand
2. Thorough competitive analysis	2. Online-friendly offerings
3. Significant financial investment	3. Reliable customer service
4. Cultural transformation	4. Cross-channel coordination
STRUCTURE	**SYSTEMS**
1. Internal investment	1. Modernized internal processes
2. Integrated management teams	2. Incentive-laden HR practices
3. IT know-how from within	3. Aligned performance measures
4. Strategic partnerships	4. Improved customer management

A more in-depth discussion of the model, dedicating one chapter to each of its components. Implications of these guidelines in retail service, and manufacturing industries, and the relationship between these guidelines and prominent cases of e-com-merce success and failure.

This book summarizes what has been learned from e-commerce implementation. As with most new technologies and most new business models, the experimentation leaves some companies in strong competitive positions and others in bankruptcy.

E-commerce has been no different. Only now can we try to analyse the recent attempts at success and summarize those characteristics that seem to work. It relies on well-accepted principles of successful business practice.

But, many of the early entries in e-commerce ignored those principles. The development of e-commerce in the traditional literature and practices of leadership, strategy, structure, and systems and summarized the characteristics of success.

CORPORATE AND FUNCTIONAL E-COMMERCE LEADERSHIP

Success in e-commerce has become almost synonymous with the names of a few CEOs and leaders of successful companies, such as Michael Dell, Jack Welch, and Jeff Bezos. In the absence of clear guidance on e-commerce strategy and implementation, a cult of personality has developed in popular press discussions of e-commerce.

Without a clearly defined approach and methodology for the formulation and implementation of an e-commerce strategy, this kind of leadership-worship was the closest anyone could come to defining what actually led to e-commerce success for these companies.

Now, we have the opportunity to step back and appreciate the full range of critical factors that contributed to early cases of e-commerce success. Leadership is one factor, but leadership shouldn't be any more or less important in e-commerce than in any other aspect of business strategy.

Still, it makes sense to discuss leadership as a precursor to formulating strategy and designing structure and systems.

The special conditions associated with e-commerce make the discussion of leadership excellence especially critical. The individual roles of the CEO, CIO, and CFO concern more than an organization chart or delegation of responsibilities. In e-commerce, the coordination between these leaders becomes as important as their actions. Failure to achieve this coordination will undermine any hope for corporate e-commerce integration.

We can identify the aspects of leadership that are applicable to all businesses wishing to implement an e-commerce strategy. Leadership occupies the first link between the inputs of the traditional business and the subsequent process elements of e-commerce strategy, structure, and systems. Placing it here emphasizes the role that leadership plays in moving from traditional strategy, structure, and systems to those in e-commerce.

Leadership is about both people and actions. Each of the major leadership roles in a company—including the CEO, the CIO, and the CFO—requires a person with a positive, reasoned approach toward e-commerce.

Just as the CFO should not trivialize the importance of IT, neither should the CIO exaggerate the role of technology over strategy. These leadership roles require technical competence related to the business operations, IT, and e-commerce, as well as a positive attitude. Knowledge and experience in the uses of technologies and an understanding of the implications of the use of technology in specific business operations are necessary for e-commerce leadership positions.

Some major assessments must be made by the company's leaders before they can consider the formulation and implementation of an e-commerce strategy. An assessment of competitive position is often particularly challenging in a dynamic e-commerce environment.

Strong traditional competitors may be currently irrelevant if their e-commerce strategy is undeveloped, but that can change quickly. Weaker traditional competitors may be able to use e-commerce as a catalyst to make the gains they couldn't make in traditional brick-and-mortar business. Pure-play Internet companies may already have established themselves in the industry or may be in the process of moving into the industry. Disruptions in the marketplace can cause additional challenges.

Thus, to assess the proper role for e-commerce, leaders must evaluate the nature of the company's offerings, traditional strategy and business models, and the geographic scope of the company.

Though current capabilities may be limited, opportunities for growth in revenue and reductions in cost must be assessed. With the data, leaders can then properly evaluate the appropriate levels of investment and potential returns. Leadership requires some initial steps to prepare the organization for a transition to e-commerce.

Some changes are of such importance that they must be addressed early in the evaluation of e-commerce strategy formulation and execution, especially discussing basic e-commerce functionality and communicating the potential impact of e-commerce on company operations.

First Stage E-commerce Leadership Requirements

Senior corporate leaders must complete the following first stage e-commerce leadership requirements:

- Assessment of the company's e-commerce competitive position
- Assessment and communication of the value of e-commerce to corporate, business unit, and functional operations and necessary technical and integration issues
- Creation of a company culture conducive to the introduction of e-commerce

The following sections highlight each of these aspects of e-commerce leadership with stories of companies that took the first step toward success or failure before the first strategy was ever formulated.

Other discussions and company cases illustrate how leadership impacted the e-commerce successes and features.

LEADERSHIP ROLES

The CEO

In the late 1990s, spin-offs were a popular strategy for e-commerce ventures. Leadership consisted of finding someone, often from outside the company, who would lead the e-commerce venture. Leaders for these ventures were frequently selected because their resumes included technology experience, often without considering their understanding of the business or its environment. The CEO of the brick-and-mortar company, on the other hand, was regarded only as a sponsor, with little involvement expected.

We now know that the appropriate role for the CEO undertaking an e-commerce venture is a highly proactive one with a strong level of commitment and a vision of e-commerce within the company. Instead of delegating the responsibilities of e-commerce to an outside "expert, " leaders must take the steps to transform the company into one that can utilize and profit from e-commerce. These e-commerce transformations are part of an ongoing process that is certainly not complete when a company successfully establishes an e-commerce foothold.

Cisco CEO John Chambers has kept Cisco at or near the top of the market through considerable market fluctuations and changes in the nature of e-commerce, through his willingness to change Cisco according to the demands of the market. Similarly, Amazon CEO Jeff Bezos has consistently altered prices on books and other products to meet competitive challenges. He also began strategic alliances with other merchants such as Target and Toys 'R' Us to better serve Amazon customers and improve profitability. This flexibility is one important key to success in the ever-changing world of e-commerce. Monitoring company and industry changes, along with the constant technological improvements in e-commerce, are critical leadership issues.

CEOs do not need to become technology experts. Instead, CEOs need a basic understanding of how e-commerce works and, more important, how it affects current and potential business models and processes.

This knowledge can be easily obtained through interaction with the CIO and senior IT personnel or by interaction with e-commerce savvy leaders at other companies. At Merrill Lynch, the impetus for e-commerce came from the CIO, who convinced a skeptical CEO of the merits of an e-commerce venture through persistent discussions of technology and strategy.

The CEO must also be convinced of the specific potential benefits of e-commerce to the company and begin to take action for the implementation, demonstrating commitment in both communications and actions.

For a successful transformation, the CEO must express the appropriate attitude, personal commitment to e-commerce, and understanding of the technical issues to make it clear that the CEO is not ceding leadership to the IT specialists. E-Bay CEO Meg Whitman is credited with transforming e-Bay from an "online flea market" to a "virtual, self-regulating global economy."

Leadership is also demonstrated through the commitment of financial resources, including adequate funding for the IT department and the modernization of the company's information systems. E-commerce and IT should be seen as value creators rather than cost centers. The CEO must be also committed to a leadership role in IT planning, facilitating communication between IT and business units and challenging the IT department to maximize business functionality.

The CEO must also emphasize a long-term commitment and ensure that the other senior corporate and business unit leaders are also fully committed to e-commerce. The role requires collaboration of the CIO, CFO, and business unit leaders and a vision for the entire organization. The role of coordination, communication, and motivation with business unit leaders is critical.

The business units ultimately have the major

responsibility for execution, as it is the business unit leaders who find opportunities for e-commerce value creation. The CEO must take the lead in driving the integration process.

The CIO

The rise of e-commerce has brought far more attention to the role of the CIO as an integral part of the senior management team. Companies that have previously treated their CIO as a technologist face the largest changes as they prepare for e-commerce. For e-commerce to be fully integrated, the CIO's place in the organizational structure must report directly to the CEO or COO.

Without direct access to the CEO, the CIO plays a lesser role in influencing strategy, which may push IT and e-commerce into the position of a cost centre. Such factors contribute to the finding that CIO tenure is quite short, compared to that of CFOs.

Even in companies whose CIOs already play an important role in senior management, CEOs should continuously work to increase coordination and interaction between the CIO and other key members of senior management, to increase the visibility of e-commerce initiatives.

The CIO should provide both information and analysis and should have a relationship with the CEO that empowers the CIO to challenge both strategic direction and technology usage. Merrill Lynch faced a severe loss in margins as Schwab began to pass Merrill in market value in late 1998 and 1999. It wasn't until then-CIO John

McKinley convinced his CEO to fully embrace online trading while using the company's IT budget to develop its Web site that the company was able to reestablish itself after being a late mover in e-commerce. When Mattel Inc.'s Joe Eckroth took over as CIO, he immediately transferred toy design online to allow virtual models to be zipped electronically to all of the company's factories, cutting development time by 20 percent.

In addition, Eckroth installed Mattel's $2 billion licensing programme online to automate and expedite the licensing approval process and significantly increase profitability.

To improve the decision-making process in organizations as well as to obtain increased resources for e-commerce, the CIO needs to provide more complete measurements and analysis of the benefits and costs of the business impacts of IT and e-commerce investments. It is important that potential projects are analyzed in a strategic context, and the financial payoffs are clear. More generally, the CIO has a large stake not only in directing business change but also in taking on the role of educator for the CEO and CFO.

While senior business leadership should still undergo specialized training to gain a basic understanding of the technologies associated with e-commerce and IT, the CIO should be capable of explaining the business implications of technology to internal and external partners so that the company makes sound business decisions based upon adequate knowledge.

As with the CEO, it is not necessary that the CIO have a specific resume or previous experience in e-commerce. Certainly an understanding of the technology side of e-commerce is necessary. The most important skills for a CIO include the ability to complete an accurate technology risk assessment, to objectively gauge strategic benefits of technology, and to manage the complications of both the technical and the human sides of an e-commerce implementation.

The nontechnical components of an e-commerce implementation are far more challenging than the technical ones. The CIO must have an integrated view of the business and be able to communicate that view to the senior corporate managers, the business unit leaders, functional staff, and many others both inside and outside the company.

The CFO

Many studies have shown high levels of conflict between CFOs and CIOs, and e-commerce is purported only to increase that conflict. The long-term and nonspecific benefits of IT projects, especially those relating to e-commerce, are often seen as anathema to the strict measurement standards of the archetypal CFO.

That conflict, however, arises from a misunderstanding of the proper roles of each position and often from a lack of rigorous analysis. For e-commerce to be successful, the CFO must be more sensitive to the challenges of IT and e-commerce, and the CIO must complete more comprehensive financial analysis of e-commerce projects to better articulate the likely costs and benefits.

A formalized approach to understanding and measuring the payoffs of e-commerce activities. The analysis of the causal relationships between e-commerce investments and financial payoffs provides a new basis for discussion between CIOs, CFOs, and CEOs. It also permits e-commerce to fit more effectively into the traditional resource allocation decisions made in the CFO's office.

When the CIO's reporting responsibility is to the CFO, the wrong message is communicated to every aspect of the business, from investors, to employees, to customers, especially in an e-commerce context. The CFO must recognize IT's strategic role and its vital role in bringing about business process changes. The CFO must also take the lead in helping the CIO with the methodology, of measuring the payoffs of e-commerce investments. It is only in this way that IT and e-commerce are seen as value creators and can compete effectively for resources within the company.

The CFO need not have the same content knowledge of IT as the CIO, or even the CEO. A modicum of technology understanding, however, is likely to strengthen the CFO's relationship with the CIO and can lead to better-coordinated analysis of project benefits. Alignment is likely to be strongest when the two leaders can move beyond their specific domains and focus on the strategic context. This united front usually also improves the coordination with business unit leaders and improves decision making. For e-commerce to be successful, business leadership must be able and willing to expand their essential functions within the company.

While old responsibilities are not to be neglected because of the addition of e-commerce, the new demands of e-commerce are of such importance that senior leaders must assume additional expertise and responsibilities.

DETERMINING COMPETITIVE POSITION

There is little consensus on the importance of timing in e-commerce. Traditional perspectives on first-mover advantage were popular at first, but proved to be an unreliable predictor of success. Companies that consciously employed a "follower" strategy had equally mixed results. Few companies have, at this point, a legitimate opportunity to be the first mover in any broad sector. If a company is not yet online, it is a near certainty that some competitor, broadly defined, is.

This fact makes it critically important that a company complete a rigorous analysis of its competitive position before designing an e-commerce strategy. The first consideration is whether any significant pure-play Internet company is an established leader or strong presence in the industry, or in related industries.

Pure-play competitors may be more vulnerable to a strategy that exploits the company's physical, intellectual, or financial resources. In that sense, being the first mover among traditional companies can still provide an advantage, even if a company is not the first overall mover.

However, it is important to note that many pure-plays have realized the advantages of traditional business and have acted to preempt that advantage among their more traditional competitors. The two main ways of doing that have been to build a physical presence or to partner with a company that can provide one. E*Trade has simultaneously pursued both strategies, building a giant E*Trade centre in New York and introducing kiosks in Target stores. Of course, any pure-play capable of this type of investment is likely to be a difficult adversary anyway.

If the company also lags behind its traditional peers in e-commerce, the situation is somewhat more difficult. While being second, or even later, gives a company the opportunity to learn from competitors' mistakes, the disadvantages are far greater. In the early days of e-commerce, mistakes were rampant enough to neutralize the disadvantage of not being first. Now, companies who are laggards must be especially creative with their business models to overcome this disadvantage.

Perhaps the most understated consideration is the fluidity of the term "competitor" in e-commerce. To make a thorough analysis of one's competitive position, one must examine companies from many other industries, both pure-play and traditional, that have used e-commerce as a way to expand into one's own industry. A CEO must recognize both general and industry-specific trends in e-commerce well enough to predict potential competitors.

The need for cross-industry information regarding e-commerce is due largely to the blurring of industry lines that is facilitated by e-commerce and is evidenced by companies such as Amazon. The list of businesses that can consider Amazon a competitor is now almost endless. Not only does Amazon now have partnerships with many specialty retailers, but its range of offerings is so wide that many have referred to it as the "Wal-Mart of e-commerce." Any company in a retailing business would be compelled to consider Amazon a potential competitor.

This blurring of industry lines should be expected. E-commerce encourages such expansion because of the potential for supply chain improvements and the economies of scale associated with product heterogeneity. In particular, the phenomenon of offering related business services is an avenue for cross-industry expansion. Office Depot's foray into small business services and Bank of America's home financing and improvement services are just two examples.

Expansions into e-commerce come from many directions. Sometimes initially motivated by cost reductions and sometimes by revenue imperatives, the cost of entry into broader e-commerce utilization is often small and brings new challenges to both traditional and pure-play Internet companies.

For some local companies or certain industries, competition may not be a traditional primary concern. Although such instances are rare and confined mostly to small businesses, some businesses have geographic restrictions that limit the customer base. The grocery business has been a prime example. Nearly every company that has experimented in grocery delivery online has initially restricted delivery to a small radius, from either the physical store or the warehouse.

The reasons are numerous. Perishable items obviously require short delivery times and distances, and low-margin items cannot justify large shipping costs. The small delivery radius has shifted from an experimental position to an industry standard. Even companies such as Tesco, which have greatly expanded their online operations, have done so by increasing the number of physical stores from which to make deliveries. As a result, competition has been somewhat minimal among grocers.

Grocery chains, especially in the United States, vary greatly by region. Very few chains are national enough even to justify the strategy followed by Tesco.For most companies, however, competitor analysis is an essential input for determining the appropriate e-commerce strategy. Such analysis, along with the CEO's leadership in forecasting e-commerce trends and technology and changes in business opportunities, is vital to properly gauging that position.

TRADITIONAL FIRMS BEGINNING AN E-COMMERCE VENTURE

Among the competitive concerns that brick-and-mortar companies must consider are:

- Pure-play e-commerce competitors
- Traditional competitors that have already moved into e-commerce
- Outside companies using e-commerce to establish a foothold in a new industry
- The limitations, geographic and otherwise, of these competitors

These factors are all part of a broad, comprehensive

analysis of both competitive positioning and customer needs. The list of potential competitors is endless. They include both the traditional brick-and-mortar companies and the new pure-play Internet companies. The analysis requires an evaluation of both the current landscape and the future customer needs and how they are likely to be served. Cannibalization and disruptions in the marketplace are likely to continue. It is critical that leaders continually monitor developments within and outside their industry for these developments.

DETERMINING E-COMMERCE ROLE AND INVESTMENT

Understanding competitive position is necessary but not sufficient to formulate the e-commerce strategy. Companies must also determine the appropriate role for e-commerce inside the company and the level of investment to be made. Thus, the external positioning must be supplemented with an internal analysis of company fit.

The fit may be related to items such as organization structure, product type and mix, customer type and mix, channels, geographical breadth, and financial resources. Thus, every company utilizes e-commerce by directly selling goods or services on the Internet. Some find profitability in supply-chain management, procurement, marketing, and providing general information online.

That decision may become obvious before any significant strategic planning or may be determined after a fuller examination of the facts. But, a full examination of the broad opportunities must be completed and becomes an important input to the investment decision.Among the most important issues is the amount of resources to be committed to e-commerce. As companies examine reports of competitor investments, companies often question whether the size of their commitment is adequate.

Though the late 1990s saw some reckless spending on e-commerce without any justification of an ultimate payoff, current approaches to e-commerce require a carefully determined return on investment, as determined by a methodology. But, the investment must follow a serious commitment to an e-commerce strategy and should not waver with modest changes in either the technology or the business environment.For companies selling online, the geographic scope of sales efforts is also a consideration.

Selling overseas creates numerous challenges, many of which are known to traditional business but are complicated further by e-commerce. Demographics of Internet users, online payment mechanisms, online marketing, and patterns of online buyer behaviour all vary greatly by country and may present too many permutations for a nascent

Internet venture to handle.A company may be understandably hesitant to begin global e-commerce immediately, even if its traditional business contains a global component. Some companies have chosen to limit the geographic scope of the venture until it has proven feasible and profitable on a domestic scale. The wisdom of such a limitation has been shown clearly in the case of grocery stores such as Tesco.Among the geographic considerations for an e-commerce venture are:

- A Web site can be viewed from anywhere around the world. Companies should be equipped to handle such a change in market size, or be prepared to explain the reasons for necessary geographic limitations.
- Product type is a key factor in any geographic consideration. Customers have far different expectations when using the Internet to order computers than when ordering groceries.

PREPARING IMPLEMENTATION AND ALIGNING COMPANY CULTURE

Most laggard companies do not have the luxury of delaying the implementation of e-commerce until the company culture is sufficiently prepared. Instead, company leaders must constantly reinforce the importance of IT in order to build the appropriate culture for e-commerce. As their personal behaviour and attitudes often send the strongest messages, private behaviour must not undermine or contradict public statements about company commitment to e-commerce ventures. Senior managers must reinforce the message that while technology itself is not a strategy, it remains a tool with strategic implications, and that the introduction of technology does not change the role of every contributor to the success of the company. Leadership must also choose the proper motivational tools, including incentives, coaching, and creating stretch targets.

For an e-commerce venture to be successful in a traditional company, senior managers must also impart a number of clear messages on company strategy and its value proposition. Instead of trying to create a unique culture for units handling the e-commerce venture, the company must create a culture conducive to integrating e-commerce throughout the company. Attitudes of either "the Internet changes everything" or "the Internet changes nothing" should be avoided, and a much more moderate position endorsed. Employees should not feel threatened or overwhelmed by the introduction of e-commerce.

The purpose of the e-commerce venture must also be carefully outlined to all employees, with a focus on the benefits of integration and the notion that e-commerce is typically a new channel for business, not a new business. People in each business unit must be apprised of the way e-commerce interacts with their current work and how best to develop that relationship to maximize integration benefits. At GE, this was achieved in the form of a company-wide initiative called Destroy Your Business, which required business units to analyse the impact and potential pitfalls of e-commerce on their business. Its associated programme, Grow Your Business, required units to formulate solutions to each of these problems.

Belief in the value of IT must be instilled throughout the organization, and resistance to IT generally, and to e-commerce specifically, must be handled through education that emphasizes the functionality of these endeavors and their importance to long-term corporate success. Training programs must ensure that everyone, especially those employees who directly interact with customers, understands basic e-commerce concepts. Senior management is not immune to these requirements and must lead by example in this area with both public statements and behaviour.

Finally, a sense of urgency must be created throughout the organization, and business decisions should reflect that urgency. The pace of e-commerce is faster than that of traditional commerce, and easing into an e-commerce venture is not a promising strategy. In all areas that impact e-commerce, aggressiveness should be rewarded, and the value of speed should often supplant cost considerations.

Many of these considerations must be addressed by specific changes in the company's systems and business processes, but the CEO should be prepared to create this orientation long before strategy implementation begins. Without strong leadership in the early stages, the changes in systems will be too drastic to implement the e-commerce strategy in a timely manner. Thus, to create a proper culture for e-commerce, companies must recognize that:

- Attitudes are as important as company policies regarding e-commerce. Company leaders must not only work to make an e-commerce venture a success, but show that they actually believe in the venture.
- E-commerce should be treated as a new channel for business, not as a revolution for the company. Employees need to be encouraged to embrace e-commerce instead of fearing it.
- The goals of the e-commerce venture need to be clearly outlined for everyone in the company.
- Aggressiveness in e-commerce should be rewarded.

E-commerce represents a major transformation, and the general principles of organizational change management are as applicable as advice specific to e-commerce. John Kotter's organizational change model provided a general framework for the consideration of how to approach significant change in business. As one can see, it can be easily adapted to the challenge of the changes necessary in the implementation of an e-commerce strategy.

Chapter 2

E-Commerce Technology

THE MOBILE INTERNET

The growth of the mobile Internet now exceeds that of the PC version. Mobile communications offer considerable potential to marketers because of their unrivalled combination of:

- Instant response;
- Personalized content (as each customer has a unique telephone number);
- Scope for geographical location tracking.

The potential for mobile networks is particularly high in developing countries that do not have an established wired telephone network and hence no established PC-based Internet services. In the Philippines, for example, SMS messaging has recently taken off rapidly, and mobile Internet services therefore offer huge marketing opportunities in these emerging markets.There has been a lot of hype recently about the potential of location-based technology in particular. However, current services are very basic, and it is important to remember that there is some way to go before they become sufficiently reliable and useful to have a broad appeal.

For example, variations on the scenario whereby a customer is called on their phone and advised of a special breakfast offer just as they walk to work past a Starbucks outlet, have been heralded as the ultimate in personalized promotional campaigns. There are a number of practical difficulties, though, such as customers' reluctance to be bombarded with intrusive advertising messages and the challenge of communicating effectively with the wide range of mobile devices and standards currently in use.The usefulness of wireless devices has recently been improved by new standards such as Jini and Bluetooth that connect wireless devices to other electronic products:

- Jini (www.jini.com) allows mobile phones, PCs and personal digital assistants (PDAs) to collaborate as part of an intelligent network, without the need for the correct device driver to be added to the operating system before a new device can be used.
- Bluetooth (www.bluetooth.com) is particularly useful for linking mobile devices because it does not require any wire connections. For example, it could allow a user on a mobile in a car to transfer data from an office PC directly to a home printer.

Keynote systems (www.keynote.com) recently launched a mobile performance measurement service to compare the services offered by all the major UK networks. It can measure delivery times, network comparisons, handset performance and geographic availability, thereby allowing content providers, networks or manufacturers to judge how successful their services have been. It also allows consumers to benchmark performance and make informed purchase decisions. In addition, for a detailed comparison of the characteristics of different mobile technologies, see Smith and Chaffey.

Mobile phones are now rapidly evolving and becoming 'pocket portals' that provide a range of personalized services including email and text messaging with just one monthly bill. Before discussing some of the recent and pending innovations in this area, we shall review developments over the past two or three years.The first mobiles to offer Internet access, using Wireless Application Protocol (WAP), were introduced in 1999. The information displayed had to be especially formatted for a small screen area, and the limited functionality fell well short of the often extreme levels of industry hype.

The telecommunications industry broke one of the central rules of marketing, which states that promotional campaigns should 'under-promise' and 'over-deliver' rather than the other way round. Users found that navigating between pages on a mobile phone could be an extremely laborious process, for which they were paying by the minute for connection charges. During 2000, many early users abandoned mobile commerce after disappointing experiences.

While mobile commerce is useful for 'distress' purchases such as parking, actually browsing the Web on a mobile phone is hardly a straightforward and stress-free experience. However, there have been successes to date, notably with mobile banking and gambling services.'Second-generation' mobile phones introduced early in 2001 offer faster connection speeds and are starting to carry advertising. High response rates are currently enjoyed by advertisers, and the most successful campaigns have been run by companies such as the *Sun* newspaper, which has used the mobile channel to advertise competitions being run in the paper itself.

In other words, the *Sun* is using online advertising to drive its traditional core business - which is offline newspaper sales. Mobile advertising still represents a very small percentage of company promotional spend in comparison with more traditional media such as radio and television, but the figure is increasing. Business services via mobile channels are currently few and far between, but early experiments are under way with order placing, stock-checking availability and order tracking to facilitate supply chain integration.

The much-hyped but still awaited third generation of mobile communications (3G) is expected to deliver sound and images and be 'always on'. Auctions held in 2000 for the licences to operate 3G services netted the UK government over £20 billion, but since then the share prices of the 'successful' telecommunication firms that purchased them have been severely dented.

The technology competing with WAP is called Short Message Systems (SMS), and it is currently by far the more successful in terms of user numbers. SMS is a derivative of numeric paging technology, which has been in existence for many years, updated for two-way communication. To illustrate the rapid growth of SMS, consider the following figures:

- In 1998, mobile phones had a 20 per cent market penetration in the UK and some *1 million* text messages were sent.

As with the growth of the PC-based Internet, it seems that communications with staff and customers are currently adding most value at this early stage, while the widespread acceptance of mobile transactions is still some way away. One must also bear in mind that not all these applications will be relevant to all companies all the time, and in most cases they will complement rather than replace existing channels.

The key skill for marketers is to focus on the particular aspects of mobile marketing that will add value to customers in their specific industry contexts. We will now examine each of these areas in turn, drawing upon a number of examples to illustrate this important point.

CONTENT PROVISION AND ADVERTISING

Mobile advertising is expected to grow exponentially following a slow start in the difficult economic conditions of 2000-1. The long-anticipated 3G technology will offer far more scope for creative advertising than the small black and white text-only screens that have dominated the market until recently. It seems to be commonly accepted that busy professional people do not want their important business interrupted by marketing messages on their mobile phones.

However, we all at least tolerate advertisements while watching movies ... so firms that specialize in placing advertisements on mobile firms are at the moment focusing their advertisement placement on mobile entertainment services rather than on business ones. Placing adverts in mobile games that users are playing when they have time to spare is likely to be more acceptable than if a user is interrupted while trying to link up remotely to a company for business purposes.

In exchange for the entertainment value in the game, it is reasonable to expect that the customer will tolerate (and, companies of course will hope, respond to) the advertising message. For example, Stone reports that Mobliss, a US-based wireless marketing agency, worked with Tribune Media in turning its 'Jumble' brand (a scrambled-word game) into a multi-player wireless game.

It was also an effective advertising tool because the words used in the puzzles could be directly related to the advertiser's company or product. The advertisements can be displayed as either graphical images or text and themed to correlate with the creative campaign that the advertiser is running offline. In either case, with mobile Internet access, customers also have the ability to click a button and be connected directly to the advertiser's call centre.

Mobliss has also launched a snow report system at www.mysnowreport.com where customers can go online and build in their preferences for particular resorts. Then a text message detailing snow conditions can be sent to the customer's phone.

By forming partnerships with companies like the travel agency Moguls that are trying to reach the skier demographic (high income, high expenditure), a customer is able to check out the snow conditions at a resort, and then follow an advertiser's link that is offering a discounted package trip to that resort.

Then another link will connect the customer to the call centre to speak to a ski-travel agent. In these circumstances, the customer is more likely to perceive the advertisement as a benefit rather than as just a nuisance.

Targeting is very effective because if a user is enquiring about snow conditions, then almost by definition they are themselves a skier. In addition, the fact that the overwhelming majority of people currently using mobile Web services are males aged 20-39 with incomes over £30,000 is of course very appealing to advertisers.

Traditional magazines have been experiencing a fall in advertising revenues over the past couple of years due to the global economic slowdown. The ability to offer interactivity through SMS can make a publication more appealing to companies seeking to place advertisements, while at the same time winning new readers for the magazine itself.

So, for example, a company seeking to run a mobile advertising campaign to promote its brand could:

- First, rent a database of readers of a particular magazine that fit the demographic profile of their target group;
- Second, send text messages promoting a competition linked to the brand that is set out in the paper-based magazine.

Stone (2002) reports that a few companies have begun sending coupons as messages to wireless devices in order to unload 'perishable' services such concert seats or restaurant tables. He describes the example of PlanetHopper, a small company based in New York, which is focusing upon the entertainment industry.

It has partnered General Cinemas, theatres and Shecky's guide to bars and clubs to provide the wireless coupons. By advertising in cinemas and in some 200 New York bars and restaurants, it drew some 20,000 users who opted in to get the promotional messages. The key to success is 'opt in' messaging, as people's tolerance of spam messages falls. *The Economist* (2001) recommends that to avoid giving offence, mobile advertisements must:

- Be optional (meaning actively requested by users);
- Be personalized;
- Be moderate in volume;
- Be free to the recipient;
- Offer a means to unsubscribe.

The article goes on to report on a recent initiative by a mobile advertising company called the Mobile Trial, in which advertisements as text messages had an average response rate of 10-20 per cent. This is much higher than usual rates for direct mail (3 per cent) and Internet banner advertisements (less than 1 per cent).

MOBILE COMMERCE

Mobile commerce - meaning the actual purchase of items from the mobile Internet - is expected to grow rapidly over the next few years.

(www.forrrester.com) suggests that worldwide revenues could reach $200 billion by 2005. Be warned that we have heard wild projections before - in connection with the potential revenues likely to be generated by dotcoms, for example - so do not read too much into these figures.

Before getting carried away in another round of Internet euphoria, think about the recent high level of negative publicity about mobile theft, which highlights the problem of security. Steps have recently been taken by the major market players to address this issue.

In early 2002, a common database of stolen phone numbers was established so that the handsets could be disabled to prevent unauthorized purchases being made. Remember also that many people are still reluctant to undertake PC-based commerce, let alone transact through a mobile phone.

Growth in mobile commerce is likely to be driven by alliances between banks and telecommunications companies. Both parties have particular strengths which if brought together can add considerable value. Banks have a banking licence, credit verification skills and an established retail network. Mobile operators provide a modern brand image and the infrastructure of a mobile network.

Both have a large customer base upon which to draw. While some companies (notably Vodafone) have made public their objective to provide financial services when restrictions on the allocation of banking licences are lifted (in 2002), others believe that the partnership route is the way forward. So far, banks have taken a cautious approach and built their mobile capabilities for small numbers of customers on a trial basis.

They now face the challenge of scaling up the infrastructure to cope with larger volumes of users. Abbey National, for example, offers e-Banking via the Genie mobile portal, which can be accessed by WAP phones over any service network. According to Bansal (2001), the bank's strategy is to develop partnerships that enable it to offer electronic banking across all technology platforms.

These alliances offer customers the security of dealing

with an established brand, which can be significant in building the necessary trust for mobile banking to really take off.

INTERNAL COMMUNICATIONS

Remote workers can use wireless devices to access office systems and marketing information held on the corporate intranet. Such services are useful for logistics companies needing to keep track of their drivers' location and also to send SMS messages with reminders and alerts, for example of schedule changes or traffic problems. Salespeople operating in the field can update customer records or request specific information automatically. Although the potential for the mobile.

Internet to enhance communications between staff or between staff and customers is considerable, adapting the corporate security systems to allow access through the mobile environment can be a significant headache, as can the practicalities of integrating mobile channels with existing IT systems more generally.

MOBILE CHALLENGES

Leung and Antypas (2001) note how the current mobile landscape resembles the first-generation Internet in the mid-1990s in terms of the key business challenges:

- *Bandwidth.* Many innovative services such as real-time video streaming will not be feasible, given the limited bandwidth currently available, and will remain what the authors refer to as 'pipe dreams' for the foreseeable future. The problem may be eased somewhat - although by no means fully addressed - by the arrival of 2.5G and 3G handsets promised for 2002.
- *Interperability.* Cellular carriers currently have different systems and standards that are not compatible with each other. GSM (Global Service for Mobile), TDMA (Time Division Multiple Access) and CDMA (Code Division Multiple Access) are available on different carriers in different areas, meaning that

communications with customers may need to be channelled through each carrier for its specific area.

- *Equipment.* The mobile cannot compete with the desktop in terms of display, computing power and keyboard facilities. The displays are currently available only in black and white, and support very limited animation. There are no cookies to recognize passwords and personalize greetings, and if the Internet connection is broken, then access cannot be resumed from where it was last used because the application will restart.

DIGITAL TELEVISION

Interactive Digital Television (iDTV) looks similar to PC-based Internet but is delivered through a television set and can be operated using a remote control. From a standing start in 1999, market penetration by 2002 is currently around 40 per cent of UK households and is projected to rise to 95 per cent by 2010, according to a Netpoll survey. Leading providers include Sky Digital, ON Digital, Telewest and NTL.

One of the key drivers for this surprisingly rapid growth has been the provision of free set-top boxes by these platform providers. Services currently provided include home shopping, email, video, banking and travel. Forrester Research (2001) predicts that more people will access the Internet through a television than through a PC by the end of 2004.

Advertising through this mechanism can be interactive, as viewers can respond immediately to request further information or to sign up for a promotion. Digital television has helped increase the fragmentation of viewers, as there are over 200 channels now available in the UK.

This means that advertising can be easily targeted to tighter niche audiences, for example through exposure on sports, cooking or health channels. Advertisers can develop their own television channels in order to incorporate content provision and communicate with their customers less intrusively. For example, the PC version of Boots' digital health channel, Wellbeing, is also automatically accessed if you type in 'www.boots.co.uk'. Specialist digital television channels also provide more focus for sponsorship deals. Domino's Pizza, which is represented on satellite, cable and the Web, is one of the early success stories of iDTV. e-Commerce transactions represent 4 per cent of its total business. Management credit the firm's sponsorship of *The Simpsons* as pivotal in building Domino's iDTV business. This activity has given Domino's a brand recognition figure of 98 per cent in multi-channel homes.

The UK government is currently pushing for total digital television penetration, and there has been talk of switching off the analogue signal by as soon as 2010. By the end of 2001, the number of digital television owners in the UK reached the same level (36 per cent) as the number of Internet users in the country for the first time, according to e-MORI's Technology Tracker (www.e-mori.co.uk).

While the number of new users seeking Internet access is levelling off, digital TV ownership more than doubled in 2001. In social groups AB and C1, PC-based Internet access far outweighs digital television ownership, but the ratio shifts in social groups C2 and DE, in which twice as many households have digital television as have Internet access via PC. The relationship between social class and choice of Internet access mechanism is illustrated in Figure 7.5.

Fewer than half of digital television owners have so far used interactive services such as shopping, banking, gaming or email. This is because PCs have been traditionally viewed as information tools and are a logical choice for accessing the Internet and using online consumer services. The television, however, is viewed as an entertainment tool, and the biggest driver for digital adoption so far has been improved picture quality and a greater choice of channels, with little attention being paid by consumers to the advantages of interactive services.Smith and Chaffey (2002) note the following advantages of iDTV to marketers:

- Direct-response mass-market advertising;
- Highly targetable;
- Moving buyers through the complete buying process;

- Audience engagement through interaction;
- Brand-building and positioning reinforcement;
- Brand-building through community-building;
- Customer service - reduction of bottlenecks;
- Security – less risk associated with TV than Web sites;
- Controllable - highly measurable;
- Cost savings.

These authors go on to recommend five key steps to making iDTV work in practice:

- Start small; test out advertisements first on a small scale and see what reaction is gained.
- Develop your own content area or micro Web site linked to iDTV.
- Design for the lowest common denominator to maximize the number of people who can make use of your service.
- Grow your offer over time to include purchasing or personalization.
- Form partnerships or build a team for the future to ensure that the necessary skills are available.

However, despite the rapidly increasing volume of viewers, actual purchase transactions have been slow to take off. Forrester Research notes that many retailers currently using iDTV as a channel to market are planning to pull out when their contracts come up for renewal. The main reason for their dissatisfaction is weak sales. The Forrester Research report points to a poor visitor-to-purchase ratio of only 2 per cent. Also problematic is the location of transactional sites within 'walled gardens', which are dedicated interactive channels that are separate from programme content.

The challenge is to find ways and means of driving consumers to these interactive channels and encouraging them to carry out transactions. Although a shake-out of unprofitable business is probably inevitable, the iDTV medium is slowly evolving, costs are falling and interactivity becoming less 'clunky', suggesting that opportunities will present themselves to companies prepared to take the longer view.

'Push' technology is the name given to a broad spectrum

of products that automate the delivery of information to the user. Many Web sites are currently based upon 'pull' models, whereby users seek out the information in which they are interested. In contrast, push technologies create automated communications relationships whereby products can be aimed at users who have expressed an interest and given permission to be sent targeted material.

V-Commerce (short for 'voice') allows users to conduct self-service transactions alternately using the web and the telephone. This initiative is being led by the V-Commerce Alliance, which consists of a number of Internet and telecom companies.

For example, a consumer would be able to make an airline reservation over the Web, and then later call a specific number to obtain departure gate or frequent-flyer information - or, before ordering a new computer online, speak to a customer service representative to check which model would be most suitable for their requirements.

Speech recognition is becoming increasingly common in US call centres, particularly in the banking and airline industries. It is also being adapted as a 'hands-free' input device for cars in Europe and Japan, as the motor industry recognizes that voice is the safest way for drivers to interact with in-car technologies (The Economist, 2001b). Nissan already sells a premium model that uses voice instruction to control audio, temperature, navigation and lighting. The new technologies promise to deliver access to information and services on a permanent basis anywhere that there is a telephone connection.

It is only in the past year or so that the necessary computing power has become small and cheap enough to fit into mobile devices in a cost-effective way. In addition, the (admittedly slow) spread of broadband access to the Internet in public places is fuelling the demand for instant information. What is also generating interest is the way in which speech recognition is improving the quality of information services by eliminating the need for telephone queuing and badly designed menu-driven voicemail systems.

Apart from call centres, other opportunities for telephone-based services using speech recognition include:

- Self-service banking;
- Catalogue ordering;
- Weather and stock market reports;
- Email collection;
- Virtual personal assistants (VPAs).

In order for the telephone and the Internet to be merged effectively, common industry standards need to be achieved so that Web pages can handle voice. In October 2001 the World Wide Web Consortium (www.w3.org) - a voluntary organization that sets international standards - released a draft version of VoiceXML for this purpose. At the same time, however, a new platform was created by such key players as Microsoft, Intel and Philips to develop a rival standard called SALT (Speech Application Language Tags). It remains to be seen which of these will prevail.

Virgin plans a new service (www.virginunlimited.com) that aims to sell everything from cars and toasters to holidays at big discounts. It will offer postcode-specific advice on financial services and household utilities at the lowest prices. In order to provide this service, the company has established partnerships with a number of consumer durable wholesalers and also providers of specialist niche products. Consumers will be able to ask product providers to compete for business by stating their requirements. The company that offers the best price and terms will win the order.

Consumers are often frustrated at having to deal with different service providers for each channel, which necessitates separate billing arrangements, passwords and email addresses. Consequently, they will migrate to services that allow them to personalize a single service for use on multiple devices. Looking ahead, Java TV (still at a very early stage of development) will bring together television and computing technologies to enable broadcasters to deliver value-added services to a range of Java-enabled devices.

This means that the Internet will be rendered 'device independent' and customers will be able to switch their viewing from television to PC or mobile - anywhere and at any time - as their circumstances dictate. The organizational challenges associated with developing and integrating effective multiple channel operations should not be underestimated.

CHALLENGES OF MULTI-CHANNEL MARKETING

The usage of various Internet access mechanisms has developed over the past few years. At this early stage, companies need to address a number of challenges when considering the development of multi-channel strategies that allow customers to access online content from a range of devices:

- The extent to which they should invest in these relatively untried technologies, with little indication of likely customer demand or long-term prospects for making money.
- The need to 'repurpose' content for each tool. For example, trying to display a Web site on a WAP screen means that graphics and pictures are lost, and different coding is required.

  Smith and Chaffey also note that switching between PC and iDTV is problematic because Web sites are designed to be viewed in 'lean-forward mode' from two feet away, but iDTV in 'laid-back mode' from more like eight feet away. Navigating with a mouse is also very different from navigating with a remote control device.
- The unique properties of each medium in terms of the user experience delivered. For example, mobile transactions are likely to be for low-value or distress purchases, because the amount and quality of information that can be displayed to the customer on screen is limited. In contrast, the PC allows huge volumes of data to searched and displayed, and so is best suited to situations where the customer wants to carry out extensive research before making a purchase. Digital television offers yet another

dynamic; although it is still in its infancy, early usage suggests that purchases may take place in a more collaborative, impulsive and social context than through the other channels.

- Whether they should offer all their products or services across each medium (and if so, the extent to which customization is necessary and/or appropriate) or 'mix and match' according to the characteristics of each channel and the specific message to be delivered.
- The need for *integrated* online and offline marketing campaigns. Smith and Chaffey (2002) describe how MTV asked viewers to send in SMS text messages to provide comments and vote for their favourite video. MTV then played the winning video together with the comments live.
  The event was promoted through offline magazines read by the target audience, and the paper-based advertisement demonstrated a text message on a phone explaining how to take part.
- How to manage the necessary internal information processing that will allow the company to achieve a unified view of customer activity across all channels. For this to work, a central database is necessary to provide up-to-date customer details to all channel operators. Remember that customers' expectations are continually rising and they may expect to use a combination of channels to effect just one single purchase ...

It should be clear from this brief discussion that the technical ability to offer multi-channel access is just the starting point. Considerable investment needs to be made in the back-office computer systems and business process integration necessary to actually make it work in practice. The difficulties are even greater for small firms with limited financial resources, or those with legacy computer systems that cannot be easily integrated.

However, for those that succeed, the potential for

combine multi-channel offerings with *personalized* content provides an enormous marketing opportunity.

THE GENIE MOBILE INTERNET PORTAL

Genie was launched in 2001 as the world's first exclusively online mobile service. Genie's UK mobile service operates on the BT Cellnet network and is therefore now part of O2. BT Cellnet is one of the largest UK mobile networks, with over 8 million customers, and offers 99 per cent coverage of the UK population. Genie is the UK's leading mobile Internet company, with over 3 million registered users of the Genie Internet portal.

It provides free text messaging and free access to WAP. The mobile Internet is the technology that allows users to view information, play games and manage personal email via a WAP phone. WAP stands for Wireless Application Protocol and is the worldwide standard enabling WAP mobile phones to access the Mobile Internet. Genie Mobile Internet provides a number of services available on WAP phones:

- Email - the ability to read, reply and forward emails;
- M-Commerce - you can now buy books and CDs;
- Information - the latest sports scores, current news and gossip;
- Enquiries - flight times, cinema times;
- Entertainment - games, competitions and reviews.

Mobile phone and Internet services are integrated so that customers can access information on a PC or via mobile phone.

The Genie portal itself runs at significant loss, but its services appeal to the key market segment of early-adopter mobile phone users. Members of this group are predisposed to purchasing new gadgets, understand the rapidly developing terminology and issues surrounding mobile developments, and also happen to spend the most money on mobiles.

Any mobile user can register on the site - they do not necessarily have to be using O2 networks. By permission-based marketing to these registered Genie visitors, special deals can be offered to get them to switch to the O2 network. At this stage of market development, the key selling points as far as users are concerned relate to content (in the form of information and alerts about share prices, skiing conditions, sports results, etc.) rather than transactional commerce.

The Genie brand has high awareness ratings despite low advertising spend. According to *Campaign's* dotcom weekly awareness survey, Genie is ranked tenth in the UK, with an awareness rating of 27 per cent, just behind the Easy Group on 32 per cent and ahead of Wellbeing on 20 per cent. Genie is promoted on the major portals such as Google, MSN and Yahoo!, and pays for prominent placements on search engines so that a banner is invoked should a surfer conduct a search for 'mobile phone', for example.

Genie aims to leverage value from its mobile services by offering customers special deals through partnerships with banks and ISPs as part of a 'closed' network. This business model is superior to many 'open' network portals because partner firms will either pay for preferential access to Genie customers or at least provide content for free. Genie customers who want to access services from companies outside the partner network have to pay extra for the privilege. To illustrate how this works, consider the example of mobile banking.

Genie provides secure links to eight leading banks to enable customers to access their bank accounts via their mobile phones on the O2 network. Within the next twelve months, customers will also be able to trade stocks in this way. Hence there is scope for the major stockbrokers to be 'plumbed in' to the partnership to make the entire contact, share purchase and payment transaction from the bank account a seamless and immediate process for the customer.

If such a service is available, why would a customer want to look elsewhere for a stockbroker? Stockbrokers, therefore, will pay for a preferential placing in the Genie portfolio, and indeed several may compete with each other - with the best positions on the listing commanding the highest fees.From the partner firms' perspective, there are three key drivers for associating with Genie:

- To obtain additional revenue from existing customers

by offering an alternative channel to access the company;

- To expand the customer base by appealing to new market segments (for example people who use their mobile phone to bet with Ladbrokes through the Genie gateway have a very different demographic profile from that of Ladbroke's traditional customer base relying upon the firm's network of betting shops);
- To reduce the costs of servicing their customer base. This is the key driver for banking partners, for example.

To illustrate the potential of mobile services to reduce costs (and in some cases change the partner firm's entire business model), consider the example of a recruitment agency for temporary staff. In the past, such a firm would rely upon a team of office-based employees to make telephone calls to perhaps hundreds of registered individuals to advise them of newly received employment opportunities and sign people up as required.

This could be an expensive and time-consuming exercise if large numbers of staff were required. By sending a text message simultaneously to the entire labour pool database requesting those interested to call in and sign up for the job, the entire cost structure of the business is altered. The staff employed to recruit would only have to answer calls from people accepting the work, rather than make a large number of outgoing calls touting for business. In the near future, the acceptance procedure will also become Web based, thereby reducing the need for human intervention still further.

THE MARKETING MIX

The idea of the marketing mix has been around for many years - well before an 'e-' came in front of Marketing or anything else. As far back as the first half of the twentieth century, the job of the marketer was described as a 'mixer of ingredients'. Marketers devise strategies and tactics aimed at providing satisfaction and adding value for customers. The various elements are blended into a 'marketing mix' - a phrase first coined by Neil Borden (1964) of Harvard Business School.

The marketing mix can be defined as the blend of tools and techniques that marketers use to provide value for customers. It is most widely known as E. Jerome McCarthy's (1960) '4Ps': Place, Product, Price and Promotion. 'Place' is not quite self-explanatory, but refers to the routes organizations take to get the benefits of the product or service to the intended customers - channels of distribution.

Product' means both tangible product and also 'service' and all the ways in which an organization adds value. 'Price' means not just the price charged, but also all aspects of pricing policy, including, for example, distributor margins. 'Promotion' is not just the more specialized 'sales promotion', but also every way in which a product is promoted to customers - from print advertising to Web sites.

The 4Ps are used as an approach to marketing planning that, according to later editions of McCarthy's still-popular *Basic Marketing*, has worked for millions of students and teachers. The prominence of the 4Ps derives largely from Kotler's and colleagues' focus on these as central to marketing strategy (*Marketing Management* and *Principles of Marketing* texts - the early US editions of which were widely accepted as the basis of marketing teaching).

In recent decades, there have been numerous attempts to update and revise the marketing mix. For example, Jefkins (1993:37) pointed out that the concept of 4Ps is no more than a simplifying convention that 'loses sight of the chronological sequence'. He devised a more realistic twenty-element mix that attempted to describe the marketing process sequentially, starting from conception, through pricing, product, distribution and sales to maintaining customer interest and loyalty.

Some marketers assert that there are '5Ps' of marketing, with the fifth being 'People'. 'People' has two meanings in this context. First, customers are people, often buying according to emotion and whim. Without these fickle customers, we have no business. Second, people make it happen. Without people to put marketing plans into operation, nothing happens.

Booms and Bitner (1982) proposed that for marketing services, the marketing mix should be extended to seven, by adding 'Process' and 'Physical evidence' in addition to 'People'. For a service, where there is no tangible product, the process of providing the service is all-important. Similarly, a service cannot be sampled. The provider needs to present evidence of the quality of the process.

With an increasing 'service' element in the added value of most production activities, the '7Ps' approach is becoming more widely accepted. The e-Retailing book in this series will return to the '7' approach. For simplicity we shall use the better-known '4' here as a framework for examining online marketing operations. The operational aspects of the other three will be incorporated where relevant.

In recent years, what marketers actually do has changed radically. Some authors have questioned whether the old idea of the marketing mix can still be valid. The challenge is based on a shift of emphasis towards relationship marketing and customer relationship management (CRM), aspects which are fundamental to marketing the e-Business. The CRM approach has many advantages, we focus on the well-tried 4Ps as an aid to classifying marketing tactics, e- or otherwise.

One development has merit as being descriptive of the way marketers think about the customer. The '4Cs' (Lauterborn 1990) imply more emphasis on customer wants and concerns than do the Ps. 'Place', rather than implying managements' methods of placing products where they want them to be, can be thought of as 'Convenience for the customer', recognizing the customers' choices for buying in ways convenient to them.

Product', rather than being something that a company makes, which then has to be sold, can be thought of as a 'Customer benefit' - meaning satisfactions wanted by customers. 'Price' may be what companies decide to charge for their products, but 'Cost to the customer' represents the real cost that customers will pay, including, for example, their own transport costs. Finally, 'Promotion' suggests ways in which companies persuade people to buy, whereas

'Communication' is a two-way process also involving feedback from customers to suppliers. In the sections that follow, we consider the operational aspects of marketing the e-Business. While using the better-known 4Ps for our headings, we draw attention to differences in approach implied by the 4Cs.

PLACE

'Place' (Convenience in the 4 Cs) means the elements of the marketing mix that marketers use to enable customers to access the benefits of a product or service. Traditionally, this has meant 'channels of distribution' through (e.g.) various wholesaler and retailer combinations. Viewing from the 'convenience for the customer' (4Cs) perspective gives a more customer-orientated focus. This is a vital decision area for the e-Business for three reasons.

First, relatively small local companies can widen their market and even export. Second, many e-Businesses aim to gain competitive advantage by using e-Systems to de-layer the distribution chain. For example, Dell (www.dell.co.uk) supplies customers directly, rather than through distributors, wholesalers or retailers. Third, distribution is an area where some e-Businesses have been severely criticized for failing to deliver customer service.

Place elements of the marketing mix have been changing rapidly over recent decades, and these changes impact in many ways on the marketing operations of the e-Business. First, the growth of retailer power has involved major retailers taking more control of their supply chains. The involvement of wholesalers has been reduced, tending to give way to contract logistics (under retailer control).

At the same time, supply chains have become more efficient, with computer network links between suppliers and retailers - many still based on EDI. Predating the Internet, EDI is based on privately owned third-party computer networks. Stock levels have been reduced using techniques such as JIT and Enterprise Resource Planning (ERP). Control of the physical distribution, ordering, invoicing and payment systems, particularly for major retailers, is often still carried out using EDI networks such as Tradanet (www.gegxs.com/gxs/products/product/traser). Increasingly, though, retailers such as Tesco are allowing Internet access to their suppliers for real-time electronic point-of-sale (EPOS) data. Trusted supplier partners can thus respond more quickly to changes in customer demand.

PRODUCT

'Product' is equivalent to Customer benefit in the 4Cs. In fact, people do not buy 'products' as such, but rather solutions to problems, or good feelings. The oft-quoted example is of a company selling the 'product' of an 8-mm drill bit. What the customer actually buys, though, is 8-mm holes. The customer is not interested in features of the drill such as the grade of steel used, only in whether it will solve the particular problem: drilling through plaster, mortar and brick, for example.

Online catalogues selling B2B might well describe this as 'tungsten carbide tipped' in the realistic expectation that trade customers will fully understand the purpose. When selling B2C, a description more in line with customer wants should be used, say 'for drilling masonry for wall plugs and similar'.

When buying online, customers are far less likely to request help than they are in the store, cash-and-carry, buying via telesales or even when placing a formal written order. Rather, when buying online, customers who need help in understanding a product are more likely to abandon the transaction and find an alternative supplier, or even buy through a different channel. e-Businesses, therefore, need to be particularly careful about describing products clearly in customer benefit terms.

The second reason why customers buy products - to get good feelings - is also apt for the e-Business. Other channels such as the retail store or the face-to-face salesperson are often much better at identifying and satisfying customers' emotional needs and wants. The physical store uses atmospherics in the attempt to change mood and give shoppers a pleasant emotional experience when buying. Emotional cues may include visual (decor), olfactory (perfume), touch (smooth and cool or soft and cuddly) and oral (music) cues. Similarly, the sales representative selling face to face has the opportunity of using verbal and non-verbal (body language) communication to build personal relationships with customers, enhancing the emotional value of products.

In trying to replicate the physical buying experience, the e-Business is at a disadvantage. On the other hand, with transaction data ready-digitized, the e-Business is well placed to enhance product value using CRM techniques. For example, data-mining can be used to build a picture of products most likely to be wanted by individual customers. Products tailored specifically can be offered proactively. Amazon (www.amazon.co.uk), for instance, uses such a system to match new books to existing customers likely to be interested in them.

The Internet, though, has the advantage in selling information-based products, including market information, business application and games software. For example, to find information on size and trends of consumer markets, there is no need to purchase a heavy paper-based report; the information can be downloaded from suppliers such as Mintel (sinatra2.mintel.com).

PRICE

'Price' is equivalent to cost to the customer in the 4Cs. Pricing decisions generate revenue, whereas the rest of the marketing mix involves costs. Pricing decisions are particularly critical for the e-Business as there is a customer perception that prices should be lower online than otherwise. Many organizations (e.g. Eurotunnel; www.Eurotunnel.com for car crossings from England to France) apply a standard discount for online purchase.

In some cases, customers can make much bigger savings buying online. For instance, to buy tickets from a travel agent in the UK for the Calgary Stampede rodeo in Canada (www.calgarystampede.com/stampede) is likely to be expensive, as the agent will probably sell these only as part of a package. Tickets can be booked directly via the Internet at a substantial saving. Some e-Businesses sell almost solely on the basis of price. For example, emagazineshop (www. emagazine shop.com) sells a wide range of the magazines normally available at newsagents'.

Subscription prices are normally lower than newsagents, but emagazineshop offers lower prices still. The most popular magazines are discounted by at least 20 per cent, more specialist ones 10 per cent. This is a rare example of a pure-play dotcom, founded in 1997, that has survived the dotcom crash and is growing steadily, now employing 25 people.Despite the Internet facilitating de-layering of intermediaries, it is still not automatic that costs will be less for selling online.

Someone still has to carry out functions such as breaking bulk and physical delivery - and for online sales these can be even higher than for offline (many small orders delivered to individual customers rather than fewer, larger deliveries to a store), with consequent loss of advantages of economies of scale. Hence, many suppliers selling on the basis of cheap prices, even successful ones like Amazon (www.amazon.co.uk), struggle to make a profit on their e-Operations. Again, this is an area where the success of emagazineshop is an exception.

Not all prices are lower on the Internet. As already mentioned, the cost to the customer includes not just the selling price, but all the costs of buying. To buy from a (bricks) grocery supermarket incurs transport costs, and also the notional cost of the value of a customer's travel time. Tesco (www.tesco.com) is able to make a charge for home delivery, which its many e-Customers must consider represents good value.

The Internet is an ideal medium for operating a mechanistic market. For the customers, this means quick and easy access to the 'best' deals. For sellers, this should in theory mean a level playing field, where products offered at a competitive price sell, regardless of issues such as the size of the organization; hence the suitability of the Internet for electronic trading exchange.

The level playing field idea, though, has hit some snags

when translated to practice, and price-based services have achieved no more than modest success to date. A number of buying services are available such as Shopsmart (uk.shopsmart.com), the leading consumer price comparison site, and ComputerPrices (www. ComputerPrices .co.uk), which finds the cheapest computer kit in the UK. Priceline (www.priceline.com) is an alternative price-based service that creates a market or reverse auction.

Enter the price you want to pay for a wide range of services like flights or hire cars and the system searches for suppliers willing to sell at that price - but the customer cannot choose the (say) airline for their flight. The company does, however, guarantee that it will be one of the top airlines. Most UK customers, though, prefer to have more control over what they get, rather than buying purely on price. For most e-Businesses, pricing remains as for non-electronic strategies; that is, based on the complex interaction of all elements of the marketing mix and value.

Marketing pricing is still what it was, the price that customers are willing to pay, based on considerations such as the company, brand, reputation and product. The difference that e-Commerce makes is that pricing and competitor information is faster and more transparent, meaning that market forces also tend to act faster and perhaps more efficiently. There is thus a tendency for prices to converge at lower levels.

PROMOTION

Promotion' is equivalent to Communication in the 4Cs. First thoughts on promoting the e-Business must be that it is unnecessary - the business can rely on its super Web site. Having built that Web site, it can sit back and wait for customers. Of course, we quickly realise that there is more to it than that.

Why should visitors come to our Web site? If surfers do find it, are they our potential customers? In practice, it is likely that we will have to be more proactive in promotion, integrating e- with other communications channels.

For many businesses, selling predominantly both on- and offline, the Internet is just one of a wide range of communication channels. The 'process' of integrating the communication tools is vital.

People' play a vital part in the marketing communication process, even (or perhaps especially) for the e-Business. Customers want human contact, and those businesses that can provide a real human to interact with a customer quickly - whether online, via email, over the telephone or even face to face - are more likely to succeed than some of the faceless, e-only operations that have been getting a reputation for poor service.

Similarly, though, those e-Businesses with customer-friendly systems that effectively mimic human interaction (www.google.com) and Amazon (www.amazon.com)) tend to be more popular than the more mechanistic sites. The People aspect is also important for e-Businesses in tailoring offers to the individual customer. For example, Amazon emails details of new books to customers whose profile makes them likely customers.

MAKING BANNERS WORK

Recently, a perception has arisen in the marketing world that banner ads are not cost-effective. Despite this, online advertising expenditure is still growing, and has now reached well over £150 million per year (£30 million more than cinema advertising, for example).

The interstitial, a pop-up that interrupts browsing to show an ad, is a much more active form of advertising. Some people using the Web for a specific purpose find these irritating, though. Online advertising company RealMedia (www.uk.realmedia.com) is using a less intrusive system called adPointer. This generates an ad when the cursor has not moved for a specific time.

Schemes that provide users with incentives to look at advertisements have been around for some years, but in the UK, Bananalotto.com (www.bananalotto.com) has raised the stakes by offering the chance to win £1 million as you click the banner ad. KPE, the media and entertainment consultancy, developed around ten games for its clients. Managing Director Paul Zwillberg says, 'So much of the Internet has been characterized by repurposing things that worked well in print or on TV.

Advergaming" is ... a new combination that's made for the medium.... You take one of the most popular uses of interactive content and marry it with tried and tested advertising models like brand association, trial or data capture and you get something really wonderful.'

BRINGING THE MARKETING MIX TOGETHER

The 4Ps are a useful framework for designing e-Marketing strategies - and have the benefit that they are clear and familiar to most managers. Successful e-Businesses bring together the elements of the marketing mix into an integrated offer representing value to the customer. This can be illustrated, for example, by outlining aspects of the 4Ps of the marketing mix of the office supplies company Quill (www.quillcorp.com).

PLACE

Customers are offered the convenience of easy ordering - not just by Web but via many other routes, with expert personal assistance readily available by telephone. We have personally tested the service and found it fast and reliable. A particular benefit is the UPS (courier service) order tracker so that customers can track the delivery status of their order.

PRODUCT

Quill offers a wide range of office and computer supplies, furniture and speciality products. The main selling point is the very wide range available from stock - almost everything imaginable for the office. This is a 'hypermarket'-type approach, offering customers far more choice than would be expected from most traditional suppliers.

PRICE

Competitive, discount prices can be offered. Low price

levels are sustainable because of the e-Efficiency of the business, and also the economies of scale arising from successfully selling large volumes.

PROMOTION

Quill is promoted by a wide range of integrated marketing communications of which an affiliate programme and e-Newsletter are central.

E-Commerce uses the Internet and the World Wide Web technologies. The evolution of the Internet and World Wide Web to their present state and provide details of the current state of those technologies that enable e-Commerce. These include digital networks and their protocols, which form the basic system technologies required to develop an e-Commerce system, and the client-server architecture and World Wide Web in particular.

As the basis of commerce is transactions between buyers and sellers, e-Commerce requires interactive digital technology that can facilitate transactions over the Internet. Consequently, also introduces interactive technologies such as JavaScript and methods of exchanging data between systems. It also looks at how the Internet, World Wide Web and interactive technologies need to be configured to enable electronic commerce that is secure. Finally, current developments in Internet and World Wide Web technology are considered in terms of their future impact on e-Commerce.

THE INTERNET AND THE WORLD WIDE WEB

Prior to the Internet, World Wide Web and its associated technologies, the impact of technology for the purposes of business transactions had been peripheral. The Internet and the World Wide Web have fundamentally changed commerce. Commerce's basic mode of communication, written and verbal communication between a business and its customer or business and its suppliers or partners, remained unchanged since Adam Smith's first observations on economic markets.

Electronic communication, in the form of digital mainframe computers and microcomputers (personal computers) connected to the Internet, has radically transformed commercial activity for customers and businesses alike. The transformation has been so fundamental that new terms such as 'e-Commerce', 'e-Business', 'e-Markets' and the 'new e-Economy' are freely used to describe the modern phenomenon of Internet-based commercial activity. e-Commerce may be described as the sharing of product and service information, developing and maintaining human commercial relationships, and transacting business over the Internet and the World Wide Web.

Technologies such as telephony have influenced business activity in the past, but their influence has not been revolutionary. Such technologies have not fundamentally changed how businesses organize themselves and how they interact with their customers, suppliers or partners. In contrast, the Internet and the World Wide Web have revolutionized business activity.

- Provides an introductory description of the current IT, Internet and World Wide Web technology underpinning e-Commerce;
- Comments on its implications for business and e-Commerce;
- Explores potential future developments in Internet and World Wide Web technology that will affect e-Commerce.

This introductory reading on e-Commerce technology should enable you to describe Internet and World Wide Web technology to enable e-Commerce. Critically, the reading should enable you to state and understand the main elements of an e-Commerce system architecture and assess e-Commerce security technology for confidentiality and payments.

Memex

The Internet's evolution has encompassed over fifty years of technological and conceptual development. The original concept of the Internet is attributed to Vannevar Bush. He worked in a team of engineers during World War II in the United States. His experience of working in an expert team of scientists led him to think about the problem of processing and sharing information among the team. His solution was the invention of a machine called Memex (MEMory EXtension). He envisaged that Memex would work like the human brain, which finds information by association. His ideas provided the conceptual framework for subsequent work on developing the technology of the Internet and World Wide Web.

ARPAnet

The Internet began in 1969 as a communications medium project of the US Department of Defence, and its associated academic and research agencies. It needed a network of computers to enable collaborative work among the different agencies. In its original form, the Internet consisted of a decentralized digital network that connected defence, research and academic mainframe computers.

This network was called the ARPAnet after the agency that led the project, the department's Advanced Research Projects Agency (ARPA). The purpose of the ARPAnet was to connect various government and related computers, and in the event of disaster or war to preserve the integrity of information passing between these important government agencies. ARPAnet was privatized in 1990, and as it was gradually released to the public domain it began to be transformed into the Internet that we know today.

The World Wide Web

Around the same time, Tim Berners-Lee, a research scientist working at the European CERN physics lab in Switzerland, conceived the World Wide Web and released it to the public domain in 1991. The problem that Tim Berners-Lee faced was how to share research knowledge among scientists who used different brands of computers and associated software at CERN. He developed the method of hypertext link for connecting information stored on different computers. In his words, his motive for inventing the Web was: 'If everyone had the same information as me, my life would be easier.

The original idea for linking electronic documents was Ted Nelson's. He coined the term 'hypertext' in the early 1960s. Marc Andreessen developed the first graphical browser for the Internet. It enabled people seeking information on the Internet to find it quickly and efficiently.

A major effect of the Internet and the Web over the 1990s was to enable executives and business strategists to develop new ways of doing business electronically. These new electronic approaches are termed e-Commerce 'business models'. Business models that combine the use of the Internet and Web technologies with fundamental business transformation are referred to as 'e-Business'.

The term e-Business is used to describe a business that shares its production or service information with customers and business suppliers or partners, fosters the development of customer relationships electronically, and enables business to be transacted from personal computers or other electronic devices, such as mobile phones or personal digital assistants (PDAs). One of the most successful e-Commerce business models is the US company Dell Computers.

It has a $14 million per day Internet-based revenue stream, or a quarter of its total revenue. Though a survey by NOP in 1999 revealed that only 15 per cent of the companies surveyed used the Internet for making online sales, Gartner Research predict that 97.5 million US users will adopt e-billing and online account management by 2005.

INTERNET AND WORLD WIDE WEB TECHNOLOGIES

The microcomputer or Personal Computer (PC) forms the basis of e-Commerce. The Internet would not have the wide reach that it has into peoples' homes in the absence of the PC. Most office PCs are linked to a computer network and PCs at home are connected to the Internet via modems or dedicated data transfer cables.

Local area Networks and Wide area Networks

PCs on local area networks (LANs) and wide area networks (WANs) are connected to the Internet. LANs and

WANs are digital computer networks that connect PCs to enable sharing of information between separate computers. LANs are limited to a geographical area such as an office, whereas WANs connect computers over a wider geographical area. The computers on a LAN or WAN share information in the form of addressed packets of data.

The capacity of a single computer is increased by connecting it to a LAN or WAN, as it can share computer programs and information. A computer that is linked to a network can download and use computer programs and share storage and printing facilities, and take advantage of network capabilities for sending and receiving data and information.

Client-server Architecture

A computer on a LAN or WAN that provides resources like application programs or printer connections is known as a 'server'. A server provides other computers known as 'clients' on the LAN or WAN with software and other resources. This set-up is called client-server computing architecture. A server that is linked to the Internet is called a 'host computer'.

A server computer is capable of running server software, which needs to be compatible with the network operating system. The client and server are independent and perform specialized tasks to process information and run computer applications.

If you use Microsoft Word on your computer, the client, it is probable that a server will have provided the Microsoft Word software for you to use. The client-server architecture is the basis of the Internet too.

The Internet and Protocols

The Internet is the sum total connection of LANs, WANs and stand-alone computers around the world. The term 'Internet' is short for 'inter-networking' or an interconnected set of networks. It is the global network of computers, whether the computer is on a LAN in an office, or a WAN in an industry extranet, or an independent computer in a private home. An

Internet-connected computer is known as an Internet host computer. The Internet is also known as the 'Net', the 'Information superhighway' or 'Cyberspace'.

The set of rules for moving information over the Internet is called a 'protocol'. The transmission control protocol (TCP) is used for sending large amounts of information between host computers on the Internet. Vinton Cerf wrote the basic ideas for TCP on the back of an envelope over lunch, and in 1983 the core protocols of the Internet transmission control protocol/ Internet protocol (TCP/IP) became the standard protocol for transmitting information over the Internet.

Intranet

An intranet consists of networked internal connection of computers owned by an organization and makes use of Web technology. An intranet may be mounted on a LAN or a WAN. An intranet makes use of Internet technology such as TCP/IP, HTML, Java and HTTP to make it interoperable and to provide it with Web capability. The basic elements of an intranet are a computer network, a computer designated as a server containing server software and the Internet protocols TCP/IP.

An intranet offers several benefits to an organization: improved sharing and communication of information, open standards and cross-platform collaboration. For example, a car manufacturing company may connect its information systems on purchasing with its accounting information systems to form an intranet for sharing and processing information between two departments in the company.

An intranet is a company's own internal information transfer system that offers: e-mail, communication among different computers, connection to remote offices, a Web browser interface and special-interest news groups. For e-Commerce, an intranet is used to provide a corporate image and unified 'experience' for a customer that combines product information, ordering and customer care.

Extranet

An extranet is used for business-to-business (B2B) e-

Commerce. It is the networked connection of computers of two or more companies. It is a private communication system to support trade and is used for communication and transactions between business partners, suppliers or special customers. For example, a car manufacturing company may connect its computers with its various suppliers of components for the cars it makes. Another example is the airline industry's OneWorld network, which enables customers to transfer seamlessly between airlines to reach their destinations.

Design principles

Intranets and extranets share the same design principles formulated for the Internet. The Internet design principles are:

Interoperability. There are varying operating systems that control computer functions on the many different computers on the Internet. Normally a given operating system cannot communicate with a different one. A standard to enable varying operating systems to communicate with each other was introduced by the US Department of Defence, which originally financed the Internet. Interoperability means that independent implementations of Internet protocols can work seamlessly.

Consequently, operating system developers such as Microsoft or Apple incorporate software into their operating systems that enables them to operate with other computers over the Internet. Internet-compatible systems use the TCP/IP common protocol for communication. Interoperability for e-Commerce means that companies and customers do not have to purchase and upgrade software from the same vendors. Their computers will be able to communicate over the Internet because of the standard protocols.

Layering. The Internet can be regarded as a series of layers of software. The structure of the Internet is layered. It is a five-layer system consisting of: interconnect level (National Access Points, NAPs), national backbone providers, regional Internet providers, local Internet service providers, and the business and consumer market.

The bottom layers of software, interconnect and network,

are concerned with operating the computer hardware. The higher layers, business and consumer market, come closer to the needs of the person using the Internet.

The most relevant layer is the layer that processes the information required by the Internet user; this is called the 'application' layer. These different hardware and application layers need to communicate with each other and they do so by using well defined interfaces. The Internet layering standard has resulted in increased reliability of Internet software and it is invisible to the Internet user.

*Simplicity.*The layering has resulted in simplicity of software design. Each layer is concerned only with its own functionality, making its design simpler. For example, the layer concerned with physical devices like mouse operations are hidden from the higher layers that process information. This kind of simplicity has contributed to increased software reliability too.

Uniform naming and addressing. Each Internet host computer has an Internet Protocol (IP) address that uniquely identifies it on the Internet from the millions of other computers also on the Internet. The IP address is expressed in a uniform format or 'dotted quad'. An example is: '17.10.2.3'. As the dotted quad is not meaningful to humans the domain name system (DNS) is used to provide a symbolic name for the dotted quad. An example is: 'sol.brunel.ac.uk'. The DNS is capable of translating the symbolic name into the required IP address to enable Internet operations.

End-to-end protocols. The Internet does not process information. It enables the transfer of 'packets' of information between computers. This is called end-to-end protocol. The Internet enables the transfer of information or 'content' of the packet. The transmitting or receiving computers, known as the 'end' system, do the actual processing of information.

The combined use of the Internet, intranets and extranets by companies has resulted in the term 'virtual organization' or 'networked organization'. The virtual organization is to be contrasted with the physical organization; the latter is restricted by geographical, physical space. Companies can combine computer-networking technology with information technology (IT) and information systems (IS) to develop a network of computers that can capture, process and share information and knowledge in virtual or cyberspace, where time and space are defined differently from physical time and space.

Amazon.com may be classed as a virtual organization. Virtual organizations tend to be flatter because access to information and knowledge is potentially open to all employees who have access to a PC.

THE WORLD WIDE WEB

The World Wide Web, also known as the 'Web' or 'WWW', consists of pages of information depicted as text, graphics, sound, or video clips. A Web page may contain Java applets - Java programs that are downloaded from the server and run on the local computer.

The Web consists of over a million Web servers, and an untold number of Web browsers. What distinguishes the Web from other computer media is its ability to link Web pages dynamically; this is known as hypertext links or simply links. The Web combines computer network technology with hypertext to provide a 'global information system'.

One Web page can be linked to another by a hypertext link and the user merely has to click on the link to display related information. A link appears as highlighted on the Web page. It is this hypertext linking capability of the Web that makes it a powerful source of information. The Web is a client-server architecture system, and a Web user can access the Web servers with a Web browser such as Netscape or Microsoft Explorer.

Hypertext

A document on the Web is composed using hypertext technology. Hypertext is an electronic document system that can be read non-sequentially and interactively. The reader does not have to read it like a book, she/he can click on hyperlinks of related information. The Apollo space programme to record its documentation used a hypertext system. e-Commerce Web sites are built using hypertext documents, and other hypermedia.

Hypertext Transfer Protocol

The Web differs from the Internet by the protocol it uses to transfer information between computers. The Web uses the hypertext transfer protocol (HTTP) to connect and transfer hypertext documents stored on Web servers, also known as Web sites. All the computers on the Internet that use the HTTP protocol compose the Web.

The Web browser

A Web browser is a graphical interface for searching, accessing and viewing hypertext and multimedia files on the Web. The first browser, called Mosaic, was invented by the US company Netscape Communications, founded in 1994 by Marc Andreessen. He set himself the problem of transferring sound and pictures over the Web. His solution was the first graphical Web browser.

It allowed basic functions such as retrieving and displaying hypertext files. The growth of the Internet and the Web is largely because of the invention of the graphical browser which makes it easier for people to search and view information. Two popular browsers are Netscape Communicator and Internet Explorer. They are more sophisticated than the original Mosaic browser and enable e-mail messaging, HTML authoring, and extensions such as scripting, plug-in and multimedia.

INTERNET SEARCH ENGINES

The Internet is unarguably the most voluminous information store in the world. Finding information on the Internet requires complex computer algorithms. These algorithms form the backbone of Internet search engines designed to help people find the information they want. Organizations need search engines to find information about customers or business competitors or partners. Search engines are computer programs that locate specific Web pages, files or multimedia items stored on the Internet. Search engines such as Google or Autonomy use different algorithms or techniques to search for Web pages.

UNIFORM RESOURCE LOCATOR

The uniform resource locator (URL) is the address of a particular Web site on the Internet. It consists of domain names and a pathway that locates a particular host computer that is connected to the Internet. An example URL is www.yahoo.com or www.dell.com. A URL consists of the protocol that is to be used to make the Internet connection (the WWW in the examples), the name of the host computer ('Yahoo' or 'Dell') and the domain (.com). In the case of commercial companies, the name of the host computer connected to the Internet is usually the registered name of the company.

HYPERTEXT MARK-UP LANGUAGE

Hypertext mark-up language (HTML) is used to author information on a Web page. HTML documents are text files that are interpreted by a Web browser. The browser reads the HTML file and interprets the HTML instructions. The browser has to do this interpretation each time a hypertext file is loaded. A Web page can be divided into 'frames' or sub-pages.

Each frame is used to display separate but relevant information designed by the Web author. Multimedia can be facilitated by extensions to HTML or by 'plug-ins' or add-on programs that make the Web client more versatile to deal with additional media types. An example of extension is Secure HTTP that enables sophisticated encryption and decryption algorithms for sensitive e-Commerce data like payments for transactions.

It takes time to learn to write HTML code. Authoring tools are available for automatically converting documents in Microsoft Word to HTML files, ready to load on to a Web server. Hot Dog Pro, Adobe PageMill and Microsoft FrontPage are examples. A Web site consists of one or more Web pages linked together by hyperlinks. The contents of a

Web site are known as 'content'. HTML is not capable of processing or interacting with Internet users. To process data captured through a Web form JavaScript is required.

MULTIMEDIA

Multimedia is a tool capable of providing the transfer of sound and images like pictures over the Internet. Multimedia applications require lots of memory and bandwidth - the physical capacity of data cables to carry and transfer data. For example, one minute of music requires 5 MB of data. The transfer of sound and images in real time requires special software which is added to TCP/IP and HTTP protocols. On the client end, a player is required to interpret the data and render it into sound or images.

Multimedia Internet Mail Extensions or MIME is an Internet standard for multimedia Internet e-mail. MIME enables e-mail to be cast as types consisting of HTML, text, images or video. Example MIME types are: image/jpeg, video/mpeg or application/pdf.

JAVA, APPLETS, JAVASCRIPT AND INTERACTIVITY

The Internet is popular because it is interactive. Interactivity means that the Internet user (or client) can actively request information from and provide information to the server. Such interactivity is important for e-Commerce applications. CGI script and JavaScript provide interactivity on the Internet.

Java is a programming language originally intended for programming consumer electronic devices like microwave ovens, dishwashers or electronic clocks. As there are many manufacturers of these products, Java's developer, Sun Microsystems, designed Java to be ubiquitous, meaning that it should be operable on any manufacturer's device.

Virtual Java machines that are independent of PC operating systems interpret Java, a feature that makes it ideal for Internet programming. Java programs created for the Internet are called applets. Java applets are embedded in HTML documents.

An applet is a Java programme that is executed on the client machine. It is loaded by the Web browser and restricted to prevent security breaches. The applet is executed on a Java virtual machine in the browser.

JavaScript, originally called LiveScript, was developed independently of Java by Netscape to provide interactivity. It is used to process data captured via forms on the Internet and to create interactive Web sites, and both the server and the client side use it. JavaScript is embedded in HTML and is interpreted by a browser.

Web pages that contain JavaScript can be transferred around the Internet, because JavaScript is platform-independent or interpreted. ActiveX is a competitor of JavaScript. Scripts can be used in e-Commerce to validate service or product order form entries.

Common Gateway Interface

CGI programs are text files that consist of line or programming code similar to JavaScript; such programs are called CGI script. Pear is an example of CGI programming. CGI is used to create interactive Web sites that pass information from a Web browser to a server using a form, very useful for organizational needs. A form is a document that is created to interact with a user, take data from the user and send it to the server for processing, usually via a database.

ARCHITECTURE OF E-COMMERCE SYSTEMS

The buying and selling of products and services over the Internet is termed 'online trading'. Online trading or e-Commerce is important to businesses because it provides a flexible source of trading with customers, and with business partners.

To enable online trading, companies need to combine existing computerized transaction processing systems and information systems with Internet and Web technology. Existing computerized systems, databases, and Internet and Web technology are the basic components of online trading and form the architecture of e-Commerce systems. Computer system architecture consists of hardware and software components that are configured in terms of the needs of organizations.

Companies connect computers to a LAN, WAN and the Internet, using TCP/ IP, based on client-server architecture, to share computer software, printers or scanners. Basic Internet tools such as e-mail, browsers, search engines and protocols such as file transfer protocol (FTP) and Telnet are combined to form the system architecture for e-Commerce.

The systems architecture for a company will depend on its trading activities. A retail company will have a different architecture from a manufacturing company or a service company. As a company changes and evolves its mission or objectives, its e-Commerce system architecture will need to change too. Alternatively, the stimulus to change may come from competitors who use the most modern e-Commerce technology.

INTERNET, E-COMMERCE SYSTEMS AND INFORMATION SYSTEMS

Some of the terms used to describe a company's involvement with the Internet are that it has 'an online presence' or it has 'a Web site'. Such terms hide the complex IT and IS that form the infrastructure that underpin e-Commerce systems.

An information system is the application of a computer to capture and process data to provide information for managers and executives for the purposes of decision making and management. A company will normally have various information systems, such as an airline reservation system or an inventory control system. These systems will be linked to a corporate database that stores relevant data, like product or customer details. A company's Web site is connected to such information systems and databases to provide the essential product or service information for customer and employee use.

Companies' existing client-server technology and its IS/ IT infrastructure is connected to the Internet to form part of an e-Commerce architecture. The e-Commerce architecture is based on a company's business model, consisting of the basic logic of what it wants to produce or sell, how it will market it, how it defines its customers and other fundamental business issues. IT is combined with Internet technology to enable a company to personalize its service to a customer.

DATABASES

A computer database consists of records on specific items of interest, for example customers' contact details or the products they have bought. It is a collection of data that can be queried for specific purposes such as targeting a particular customer for certain products. Databases are used to market products and services. This is termed *database marketing*. Databases are used to store data on the purchasing habits of customers and enable a company to develop a tailored relationship with its customers.

The data are then processed to provide tailored information on individual customers' preferences that are then sent information about products or services relevant to their current buying habits. Data-mining techniques are used to reprocess existing data in databases to extract previously unrealized information of potential commercial use.

E-COMMERCE SYSTEMS AND THE CUSTOMER

e-Commerce systems that interface with the customer need to be pragmatic. The selection and evaluation of Internet technology need to be appropriate to both the company's needs and the customer's ability to use the system. A good business model will assume that the customer has little interest in technology and avoid the technology trap.*Avoiding the technology trap.*

It is not user-friendly to use over-complex Internet and Web technology in e-Commerce systems. The technology needs to be appropriate to prevent prolonging the time it takes for customers' commands to be executed by the system.

WEB SITE EVALUATION SOFTWARE

It is possible to measure the popularity of a company's

Web site using evaluation software that generates log files. Such log files record the number of visitors to the site or page impressions.

They record which parts of the Web site are most popular, the times of the day people visit, record which search engines are being used by visitors and how long they spend on the site, known as the 'stickiness' of the site. These log files can subsequently be used to evaluate the performance of the site from a business perspective and the information can be used to make it easier for customers to make transactions.

INTERNET SERVICE PROVIDERS

A company wanting to trade over the Internet has to agree a contract with an Internet service provider (ISP). ISPs provide communication and hosting services for individuals and companies wanting to access the Internet. ISPs provide access to the Internet and enable Internet commerce by connecting individuals and companies to the Internet.

There are thousands of ISPs that a company can choose from, all of them providing domain name services and electronic mail. The two most popular ISPs are UUNET Technologies and AT&T World Net. Other organizations, like a bank with mainframe computers, may also act as an ISP.

ISPs also provide hosting services for Web sites by installing and operating the server computers and software for a company. The computers and software are located at the ISP's site. Transaction services such as payment systems or order capture and fulfilment are also provided by ISPs.

EXAMPLE OF E-COMMERCE ARCHITECTURE

The important considerations for designing e-Commerce architecture are the customer, the company, the company's existing information systems and how payment will be made. For example, a company with a Web site that includes an order form would need a Web server that can provide a catalogue, whose details would be retrieved from a catalogue database, and order form.

It would need to interface with an existing database to collect and record the order details entered by the customer. The payment might be transacted with a credit card whose details would be captured on the order form utilizing standard security features available on the Web.

This example shows that an e-Commerce system is composed of existing information systems, databases and Internet technology. Other sophisticated e-Commerce architectures are possible for companies that need distributed transaction processing. For example, the Open Buying Consortium (OBI) has proposed a system architecture consisting of six fundamental system components split into buy-side, the customer and sell-side activities. These components are: Browse, Request, Approve, Fill, Receive and Pay.

E-COMMERCE SECURITY TECHNOLOGY

The success of e-Commerce depends on the security of data like personal details and credit card numbers transmitted over the Internet. The domain name system Internet protocol that makes IP addresses readable by humans is insecure. Security measures need to be taken in e-Commerce systems to prevent compromising the systems. Some of these measures include building firewalls, incorporating cryptography and authentication, and using secure connections.

Firewall

A firewall is hardware and software that are used to secure a private computer network system from uninvited intruders. A firewall is used to control whether a client is permitted to connect to the private network it protects.

Cryptography

Cryptography is a science that provides secure communication over vulnerable channels. Cryptography is fundamental to the success of the Internet and e-Commerce. Governments regulate cryptographic technology because of its importance to national security.

In cryptography a message, like a credit card number, is

encrypted using a key and the encrypted message is transmitted. The receiver uses the key to decrypt the message and convert it back to its original form.

The basic elements of a cryptographic system are algorithms, protocols and key management. An example of key management is the secret-key encryption algorithms. These algorithms are 'secret' because only the receiver and sender know the secret key.

Cryptography is used to provide secure transmission of data over the Internet. Private data like credit card details or digital signatures are encrypted and then transmitted over the Internet. Cryptography can keep a message secret and act as a gateway for identifying senders and receivers. It provides the secure electronic transaction technology for credit card transactions on the Internet.

Authentication

Authentication procedures are used to establish the identity of an individual or another computer system. Authentication procedures can be hardware-or software-based. Authentication procedures make use of personal items of knowledge or possession such as secret names or birth dates. Good authentication systems make use of two-factor authentication, such as a place name and memorable date known to the user. Some banking systems make use of three-factor authentication before allowing customers to make online account transfers.

Secure Socket Layer

The secure socket layer (SSL) is a layer of security between the application and the transport protocol. The purpose of SSL is to enable secure and reliable data transmission and communication over the Internet. The SSL provides private connection, making use of encryption and secret-key cryptography.

Authentication in SSL is achieved using public-key cryptography, which consists of a private key that is never made public chosen by one participant in the data exchange, and a public key chosen by the other participant in the exchange. Either key may be used for encryption.

Reliability of data transmission is achieved by using secure hash functions like SHA or MD5. Secure hash functions check the integrity of a message. SSL is commonly used in e-Commerce systems.

FUTURE DEVELOPMENTS IN E-BUSINESS TECHNOLOGY

THE INTERNET

Just as the internal combustion engine (the motor car) and jet engine (aeroplane) have radically changed our lives, the Internet is beginning to do the same. In the short time of its existence the Internet has greatly affected business and society. The Internet's evolution and future development are set to continue.

The TCP/IP protocol is evolving with the development of IPv6, the next generation of the Internet protocol. The improvements in IPv6 are scalability, security and support for real-time media quality. Companies such as Ciena Corporation are working on improving bandwidth. They have a product called Wave Division Multiplexing (WDM) that moves data at the speed of 100 billion bits per second (100,000,000,000 b.p.s.). This contrasts with the standard modem's 36,600 b.p.s.

THE WORLD WIDE WEB

The Web's HTTP protocol is evolving to encompass better performance and flexible interactions between clients and servers. Companies compete in complex and increasingly competitive markets. They do so by following, for example, competitive strategies of product differentiation or cost reduction. Similarly, *relationships* are becoming increasingly important in business models.

Current developments in Web technology are best placed to enable companies to exploit their differences and build personal relationships with customers, suppliers or business partners. For example, the eXtensible Mark-up Language, the Semantic Web and other Internet developments are leading the way to providing tailoring capability in e-Business technology.

Extensible mark-up Language

The extensible mark-up language (XML) is gaining popularity over HTML with companies. XML offers companies the ability to define tags that uniquely describe their products, services or customer service culture. Companies can design XML tags to display price or product or service descriptions that cannot be done in HTML. In short, XML allows a company to tailor the feel and look of its Web site and order forms to its needs.

The Semantic Web

Semantic Web is the name given to developments in Web technology by the World Wide Web Consortium (W3C), headed by Tim Berners-Lee, who invented the Web. The Semantic Web enables communication of contextual data and information. Information makes sense to humans only when it is used in context. The Semantic Web enables such context to be captured in Web applications. The primary contribution of the Internet, the Web and associated technologies is to enable collaboration and sharing of information and knowledge among people.

The types of collaboration are numerous, ranging from intra-organizational to inter-organizational and across the boundary of the organization with the customer. Future technology development will focus on this collaborative aspect of e-Commerce and will lead to radically different organizational structures and patterns of interaction among and between businesses and their customers.

THE WORLD OF E-RETAILING E-RETAIL

The business of *e-retail* has been defined as the sale of goods and services via Internet or other electronic channels, for personal or household use by consumers. This definition includes all e-commerce activities that result in transactions with end consumers (rather than business customers), i.e. *B2C* rather than *B2B*. Some e-marketing activities that do not directly involve transactions, such as providing (free) information or promoting brands and image, are considered to be part of B2C but are not normally considered as being within the scope of e-retail.

Despite the *dot.com crash* of 2000, e-retailing has been growing, particularly for the 'top eight' categories that account for three-quarters of all European sales. These major growth areas comprise: books, music and *DVD* movies, groceries, sex products, games and software, electronic and computer equipment, travel, and clothes.

DISADVANTAGES OF E-RETAILING FOR RETAILERS

Retailers have been slow to take up e-retailing. This is to some extent understandable in the light of many disadvantages and problems. Retailers, for example, may lack the technical know-how, the substantial investment required or the order fulfilment capabilities. Set-up costs start from around £20,000 for a small site and up to £500,000 for a large operation ($A53,000 to $A1.4 million).

And set-up costs are only the start - Datamonitor estimates that high street retailers are spending more on ongoing costs than on setting up new sites. A continuous cost will be fulfilment and logistics. Successful e-retailers such as Next and Land's End have had the advantage of already operating profitable mail-order catalogues.

There can be legal problems. For example, if purchaser and supplier are in different countries, there may be conflict between the laws and taxation of the two countries. In Europe, the *VAT (Value Added Tax)* position is still unclear, but Richard Branson's Virgin group's e-retail operation is registered in Madeira, the country with the lowest VAT rate in the European Union (EU).

A further disadvantage is that e-selling is less powerful than face-to-face selling (it is easier to say 'no' to a computer). This viewpoint is linked to a concern of traditional high street retailers that e-retailing offers a diminished role for their expertise. For example, there are obvious difficulties with products sold by 'atmosphere' - touch, feel, smell - and impulse purchases.

In addition, consumers have a perception of lower prices online. This puts pressure on margins for e-retailing, and can lead to shoppers expecting consistent low prices in-store. Finally, aftercare can be difficult, especially if the shopper is overseas.

DISADVANTAGES OF E-RETAILING FOR RETAILERS

- May lack know-how and technology
- Substantial set-up, investment and ongoing costs
- Complex logistics of fulfilment
- e-Selling less powerful than face-to-face - uptake slow for goods selected by taste or smell
- Fewer impulse purchases
- Legal problems
- Lesser role for traditional high street retail expertise
- Pressure on margins and prices in-store
- After-sales care difficulties

ADVANTAGES OF E-RETAILING FOR RETAILERS

On the other hand, there are a number of advantages for retailers. First, location is unimportant. According to some textbooks, adapting an old saying, the three most important elements in *retail* are 'location, location and location'. The best high street locations are therefore expensive.

The e-retailer, though, can sell equally well to anywhere in the country and even overseas. Second, size does not matter - small e-retailers can compete on equal terms to large ones, can reach a larger audience than the high street and can be open 24 hours a day. For example, the independent, northern UK-based Botham's of Whitby has been a pioneer of e-retailing.

There are many other advantages. The socio-demographic profile of e-shoppers is attractive to many retailers, with higher-than-average education, employment and disposable income levels. In theory at least, online selling saves on the wages costs of face-to-face sales people and the costs of premises. The savings may be less than expected, though, as there are still costs in Internet customer contact, and packaging and delivery can be more expensive to provide.

Perhaps a more substantial advantage is the ease with which e-retailing integrates with *customer relationship management (CRM)* and micro-marketing systems - identifying and treating the customer as an individual. This, together with the easier provision of product information, leads to greater opportunities for cross-selling and selling up. Finally, the late entrants into e-retailing are largely being driven by 'if we don't, our competitors will'.

ADVANTAGES OF E-RETAILING FOR RETAILERS

- Location is unimportant
- Size does not matter
- Saves on the wages and premises costs
- Reaches a larger audience
- Higher disposable income profile than average
- Accepts orders 24 hours a day
- More opportunities for CRM, micro-marketing, cross- and up-selling
- If we don't, our competitors will

Other retailers, though, are put off e-retailing by what they perceive as consumer resistance. According to e-research company Forrester, nearly 40 per cent of UK homes are now connected to the Internet, but estimates vary from only 12 per cent (Verdict) up to 20 percent (Forrester) of UK adults shopping online. This contrasts with the faster take-up of e-business for B2B, with 25 per cent of businesses ordering online.

THE (E-)RETAIL MIX: SALE THE 7CS

The (e-)retail mix is a shorthand term for the blend of tools and techniques that (e-)retailers use to provide value for customers. It is a development of the well-known marketing mix, more specific to retail and e-retail. As far back as the first half of the twentieth century, the job of the marketer was described as a 'mixer of ingredients'. Marketers devise strategies and tactics aimed at providing satisfaction and adding value for customers. The various elements are blended into a 'marketing mix' - a phrase first coined by Neil Borden (1964) of Harvard Business School.

The marketing mix is most widely known as E. Jerome McCarthy's (1960) '4Ps': Place, Product, Price and Promotion. 'Place' is not quite self-explanatory, but refers to the routes that organizations take to get the benefits of the product or service to the intended customers - channels of distribution.

Product' means both tangible product and also 'service', and all the ways that an organization adds value. 'Price' means not just the price charged, but also all aspects of pricing policy, including, for example, distributor margins. 'Promotion' is not just the more specialized 'sales promotion', but also every way that a product is promoted to customers - from print advertising to websites.

In recent decades there have been numerous attempts to update and revise the marketing mix. One development is particularly descriptive of the way that marketers think about the customer. The '4Cs' imply more emphasis on customer wants and concerns than do the 4Ps. The 4Cs (in the same order as the equivalent 4Ps listed above) are: Convenience for the customer; Customer value and benefits; Cost to the customer; and Communication. Reflecting the emphasis of 'new' marketing on long-term relationships with customers, we include 'Customer relationships' within the umbrella of the 'Communication' C.

C1 Convenience for the Customer

'Place' (from the 4Ps), rather than implying management's methods of placing products where they want them to be, can be thought of as 'Convenience for the customer', recognizing customers' choices for buying in ways that are convenient to them.

For the retailer, 'Place' incorporates what can be the most critical decisions concerning 'location'. For the e-retailer, this is also important, as many customers prefer a multi-channel approach: browse on the Web, buy in-store or vice versa - or buy on the Web, return to the store for a refund! This perhaps goes some way towards explaining the success of *high street* and *multi-channel retailers* in e-retail, as compared to the 'pureplays'.

Physical location can also be important for the e-retailer as many customers prefer to buy from, or are more likely to trust, an e-retailer based at least in the same country, where carriage costs and maybe taxes are cheaper.

Location' for the e-retailer also means virtual location and the ease of finding the website. This entails registration with search engines, location in e-malls and links from associates.

Convenience also includes key aspects of website design, such as navigation, layout and ease of purchase. For the '*bricks*' retailer, convenience decisions include shelf space allocation and layout. The equivalent in 'clicks' e-retail is site design and page layout - for example, whether layout follows the 'free-flow' or 'grid' type of layout, or indeed a combination such as 'free-grid'.

C2 Customer Value and Benefits

'Product', rather than being something that a company has to sell, can be thought of as 'Customer value and benefits' - meaning the bundle of service and satisfactions wanted by customers. People do not buy 'products' as such, but rather solutions to problems or good feelings. Retailers and e-retailers now specify (and sometimes design) products to a much greater extent than previously, reflecting closeness to the customer and appreciation of benefits that customers want.

An essential task of retail and e-retail is selecting the range of products offered for sale - assembled for target markets from diverse sources. The wide and deep range that can be offered is one of the areas where the clicks e-retailer can score relative to the bricks retailer.

When buying online, customers are far less likely to request help than they are in the store. Rather, e-shoppers who need help in understanding a product are more likely to abandon the transaction and find an alternative supplier or even buy through a different channel. Therefore, e-businesses need to be particularly careful about describing products clearly in customer value and benefits terms.

C3 Cost to the Customer

'Price' may be what companies decide to charge for their products, but 'Cost to the customer' represents the real cost that customers will pay, including, for example, in the case of bricks retail, their own transport costs. For clicks e-retail, there are also the costs of carriage and perhaps taxes to be added to the quoted prices. High carriage charges may be one reason for the high rate of carts abandoned at the checkout. Customers also need to consider the costs of Internet and telephone access.

Consumers have a perception that prices should be lower online than in-store, and this can cause problems when customers buying via other channels realise that they are paying more than online customers. For example, Screwfix, a well-known supplier of tradesperson's supplies via paper catalogue and telesales, has a number of attractive special offers available only online.

Customers who have looked up what they want online, then telephone to order, can be irritated to learn that the extra discounts are not available when ordering by phone.

C4 Communication and Customer Relationships

'Communication' is equivalent to the final 'P' in the 4Ps: 'Promotion'. Promotion suggests ways in which companies persuade people to buy, whereas communication is a two-way process also involving feedback from customers to suppliers. Reflecting an increasing control of elements of the retail mix by retailers rather than manufacturers, retailers spend more on advertising than manufacturers do (assisted by advertising allowances from manufacturers). Retailers are closer to the customer than are manufacturers and have more access to customer feedback.

Communication is not just advertising, though, but all the ways in which retailers communicate with their customers, including, for example, marketing research surveys, public relations (PR), direct mail, *e-mail*, Internet, marketing database and loyalty schemes. Successful e-retailers often use offline advertising such as magazines and 'click here' sections of newspapers integrated with online marketing communications. Online methods include banner ads and pop-ups (often incentivized); paid-for listings in search engines and directories; and affiliate programmes.

In addition to solving problems, there is another reason for customers buying products - to get good feelings. This is a particularly difficult area for e-retailers. The bricks retail store and the face-to-face salesperson are often much better at identifying and satisfying customers' emotional needs and wants. The physical store uses *atmospherics* in the attempt to change mood and give shoppers a pleasant emotional experience when buying. Emotional cues may be visual (decor), olfactory (perfume), tactile (smooth and cool or soft and cuddly) and aural (music).

e-Retailers can create a 'web atmosphere' using, for example, music and visuals such as 3-D displays and downloadable video clips. Such enhancements must always be a compromise, on account of the need to avoid long download times.

One way of tackling the problem is to provide a 'click here for *broadband*' 'Customer relationships' is an area that successful bricks retailers such as Tesco have used to gain a major lead over competitors.

The importance of the emotional aspects of selling has already been mentioned. The sales representative selling face-to-face in the bricks retail store can use verbal and non-verbal (body language) communication to build personal relationships with customers, enhancing the emotional value of products. In trying to replicate the physical buying experience, the e-retailer is at a disadvantage.

On the other hand, with transaction data ready-digitized, the e-retailer is well placed to enhance product value using CRM techniques. For example, data mining can be used to build a picture of products most likely to be wanted by individual customers. Products tailored specifically can be offered pro-actively. Amazon, for instance, uses such a system to match new books to existing customers who are likely to be interested in them.

There has been a number of suggestions for structuring a 'retail mix', equivalent to the 4Ps or 4Cs of the marketing mix, adding other aspects that may be key to retailer success. For example, McGoldrick (2002) uses a nine-element mix. In addition to those that can be incorporated into the 4Cs framework above, McGoldrick also includes factors such as 'brand image', 'logistics' and 'information'. Most versions of the retail mix are not as 'catchy' as the 4Ps or 4Cs of the marketing mix.

Therefore we propose a simplified '7Cs' for the *e-retail mix*, adding Computing and category management issues; *Customer franchise;* and Customer care and service.

C5 Computing and Category Management Issues

The success of retailers has been founded on supplying the products that customers want, in the right sizes and quantities, at the right time and in the right place. With the growth in consumer choice has come a proliferation of products. Superstores carry 20,000-plus branded products and department stores from 100,000, and even up to one million or more. Efficient control of this degree of complexity needs effective computer and logistics systems.

Retail logistics have been changing rapidly over recent decades. First, the growth of retailer power has involved major retailers taking more control of their supply chains. The involvement of wholesalers has been reduced, tending to give way to contract logistics (under retailer control). At the same time, supply chains have become more efficient with computer network links between suppliers and retailers - many still based on *electronic data interchange (EDI).*

Pre-dating the Web, EDI is based on privately owned third-party computer networks. Stock levels have been reduced using techniques such as *efficient customer response* (*ECR* -the retailers' equivalent of *Just in Time* or *JIT*). EDI networks are expensive to install, costing at least hundreds of thousands of pounds. There is a growing trend towards the use of the Internet, particularly for smaller businesses (suppliers and customers) and smaller order quantities. Increasingly, retailers such as Tesco are allowing Internet access to their suppliers for realtime *Electronic Point of Sale (EPoS)* data. Trusted supplier partners can thus respond more quickly to changes in customer demand.Cooperation between suppliers and retailers has been key to improving the efficiency of satisfying customers while minimizing stocks and costs.

On the larger scale, this cooperative process is known as *category management (CM)*, the retailer/ supplier process of managing categories as strategic business units.

High efficiency of the computer-controlled logistics systems is largely behind the success of 'bricks and clicks' retailers such as Tesco. Ironically, deficiencies in this area have been a major factor in the failure of a number of pureplay dot.coms that have concentrated on advertising and promotion at the expense of other areas of the e-retail mix. One exception is Amazon, which is founded on efficient logistics systems and customer care and service.In the UK, Amazon is using its logistics expertise to carry out distribution services on contract for bricks retailers such as WHSmith and Toys R Us.

Apart from Amazon and the major bricks and clicks retailers, many of the e-retailers with the most efficient computer and logistics efficiency are established direct-selling businesses. For example, Quill and Screwfix, office supplies and tradesperson supplies respectively, operate established mail businesses via a paper catalogue.

Dell have been pioneers in telemarketing and direct selling since the late 1980s, demonstrating that a complex product like a computer could be sold without face-to-face contact. Much of the success has been due to investment in computer-based *mass customization* systems, along with excellent customer care and service. The company was one of the first e-retailers and is the market leader worldwide for computer hardware.

SCREWFIX

Screwfix started out as a UK trade wholesale supplier, but

also now sells extensively for DIY. Screwfix.com earned *Retail Week's* 'Retailer of the Year' award for 2002. Screwfix is an example of the successful niche e-retailer and one of few to gain favourable mentions in the *Sunday Times* (UK) survey. Screwfix is owned by Kingfisher, i.e. in the same stable as the B&Q UK DIY stores.

Although the branding, ordering and fulfilment are completely separate, the supply chains are integrated, resulting in economies of scale and buying power. Screwfix has 0.5 per cent of the UK repairs, maintenance and home improvement market, but a massive 20 per cent of the *direct* market for those products. Web sales are over £20 million per year (15 per cent and growing of Screwfix's total business). The (e-)retail mix is summarized below.

Convenience for the Customer

Express shopping: if you have the catalogue, simply type in the quantities and catalogue number, or alternatively use 'search' to find what you want. A freephone telephone number is available 24 hours a day, plus fax and e-mail options, offering improved personal interaction.

Customer Value and Benefits

Products include not only screws, bolts and nails, but also fixings, adhesives, tools, hardware, lighting, plumbing and cleaning products - the claim is 'Everything for the trade and DIY - next day', and 100 per cent stock availability of 6,000 products.

Cost to the Customer

A number of special offers are always available. Most prices are significantly cheaper than in DIY retail sheds.

Communication and Customer Relationships

The homepage has many examples of good practice, for example: Recommend a Friend - get a reward when they order for the first time; Open a Business Account; Testimonials - 'I have just received my order and felt I must congratulate you on an excellent service. Your site is well designed. The products are well laid out and the order processing excellent.' ... 'Your website is brilliant, the designer needs a big pat on the back. Well laid out, and to order online is so easy.'; and Register/Login - optional registration makes ordering quicker and easier.

There are regular communications by mail with catalogues, 'What's new' and special offers for registered customers.

Computing and Category Management Issues

Winner of best use of Supply Chain Management at the 2001 Internet Business Awards.

Customer Franchise

Without the need for heavy advertising, Screwfix has quickly built up a reputation for cheap prices, with quick and reliable delivery based on actual performance.

CUSTOMER CARE AND SERVICE

To test the service, we ordered a long, complex list of equipment and fittings at 4.00 p.m. on a Sunday. The complete, correct order was delivered by 8.00 a.m. on Monday.

C6 Customer Franchise

The most successful bricks retailers have invested heavily in quality and customer care and service in order to raise their standing in the assessments of customers. Some authors refer to the accumulated value of image, trust and branding as the retailer's 'customer franchise'.

Consumers' lack of trust has been one of the main factors inhibiting the growth of e-retail. As McGoldrick (2002) pointed out, with greater choice consumers choose the brands that they trust.

Many bricks retailers have high-quality brands with clear personalities backed by long-term corporate promotion. These strong brands give bricks and clicks retailers a head start over 'pureplay' dot.coms. *Start-up* brands must work hard on trust.

For example, one of the few pure plays to prosper, the auction site eBay, includes five levels of safeguards, including fraud protection and dispute resolution.

C7 Customer Care and Service

According to McGoldrick (2002), retailing has traditionally been classified as a 'service industry' but, for most retailers, the preoccupation with service quality and services offered is of more recent origin. At the broadest level, most of a retailer's activities deliver a form of service to the consumer, creating assortments at competitive prices in accessible locations.

These activities, therefore, all play major roles in creating customer satisfaction. More specifically for the e-retailer, good service means, for example, reasonably fast and reliable deliveries at times convenient to the shopper; the availability of telephone help; and return and refund facilities. These are aspects in which the early e-retailers have been lamentably poor, with the big majority of e-shoppers still having a sorry tale to tell.

For the bricks retailer, even in self-service settings, store personnel play a crucial role in forming retail images and patronage intentions. The e-retailer is at a disadvantage, but elements such as *click-through* telephone help, bulletin boards and chat rooms can help to make the e-shopping experience more interactive.

In general, the successful (e-)retailer sets out to make shopping more enjoyable, more convenient and/or less worrying for the customers. When buying high-priced items and those with a high 'personal' content such as cars, shoppers particularly value personal service.

Retailers such as Virgin attempt to overcome this drawback with a pop-up window with a phone number to reach a sales consultant and the working hours in which they are available.

SALE THE 7CS - THE (E-)RETAIL MIX

C1 Convenience for the Customer ('Place' from the 4Ps)

- Physical location

- Multi-channel options: browse the Web, buy in-store or vice versa - or buy on the Web, return to the store for a refund
- Virtual location and ease of finding the website: registration with search engines, location in e-malls and links from associates
- Website design: connectivity, navigation, 'shelf' space allocation and ease of purchase
- Layout: 'free-flow', 'grid' or 'free-grid'

C2 Customer Value and Benefits ('Product')

- Satisfactions wanted by customers
- Solutions to problems or good feelings
- Specification (sometimes design) of products reflecting closeness to the customer and benefits that customers want
- Selection of the range of products offered for sale, assembled for target markets from diverse sources
- Wide and/or deep range, where the clicks e-retailer can score relative to the bricks retailer
- Content: describing a compelling offer of products clearly in customer value and benefits terms
- Customization of products to match the wants of customer segments as closely as possible

C3 Cost to the Customer ('Price')

- The real cost that customers will pay, including transport, carriage and taxes
- Costs of Internet telephone access
- Customers' perceptions that prices should be cheaper online than in-store

C4 Communication and Customer Relationships ('Promotion')

Communication is a two-way process also involving feedback from customers to suppliers, including:

- Marketing research surveys
- Public relations (PR)

- Direct mail
- e-Mail
- Internet
- Offline advertising such as magazines and 'click here' sections of newspapers
- Online methods such as banner ads and pop-ups (often incentivized); paid-for listings in search engines and directories; and affiliate programmes
- Atmospherics and web atmospherics: visual (decor, colour management, video clips, 3-D), olfactory (perfume and samples), tactile (smooth and cool or soft and cuddly - communicated by visuals or samples) and aural (music).

Customer Relationships

- In-store sales representatives use verbal and non-verbal (body language) communication
- Marketing database and loyalty schemes
- The e-retailer can enhance product value using Customer Relationship Management (CRM) and data mining to tailor products specifically to individual customers

C5 Computing and Category Management Issues

- Supplying the products that customers want, in the right sizes and quantities, at the right time and in the right place
- Efficient supply chains with computer network links between suppliers and retailers
- Minimizing stocks and speed of response: Efficient Customer Response (ECR - the retailers' equivalent of Just in Time or JIT)
- Cooperation between suppliers and (e-)retailers aiming to improve the efficiency of satisfying customers while minimizing stocks and costs. On the larger scale, this is 'category management' (CM), the retailer/supplier process of managing categories as strategic business units

- Efficient logistics systems - an important component of customer care and service

C6 Customer Franchise

- Image, trust and branding - long-term investment in quality, corporate communications, and customer care and service
- Safeguards, including fraud protection and dispute resolution
- Safe shopping icons, e.g. Which? Webtrader

C7 Customer Care and Service

- Creating assortments at competitive prices in an accessible format
- Fast and reliable deliveries at times convenient to the shopper
- Availability of help; return and refund facilities
- For the bricks retailer store personnel are crucial
- For the e-retailer click-through telephone help, bulletin boards and chat rooms make the experience more interactive and add a feeling of community
- Addressing customer concerns, particularly for credit card security, e.g. displaying the 'padlock' secure site logo

The extra 3Cs of the (e-)retail mix (in addition to the 4Ps or 4Cs of the marketing mix) can therefore be seen to be particularly critical for e-retailers. The computing, category management, supply chain and delivery systems are areas in which the early e-retailers, particularly pureplay dot.coms, have been sadly lacking, affecting trust, image, and customer care and service.

The stronger brands with greater customer franchise have higher sales and potentially higher profit - for example, Tesco and Next. With few exceptions, it is already strongly branded bricks retailers with established computer and supply chain systems who are making the running in e-retailing.

Notable exceptions include Amazon and Dell, both well

known for efficient systems, quality, service, communications and interaction.

GROWTH AND PROSPECTS FOR E-RETAILING

Online shopping is growing in the UK with sales having reached £3.3 billion by 2003. This was only 2 per cent of all retail sales but is predicted to rise to 5 per cent within a year or two and to 10 per cent by 2009. Other researchers estimate the market to be even larger and growing faster. For example, IMRG (2003) estimated e-retail sales to have already reached 7 per cent of all retail sales.

Most people' will buy groceries, books, CDs and even clothes by e-shopping. Books, movies and software, high on 'factual search', are natural for e-retailing, but electronic products, groceries and clothing are also increasing. Ninety-four per cent will be at the expense of existing channels and only 6 per cent from extra growth. According to the industry body, the Interactive Media in Retail Group, there are about 4 million people in the UK who spend an average of £3,000 to £5,000 per year online.

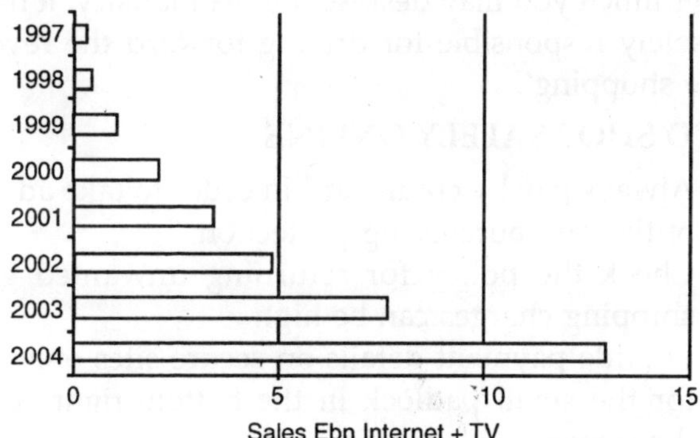

Fig. The Growth of online Shopping: Surveys, 1997 to 2003, Forecast 2004

Shoppers have long used the Internet to browse for products before buying offline, but US e-shoppers at least are reversing that trend, with 45 per cent of e-shoppers buying online after researching in stores and catalogues, according to a survey of 1,252 e-shoppers and over 80 e-retailers . This must be a worrying trend for bricks retailers, but also helps to strengthen the competitive position of multi-channel bricks and clicks retailers.According to Verdict, in 2001 grocery accounted for half of all UK e-retailing - £1.3 billion - which sounds massive but represents only 5.6 per cent of groceries.

The market leaders in their sectors were Amazon (books, plus CDs and DVD movies), Tesco (groceries), Dell (computers), Next (clothing) and Comet (electrical and electronic hardware). Though perhaps not actually an e-retailer, eBay is the leader for auctions and is the most visited of all UK websites. Average spend has risen faster for men (+15 per cent) than women (+5 per cent), leading Verdict to comment that 'the proliferation of female-orientated sites... [has] failed to motivate women to shop significantly more'.

The proportion of e-shoppers preferring to shop from e-sites run by high street retailers rather than Internet-only is soaring. The main service is travel and the main virtual product is sex (pictures, stories and video) - often absent from published statistics, but accounting for around 10 per cent of e-retailing. In the words of *The Virgin Internet Shopping Guide*: 'However much you may despise the sex industry, it has been almost solely responsible for driving forward the revolution in online shopping'.

HOW TO SHOP SAFELY ONLINE

- Always pay by credit card in order to take advantage of the safe purchasing protection
- Check the policy for returning unwanted goods - shipping charges can be high
- Provide payment details on secure sites only - check for the small padlock in the bottom-right corner of the screen
- Check carefully for extra charges. For example, goods from outside the EU may be subject to Customs and Excise duty and/or VAT

CASE STUDY

NEXT

Next is a top name in high street fashion. The first Next

store opened in February 1982 with an exclusive coordinated collection of stylish clothes, shoes and accessories for women. Next later introduced collections for men, children and furnishings for the home and now has around 330 stores in the UK and Ireland. It also franchises about 50 stores elsewhere in Europe, Asia and the Middle East.

The successful mail-order business, Next Directory, was launched in 1988 with 350 pages. The most recent catalogue now has 749 pages. Online shopping at Next began in 1999 and now the entire catalogue is available to shop from on the Internet. The mail-order expertise in order handling, fulfilment and customer care has proved invaluable, taking the business to the number one spot in UK clothing e-retailing. The entire Next Directory is available online, including formal wear, casual wear, accessories, shoes, swimwear, lingerie, men's and children's wear.

To shop online, the customer has to set up an account, which can take a day or two to arrange. There is a small charge for next-day delivery and a courier picks up returns free (or they can be returned to a high street shop). Revenue comes from its retail stores, the Next Directory catalogue, e-retailing and Ventura, which provides call centre and customer support services on contract for other firms.

The E-retail Mix at Next

C1 Convenience for the customer: The website can easily be found using most search engines. The Next website is a convenient place to shop as it is well-structured and easy to navigate and buy from, pages download fast and there is general ease of access.

C2 Customer value and benefits: There is a wider product range than can be found in the high street shops, offering all the products that are available in the Next Directory.

C3 Cost to the customer: Next does not offer online customers any discount. Customers also pay a £2.95 delivery charge no matter how large the order. However, customers do save in terms of the time and travel costs of travelling to a bricks store.

C4 Communication and customer relationships: The Next website provides communication to customers via e-mail. Customers can register to receive e-mail updates of forthcoming offers and promotions, including details of the end-of-season sale.

C5 Customer franchise: Next has a good brand name for high street and Next Directory shopping and the website has inherited this to some extent. Next claims to be attracting 700 new mailorder customers a week via the Web without pouring large amounts of cash into the online division - mainly due to the brand name. According to David Jones, Chief Executive, Next has 'spent £125,000 on its Internet site and will do £12m of sales'.

Next targets customers in their twenties and thirties who are looking for stylish but affordable clothes to take them through the next fashion trend. Quality, style and value for money are core brand values.

C6 Customer care and service: The Next website provides good customer care and service. If a customer wishes to return goods, they can do this with no extra charge. They can either take them back to a store, return them via a courier, or send them by post (Next provides a pre-paid label). Purchases made before 5.00 p.m. are delivered the following day, excluding Sunday deliveries.

At the time of writing, online purchases at Next can only be made between 7.00 a.m. and 11.00 p.m. This is a substantial limitation as one of the main customer benefits of buying online should be the ability to buy 24/7.

C7 Computer and category management issues: The supply chain systems are slick and efficient, utilizing ECR techniques to provide fast delivery from minimum stocks, keeping the customer informed of progress by an automated e-mail system.

Web Atmospherics

Next does not have sound on their website. Audio would not be difficult to add and could be important as, for example, music pleasure intensity can compensate for a lack of interpersonal contact. The Next website is not very interactive;

there is no chat group or message board and it does not sell any customized products. 'Extras' such as these could help to compensate for the lack of personal contact. There is separate login for customers who have bought online before, but, apart from this, no personalization or mass customization can be found on the site.

The Next website is very simple, which makes for good usability-something that many Internet retailers get wrong. The layout of the site is easy to navigate around for people who are not computer literate. Purchasing from the website is very straightforward, without too many click-through pages.

Visually, the Next site is appealing and sophisticated. Pictures of the products are downloaded reasonably fast. The quality and colour of the pictures of the products are excellent. The text on the Next website is short, yet contains all the required information. In conclusion, the good all-round retail mix has made Next into one of the top Internet retailers. As a result, they are now looking to start sub-contract fulfilment services for other e-tailers.

As an improvement, Next could consider introducing sound to the website. This is simple to do and can help make the purchase experience more pleasant to a customer. Adding sound to a website will not slow down the speed much as compressed files can be used which do not take up much memory.

Next will need to make sure the music is in character with their products, so needs to carry out research on what its customers would like to hear. Next could also consider using pre-recorded voice advertising on the website, as is found in many high street shops, promoting offers, new ranges, etc.

Another refinement would be to introduce a virtual changing room where items could be coordinated. This is the 'Style Builder' idea as used by Eddie Bauer. A further improvement would be to implement a system for customers to see pictures of themselves wearing different garments. Records could be stored on a database for customers to refer to later.

These kinds of ideas may encourage people to buy by

making the experience more interactive and personal.The colour quality of the website will be different on every customer's monitor.

Next could perhaps investigate colour management systems - for example, eColour, a system that sends a *cookie* that reads the monitor's output and from this advises adjustments to the monitor settings.

Finally, but perhaps of more immediate potential benefit, the Next website needs increased working hours to provide a better service and meet customer expectations of being able to buy any time on the Internet.

Chapter 3

Global Overview and Ethics

THE IMPORTANCE OF GOING GLOBAL

Globalization involves the transfer of an existing business system to other countries or the management of another business system in other countries. The terms 'international', 'multinational', 'global' and 'transnational' have been used to describe different stages in the globalization ladder of business development.

The decision of nationally based e-Commerce to go global will depend on factors such as demography, entry modes, socio-cultural diversity, as well as the approach and management style to be used when entering new markets. The United States today represents the largest national market in the world, with roughly 25 per cent of the total world market for all products and services.

The fact that 75 per cent of the world market potential is outside their national territory has been the force driving many US companies to 'go international' and even to extend further and 'go global'. With three-quarters of its revenue generated by its soft drink business outside the United States, Coca-Cola, acknowledged as the most successful global company, has driven the message of globalization further than anybody else. For non-US companies the incentive is even stronger. The two wealthiest countries after the United States, Japan and Germany, have 85 per cent and 94 per cent respectively of the world market potential.

Today there are only seven countries where English is the primary language spoken, by about half a billion people or 8 per cent of the total population, their combined economies representing only 30 per cent of the total world economy. e-Commerce companies that will continue to target this small percentage of the world market will miss out on capturing a much larger potential market.

The total global e-Commerce market is forecast to reach $1.6 trillion by 2003, a very powerful incentive for companies entering this arena. If present e-businesses have been able to achieve year-upon-year growth in visitors, sales or members using only domestic focused Web sites, then in order to sustain or increase this growth it will be almost impossible to do so without entering and servicing new markets.

According to a Nua.com survey, almost 10 per cent of the world's population has access to the Internet. The global Internet audience had grown to 580.78 million people by the end of May 2002. The survey indicated that, for the first time ever, Europe has the highest number of Internet users in the world, with 185.83 million Europeans online, compared with 182.83 million in the United States and Canada, and 167.86 million in Asia-Pacific.

The survey's findings also indicate that the digital divide between developed and developing nations is as wide as ever. While Europeans account for 32 per cent of global Internet users, only 6 per cent of the world's Net users are based in Latin America. The Middle East and Africa combined account for just 2 per cent of global Internet users; the lack of telecommunications infrastructures in those regions means that most citizens remain unconnected.

Methods of Entry into Global Markets

Until recently a traditional business has had the options of entering new geographical markets through direct or indirect exporting, new start-ups, franchising, joint ventures, acquisitions, concessions or licensing, depending on the degrees of risk and the level of involvement they were prepared to accept.

To these alternatives can be added now the virtual business via the Internet. The nationally based business will start with cautious testing of new markets, often selected with a similar culture, having a focus that is culturally and managerially 'ethnocentric' or centred around the home market. A multinational business will have a 'polycentric' orientation, i.e. a focus based on the understanding and appreciation of different operating contexts.

The global or transnational business will have a fully global strategy, focusing on maximizing the benefits obtained from economies of scale in sourcing, product standardization and marketing. Typical of global operators is their adaptable, geocentric approach, which allows them to 'think globally but act locally'.

Opportunities and Threats in Global e-Marketing

The Internet has already made a big difference in the way business operates globally, offering substantial advantages to both buyers and sellers, because it can cope with a rapidly changing environment. Many industries have further motives for embracing the Web, as it offers huge savings on their marketing and distribution costs, which in certain cases, for example the airlines, can make up about a quarter of their total operating expenses.

The Internet has made a big difference to aviation, with portable computers becoming essential in the process of booking and buying air travel. Simplifying booking and cutting out the cumbersome process of issuing card tickets can be very attractive to customers. Since 2000, an increasing number of airlines, such as Northwest and Swissair, have been offering online facilities for seat selection and check-in, as well as for booking and paying for flights.

e-Commerce will also allow businesses to learn more about their Web customers, so they can package offers tailored to their individual needs. This is what in marketing terms is called 'customer of one' and it applies to airlines, just as it does to cars or computers.

Continuing with the same example, there are distinguishing characteristics between the different levels of airline Web sites. The most basic are 'brochure sites' which offer simple static information, not much different from the printed brochures found in the bricks-and-mortar travel agents. At the next level are the constantly updated versions of the 'brochure sites'.

The third level contains sites that obtain information from the customer as he logs on and builds a profile of his travel needs and preferences. It can answer requests for information, take bookings and issue e-mail confirmation of bookings. This sort of e-Commerce transaction is now quite common, especially for the no-frills, low-cost airlines.

The next generation Web site will recognize and greet the customer by his or her name when s/he logs on and will know that s/he is a valuable customer. It will be able to analyse his travel history and suggest alternative itineraries that might suit him better.

Niche Marketing

No-frills, low-fare carriers such as EasyJet and Ryanair have been using this low-cost, high service strategy to carve out successful niches. The emergence of these new companies has increased the level of competition in the industry, putting established carriers under increasing threat of loss of business on their traditional routes and ultimately bankruptcy. One notable example is Swissair, and even British Airways has felt the pinch with the threat of its shares losing their blue-chip status.

Other examples of industries that have made good use of the trend towards personalization through the Internet are the perfume and fashion industries. Custom fragrance marketers have been established, usually family-run businesses where the Internet has radically changed the direction of this niche market.

In 2001 a number of new entrants have included Procter & Gamble with Reflect.com, Ashford.com, RomanceHer.com, Eleuria.com and Creativescent.com. The Internet is about to turn this niche market into a major profit-making category of prestige fragrance and force the major perfume companies to create custom divisions.

Nevertheless these new ways of doing business are at risk for being untested and vulnerable to sudden market downturns or fashion changes.

Small and medium-size enterprises are the main beneficiaries of the low-cost marketing possibilities offered by the Internet, which can turn them from small niche players into global ones. A fundamental change is happening in the world of Asian marketing that could prove a bonanza for struggling companies.

The Internet is providing low-cost ways for small to medium-size businesses to get their advertising message across, focusing on specific audiences. Asia has been experiencing a phenomenal growth in Internet advertising, whose potential demand has been recognized by US Internet advertising agencies.

DoubleClick Asia, a joint venture between New York-based Double Click and Hong Kong Web portal builder Asiacontent.com, has been able to track Internet users' movements by collecting 'cookies' or files embedded in users' Web browsers that log the pages they visit and for how long. This information allows marketing solution providers such as DotMedia China or Next Media to help their customers, which are local companies, to target their own local audience in a far more efficient way by posting relevant ads on their Web sites.

Another interesting sme example is Charles Tyrwhitt, a UK manufacturer of mainly shirts, but also ties and other accessories, to the exclusive ABC1 men market. The company has adopted a 'clicks and mortar' strategy, which hopefully will turn this British niche player into a global one. It will also reduce its brochure and marketing costs.

The company's strong customer service culture is being translated on to the Net, where this is so important. The firm's success lies in its ability to carry more than 3,000 lines of stock at any one time, with each shirt being offered in up to forty-eight combinations of size, cuff and sleeve. The company is able to maximize sales by targeting groups of people more effectively than could ever be done through mail order.

The key to the success of niche e-businesses is first and

foremost brand awareness. Second, expanding the customer base geographically is leading to the need for a greater product range to meet strong local preferences in style and fashion. The Internet has proved to be the perfect messenger for niche interests, serving individual tastes and diverse geographical demands.

In certain industries, such as national media, which were previously dedicated to mass markets, the Internet is offering for the first time the possibility of meeting specialist demands. As successful online newspapers in the United States reach less than 25 per cent of their local Net users, some have tried to add an interest-based niche to their regional focus. For example, the *San Jose Mercury* is concentrating its online energies to SiliconValley.com, a specialist site for technology news.

The objective is to have a network of loyal users by meeting specialist demand with detailed information. In the United Kingdom the commercial site Fish4, which is backed by local newspaper publishers, owned by the Guardian Media Group, is claiming to have reached the necessary critical mass of information to make a niche product.

BBC News online is another example where the battle between general and niche is being fought. The way it uses its huge breadth of content, both broad-brush and localized, demonstrates the diversity of its users and their demands. In just one day 98,450 different stories were read, amounting to a staggering 20 per cent of all the stories the site has ever produced.

Understanding the Global Environment

For the e-Commerce organization shaping the direction of its global expansion it is vitally important to understand the external environment as a means of identification of opportunities and threats.

An analysis of the variety of factors and environmental influences is necessary in order to allow a balance of internal capabilities and resources with the opportunities offered externally that ultimately would affect business planning and implementation within the organization.

The elements of the external environment connected with the organization can be divided into four distinct groupings, known by the acronym STEP.

SOCIO-CULTURAL ENVIRONMENTS FOR GLOBAL E-COMMERCE

Culture is particularly important for an internationally or globally oriented e-Business, especially in respect to the impact it has on buyer behaviour and all the implications related to the organization and its management.

Definitions of Culture

Culture has been defined in a multiplicity of ways and because of its diversity, there is no one universally accepted definition. Anthropologists and sociologists alike have tried hard to produce the perfect definition, which samples their opinions spanning more than a century. In very simple terms, *culture* is defined as 'ways of living, built by a group of human beings that are transmitted from one generation to another'.

Elements of Culture

In 1999-2001, according to International Data Corporation, roughly 40 per cent of the people visiting the Internet have been seeking sites in languages other than English. Yet, according to the same study, 55 per cent of US companies have done nothing to customise their Web sites for non-English speaking users.

With a total global potential e-Commerce market of $1.6 trillion by 2003, companies worldwide need to become experts fast on the cultural issues that must be met in order to make e-Commerce work. For a successful e-Commerce operation, communication between a diversity of cultures with a multiplicity of languages involves far more than mere text translations. There are a variety of other cultural factors to consider, some of which might appear inconsequential to a globally expanding e-Business but important enough to the consumer, and which could create significant problems if ignored.

Language

Today more than 50 per cent of all Internet users have a non-English mother tongue. With the dramatic expansion of the Internet, this number is expected to increase to 70 per cent by 2003. By contrast, more than two-thirds of Web pages are in English, with Japanese and German at a distant joint second position with almost 6 per cent each.

Nevertheless, past research has revealed that Web users are three times more likely to make purchases from Web sites in their own language and two-thirds of surfers will click away from a site in another language. It is expected that a fast increasing proportion of new Web sites will be in languages other than English. Asian languages, mainly Chinese, are poised for especially strong growth, owing to a fast increase in Internet penetration among Asian countries' population.

There is also an increasing trend for companies worldwide to make their current English-language sites available in several other languages. The Internet is at present dominated by English and probably will continue to be for the foreseeable future, although it remains to be seen whether it will be the universally adopted language of the Net.

Translations on the Web

Literal translations of Web sites are a minefield. Machine translations have been an attractive option for some e-Commerce organizations because they are cheap, but they have severe limitations. In circumstances where speed has been the most critical factor, machine translations have been used to understand the general idea of a received message and to send an acknowledgement of its reception with a promise of follow-up. This has been acceptable in the early years of e-Commerce development, as a strategy designed to generate goodwill and buy time. To use it for a permanent Web site is a strategy fraught with danger.

Handing the text to computer-aided translators is not enough to ensure that the meaning and scope of the Web site are achieved. Here is an example of machine-translated text which has gone seriously wrong. A news item was taken in

1998 from the German version of MSNBC about the famous round-the-world balloon race, which was about to become an international incident if not properly understood by the Chinese. It was translated with the help of a computer-aided translation service supplied by Systran and sounded like this:

One of the urgent problems of the Weltumrunder in the balloon "global challenge" solve itself now: China gave on Tuesday an overflight/flyover permission to the three balloon drivers on their Weltumseglung the message in Peking, British after information. ' It is clear from this example that human translation and adaptation are required when interfacing with international customers and the correct understanding of critical messages is required.

Tone and Formality of the Language

Business culture and etiquette used on the Net, or 'Netiquette', need to be carefully researched and understood in order to avoid embarrassing mistakes. For example in the United States it is common to see Web sites which use informal greetings for their registered users, such as: 'Welcome back, Frank!' To address using first names might be appropriate to Anglo-Saxon cultures, but it would be unacceptable in Japan, where a registered Japanese visitor to the site would take offence at such a casual greeting.

A culturally sensitive business would ensure that it used a significantly more formal greeting such as 'We are honoured by your return visit to our site, Mr Takahashi'. A survey undertaken by Ion Global which focused on the level of formality expected by different cultures in Asian and Pacific countries placed Japan and South Korea at the highest end, whereas Australia and the United States were the least formal.

SYMBOLS AND SYMBOLISM

The use of symbols on Web sites is widespread, owing to space saving requirements. Web designers frequently use icons and images; however, not all of them are exportable. For example, hand gestures could be a minefield to the uninitiated, and as they are natural they are perceived to be universal. In effect, they are culturally transmitted from one generation to another. The commonly used 'A-OK' of a circle formed with the thumb and forefinger, with the other fingers extended, is widely used in the United States, where it is considered a friendly gesture, whereas in Brazil it is considered obscene.

Similarly the 'thumbs up' sign is considered highly offensive in Iran. A palm-forward wave is a nasty gesture in Greece and Nigeria. Some very successful Web sites are designed around a particular theme which has a specific symbolic significance (such as a compass or an animal).

Special attention needs to be given to the choice of symbols, as their meanings might have different connotations in other cultures. For example, flowers have a strong symbolic significance in many cultures around the world. The rose is considered almost universally the symbol of love, although a hand holding a red rose is the symbol of socialism in Europe. The white lily is a symbol of purity, although in other cultures it is associated with death.

Colours

Similarly, colours must be chosen with care in designing a Web site for global audiences. Colours such as black, white and red have different symbolic or religious meanings throughout the world.

A Web site with a black background can appear 'cool' and 'sophisticated' to an American audience, but black is linked with death and bad luck in Chinese culture. Purple has religious significance in Catholicism, as does green in the Islamic world. User feedback during the design phase is necessary in order to avoid culturally insensitive choices.

INCOMPATIBLE SOFTWARE

Rutherford also mentions a Forrester report entitled *The Multilingual Site Blueprint,* which surveyed twenty-seven US-based multilingual site operators and found that the greatest challenge encountered was adapting software to work with other languages.

She gives the example that, to make Web software work

with Asian languages, which contain up to 6,000 characters, site operators must install Unicode, a character coding system that supports written texts in different languages.

CULTURALLY SENSITIVE WEB DESIGN

The way a home page is designed determines whether the user will stay on the site or abandon it out of frustration. There are a number of commonsense Web site development methods which will ensure the building of a loyal and satisfied customer base.

As a matter of practice, the first thing a non-English-speaking Net user will do when reaching a Web home page is to look for navigation leading to the site in a familiar language. According to Hanrahan and Kwok, the presentation of the language selector navigation is one of the key elements of the global user experience.

A popular form of this type of navigation is a pull-down menu with a list of languages and the title such as 'Language selector' or 'Choose a country'. This method might be problematic, as a foreign visitor might not be able to understand the instructions designed to lead to the pull-down menu on a page in English that might be full of information and navigation options.

Another commonly used method suggested by Hanrahan and Kwok is to show a selection of country flags representing the different Web site versions. This method is acceptable if the Web sites contain country-specific content as opposed to language-specific content, as flags represent countries and not languages. Sertain languages, such as Spanish for example, are used by majority or minority populations in a number of diverse countries.

Using the flag representing Spain to represent Spanish might confuse users from Mexico, the United States or Argentina, who do not identify with the Spanish flag. The use of flags is appropriate when the target is a specific national market and not all speakers of a specific language.

When the target market is language-specific, one recommended way to address these problems is to design navigational images and buttons showing the name of each language available written in that language and with the appropriate script. This is known as 'good user experience'.

Another aspect related to language specificity is 'text swell', which describes what happens when the translation of a word from one language to another necessitates extended (or contracted) display space. Text swell can have a considerable effect on the layout of a Web page and should be an important consideration in the design of an international Web site.

Both HTML text and text within an image can be affected by text swell, as well as the size of pop-up windows. German tends to take up more horizontal space than English, while Chinese and Japanese take up less, but need taller spaces than languages based on the Latin alphabet.

METHODS OF PAYMENT

Payment preferences vary considerably from country to country. For example, in the United States or the United Kingdom the overwhelmingly preferred method of payment is the credit card, whereas in China cash on delivery (COD) is the prevailing method.In Japan, purchases through the Internet can be dispatched to and paid for at the convenience stores called *conbini*. From a Web design point of view, it is therefore important to understand what payment options are used in the target market. No matter how appealing the product or service might appear to the consumer, if s/he is not given the right options of payment the purchasing sequence will be aborted.

Along with payment options, the online sales effort should also take into account the variety of currencies and country-linked value-added tax (VAT) systems. Research shows that customers are reluctant to commit to an online transaction in a 'foreign' currency owing to the uncertainty presented by the daily fluctuation of exchange rates.A simple solution is to add an interactive currency calculator to the site, which will give a rough idea of the cost of the product or service and give an indication if it is worth proceeding with the purchase. A better solution includes payment systems that not only perform currency calculations but also calculate VAT (valúe-added tax or sales tax) by country and product or service category.

The best systems currently available automatically update the currency conversion and táx rates, relieving the e-Commerce Web site operator of a daily burden, and can be used with any payment systems on the market. An example of a multi-currency payment system is WorldPay, launched in the United States, which offers the Web site operator the facility of offering products or services in more than 100 currencies.

With the exchange rate updated daily, customers will have the certainty of seeing the real cost of their purchases, which will give them the ability of meaningful comparison with what they can find in local stores. These customer-sensitive methods are reducing the often painful order cancellations or goods being returned, owing to customers' shocked realization when checking their credit card bills.

For example, having such a system implemented will allow the French or the Italian customer to see in euros exactly what has been charged on their Visa card, whereas the UK-based e-Commerce retailer will receive the equivalent amount in pounds sterling or, if US-based, the equivalent amount in US dollars.Taxware is offering a system solution that calculates the appropriate local sales tax (VAT) for purchases based on geographical location and type of goods or services. It can even supply VAT records to be used by customers for tax return calculations.

The combination of the two system solutions showing prices in the local currency and the local VAT provides the international customer with the complete picture, enabling a rapid and informed purchase decision online. The e-Commerce retailer offering such a facility is showing care towards the target market needs, leading to a satisfied, thus loyal customer base.

TEN EXPERT TIPS FOR GOING GLOBAL ONLINE

When developing a global e-Commerce Web site, it is

imperative to pay close attention to how users around the world are going to interact and experience the process of finding products, the reading and understanding of product descriptions, the process of adding the products chosen to the shopping cart and finally concluding the purchase. Here are ten tips from the experts:

- Use local experts for advice on culturally, technically and legally sensitive issues and the overall development of the Web site. If necessary, establish partnerships with local e-businesses to ensure that the message is appropriate to the target market.
- Conduct usability tests on the Web sites in target markets at several stages of the development process. The site needs to be tested not only for ease of use but also for cultural appropriateness, adherence to technical requirements and legal compliance in the target markets.
- The home page design should include a clear and easy method for global users on how to find the version not only in their own language but also tailored to their country.
- All product descriptions should use the appropriate measurement terms and scales for weights and sizes (feet versus metres, pounds versus kilograms, etc.).
- Product descriptions should be written in a clear and easy-to-understand style, appropriate to the target market. If product information is written in English, but is destined for a global audience, it should be clear, precise and free of jargon, abbreviations, acronyms, slang or country-specific terms.
- A product information glossary should be provided, as well as a Help feature.
- International shipping information and country options should be clearly made available early on in the product selection process. e-Commerce users feel cheated spending time choosing and filling their shopping baskets only to find out at the end that shipment will not be available to the location

requested. Differences in price, terms and conditions should be clearly stated.

- Payment options should be culturally sensitive and appropriate to the target market.
- Form fields used in the checkout process should allow for different formats for international addresses, telephone numbers and postal codes.
- And finally ... offer a currency converter!

LEGAL ISSUES IN E-COMMERCE

A comprehensive international legislation system for global e-Commerce does not exist at present and it is not expected in the foreseeable future. Even within the United States, which is so advanced in its use of the Internet, certain e-Commerce legal issues have caused significant disagreements, such as the validity of digital signatures.

While waiting for federal legislation, many states have set up their own laws, which have been widely different in substance from state to state. Organizations such as the UN conference on international trade law have been actively calling for global co-ordination of appropriate legal structures. The most important issues are copyright protection, contractual agreements and privacy laws.

E-COMMERCE GLOBAL STRATEGIES

The organizations practising in the area of e-Commerce are facing a number of d ecisions regarding their global activities. Having analysed the characteristics of the target foreign market, they now face the next stage of developing an international marketing programme.

This would include defining and selecting target segments, positioning the product or service and making the decision to modify the elements of the marketing mix to suit the conditions of the foreign market. For physical goods, the marketing mix is composed of four elements: product, price, place (distribution) and promotion. For services, the marketing mix extends to seven elements with the addition of people, processes and physical evidence.

Given the diversity of the global environment, with differing cultures, customs and competition, the decision facing the e-Commerce marketer is the degree of change necessary within the elements of the marketing mix. There are a number of pressures affecting this decision, which can be summarized as (1) staying local versus going global, (2) standardization or adaptation.

Local Versus Global

Ten years ago 'pan-European' advertising was all the rage among direct marketing companies in the United Kingdom. A precursor of global communication, it was based on a simple idea, namely that consumers in various countries fall into the same socio-demographic categories, with similar if not identical buying habits and tastes brought about by low-cost cross-border travel. It uses the same imagery, messages, product and brand positioning across all campaigns and all markets. Economies of scale could be achieved and global brands built up, as campaigns could be extended from one country to another.

More recently, globalization has received a few hard knocks, due to changes in customer tastes and timing. Some products achieved global status because they required very little effort in terms of product development in order to be successful in new markets. Others needed extensive redevelopment in order to localize their marketing mix.

A good example is basic office software such as Microsoft Word, which works equally well in most countries, once it has been localized for language characteristics. Other examples are soft drinks like Coca-Cola or imaging products like Kodak, which need only minimal changes of their global campaigns to adapt to local taste. Alternatively, cars are more of a 'lifestyle' purchase.

Consumer tastes in cars vary more widely between the United States, Germany, Japan, Italy, the United Kingdom and India. Achieving substantial economies of scale either in product development or in advertising is more difficult. Ford has been one of the manufacturers most successful in using a modular approach to car manufacturing and marketing. Recognizing that there are strong differences in consumer preferences, Ford has reduced the number of components - and thereby has achieved economies of scale - without affecting the number of options available to customers in each of the seventy-five different national markets in which Ford sells cars.

Ford manages to use a modular approach also in its advertising messages, emphasizing safety in Scandinavia, performance in Italy, design in France and handling in Germany. The Ford brand may be global, but the product and its supporting marketing effort are very much local.

For e-Commerce marketers with global ambitions, the requirements are to find out if the product or service they represent and the way of doing business can be exported in their 'domestic' forms or they will encounter consumer resistance and will need substantial adaptation to suit consumer tastes.

THE RISKS OF GLOBAL WEB MARKETING

For companies that have an established global distribution system the decision to exploit the Internet as a marketing tool needs to be considered with care. Once a Web site is established which has an online purchase facility, there is the risk that overseas customers will cut out the local distributor, place orders electronically and expect price discounts.

This was the case of Millipore Corporation of Bedford, Massachusetts, a company with annual sales of $600 million specializing in filtration products for water purification for laboratories and the detection of contaminants in semiconductor manufacturing. With a 'blue chip' list of customers worldwide the Internet clearly offered an effective medium to both communicate information and provide the customer with a purchasing mechanism.

However, Millipore faced a massive complication in that, similar to many other multinationals, it charges higher prices overseas in order to cover the additional cost of support services. Having faced the potential dilemma associated with inter-country pricing differentials, Millipore decided to postpone offering an online ordering facility and instead restrict its Web site to providing information with supporting pre- and post-purchase service activities.

Standardization Versus Adaptation

The decision whether to standardize or adapt the marketing mix elements is a major one for any organization operating outside its home environment. Standardization allows the organization to maintain a consistent image and identity throughout the world.

It provides economies of scale and is particularly valuable for maximizing impact with the internationally mobile customer. It works best within an identified international segment and with a product of well defined complexity. Global branding and the transfer of new product ideas across boundaries are both possible with standardization.

Standardization has been used successfully in running global promotional campaigns. Transferring campaigns from one country to another is almost impossible, owing to language and cultural differences. Nevertheless, the clever use of pop music as a universal language has allowed Levi's advertising to be successful where others have failed.

Coca-Cola has also succeeded with its 'one sound, one sight, one appeal' philosophy which brings it closer to a full standardization position. Benetton is still running their 'United Colours of Benetton' global campaign based on multi-cultural, universal images that appeal globally.

Adaptation is nevertheless necessary if the organization is under pressure to satisfy the multiplicity of needs of the global customer to the extent to which it will have to change the elements of the marketing mix.

CHANGING PATTERNS IN GLOBAL DISTRIBUTION

Distribution is the process by which all consumer and industrial goods are transferred from the producers to the end users. The process includes not only the physical handling and distribution of goods and the transfer of ownership from producer to consumer, but also the whole range of buying and selling negotiations between producers and intermediaries, and between intermediaries and consumers. Distribution channels are the ways and means by which goods are distributed from the producer to the end user. The traditional distribution model has been linear.

The producer is the originator of the products, which it builds or manufactures. Wholesalers and distributors bring together the products from a number of manufacturers, then divide them and transport them in small lots to resellers or retailers who deal directly with the consumers. The value added of the distribution chain has been in the dispatch, warehousing and delivering of products.

Sometimes distributors undertake the repackaging and marketing of the products. The chain of intermediaries, who are the wholesalers, distributors and retailers, adds substantial costs to the value chain, which can make the prices to the end user significantly higher than those of the producers. The Internet has been unique in its potential to revolutionize the value chain, as it enables producers to reach the end users directly.

As e-Commerce firms are developing, they will be choosing their entry and distribution modes on the basis of reducing their transaction costs even to the point of internalizing certain activities which have been traditionally performed by intermediaries. The Internet has raised expectations that, in time, producers will sell directly to end users and, in turn, end users will prefer buying direct from the producers. What is actually happening is that value chains are being deconstructed, reconstructed and transformed into value webs, giving rise to a new class of intermediaries, which are the collecting and distributing of information.

For example, companies like Yahoo! or Netscape act as information collectors and disseminators, offering e-Commerce new possibilities of doing business.

e-Commerce Distribution System

For Web-based businesses focused on competing in

global markets, there is every indication that representatives in the field are necessary in order to facilitate dispatch, the handling of returns and servicing. Companies that deal with consumer goods and have relatively low international volumes that require little service assistance may be able to dispense with any on-the-spot distribution requirements and rely on a global integrated carrier.

Global Exporting

The European Union in its present form has a larger population than the United States. Nevertheless, most of its producers and consumers live and work in a radius of 800 km, equivalent to 12 per cent of the land area of the United States, and for historical and economic reasons, transport in the European countries has been burdened with rules and regulations. For example, a trucker transporting goods from Glasgow to Athens used to spend 30 per cent of his time at border crossings, waiting and filling in up to 200 forms.

These inefficiencies are mercifully now a thing of the past. In order to move goods between EU member states only one simplified transit document is required and many of the custom formalities have been eliminated. However, consignment to countries outside the European Union is still burdened with an array of obstacles, cultural and linguistic, which lead to many companies failing to exploit the opportunities offered by overseas markets. The SME sector is affected in particular, as such companies do not have the resources to spend on overseas sales teams and trade-related computer systems.

THE CONCEPT OF BUSINESS ETHICS

Ethics is about understanding right and wrong. Business ethics is an increasingly acknowledged part of business life, and this is no less true for e-Business. The concept of business ethics and looks particularly at how they relate to e-Business. It will discuss the extent to which ethical e-Business issues are distinctive, how they result in particularly challenging dilemmas because of the need to rely on computers and evolving debates about ethics in cyberspace. In theoretical perspectives on business decision making, the dominant discourse is often focused on maximizing profit for company shareholders alone.

This perspective is increasingly proving to be inadequate. In practice, profit maximization in the long term may best be achieved by making sustainable decisions that take the consequences for trust between stakeholders (including employees, competitors, suppliers, customers, the local community and shareholders) into account. This is called 'enlightened self-interest' - where business managers take 'ethical' decisions because of the positive impact on the financial bottom line.

It is far from being the only reason for the increasing acknowledgement of business ethics. Some business people see the primary role of business as being other than profit maximization. Owner-managers of small firms, for example, have been found to be particularly concerned about the financial and personal welfare of their employees. Business and managers have increasing power as a result of their activities, and with it comes responsibility for their actions.

While there are common understandings of right and wrong in business life which we use every day and see in newspaper headlines, a detailed consideration of ethics in business cannot rely on shallow statements of how we ought to behave. It is necessary to draw on well established theories of ethics. Here the briefest of introductions will be given to some of the key ethical perspectives. Further reading on ethics is strongly recommended.

Ethical theories offer frameworks by which individuals can reflect on the acceptability of actions taken and evaluate moral judgements and moral character. The theories are normative, and outline ways of assessing good and bad behaviour, usually on the basis that decisions about moral practices can be cognitively arrived at. The purpose of the application of ethical theory is *not* to make blanket judgements about the rights or wrongs of the actions observed.

The theory enables a systematic analysis using established

structures for analysing behaviour from the perspective of moral philosophy. Ethical egoism, utilitarianism, Kantianism, discourse ethics theory and virtue theory.

Ethical egoism and utilitarianism are consequentialist theories. This means that, when considering whether an act is right or wrong, the actor considers the likely outcome of that act. Both theories suffer from the fact that outcomes can be difficult to predict and they also ignore the individual rights of others. The ethical egoist acts in a way which furthers his or her own self-interest (although it may be 'enlightened' self-interest). Faced with the possibility, for example, of copying a competitor's Web page design, the ethical egoist will weigh up what the likely outcomes will be if he or she does so.

If caught out and labelled with a bad reputation by employers, possibly even facing legal charges of violating copyright, the ethical egoist will not copy other people's work. If the egoist will not be found out and will save him or herself time and trouble while still fulfilling work obligations, then the outcome is positive for the egoist and he or she should act in order to further their own self-interest.

The theory suffers from inconsistency, since the egoist simultaneously must expect that everyone else will further their own self-interests too, which may well conflict with their own advancement. Utilitarianism promotes the notion of achieving maximum happiness for society (or avoidance of pain and pursuit of pleasure). The person acting ethically according to utilitarianism will weigh up carefully which act will result in the most positive outcomes for those individuals who will be affected by it, a kind of cost-benefit analysis for happiness.

When deciding, for example, whether to undercut the prices of high-street booksellers, an Internet-based business that bases the ethics of its activities on utilitarianism would consider all the positive and negative impacts on individuals of not making their books cheaper, and all the positive and negative impacts on individuals of undercutting.

In such an example, although a price cut might result in some job losses and reduced dividends for shareholders, the weight of advantage for many customers is likely to be widespread, hence utilitarianism might see price undercutting on the Web as ethical.

Kantianism is a very important ethical theory. Kant argued that every individual must seek to do his or her duty. He defined 'duty' very precisely as obedience to the 'categorical imperative', which is what an individual would consider to be the rational, universal, ethical action. The act is the focus of attention in Kantian ethics and an ethical act is one which complies with the categorical imperative, i.e.:

- It is universalizable - if it is right in one situation for one person, it must be right in every situation for everyone.
- It respects other people and never uses them as a means to the actor's end.

This approach is clearly quite different from the consequentialist perspectives. For Kant the consequences of an act do not matter. It follows that it is our ethical duty not to lie, cheat or steal, to keep promises and not to use others.

Table. Summary of Ethical Theories

Theory	Basis	Characteristics
Ethical egoism	Consequence-based: maximize own selfinterest	Promote own well-being above everyone else's
Utilitarianism	Consequence-based: maximize utility	Greatest good of the greatest number
Kantianism	Act-based	Act in a way which is universalizable Treat people as ends in themselves, never means to ends
Discourse ethics theory	Process-based	Consensus by full, open discussion
Virtue theory	Character-based	What sort of person should I be?

Discourse ethics theory focuses on the process by which a decision is reached. Ethical actions are those which are reached by full, open discussion including all those who are connected in any way with a decision.

For a business this means including all stakeholders actively in decision making. This is impracticable in some instances, and is not always culturally readily achievable, since some groups are more disposed to work towards consensus than others.

The Chinese government, for example, seeks to block access by its citizens to Web sites containing material deemed inimical to the Chinese Communist Party. They do so by blocking access to two Californian search engines, Google and Altavista, via Chinese internet service providers. This action, while no doubt well intentioned, also blocks the autonomy and free choice of the citizens. They have no opportunity to voice their preference, negotiate or discuss the issue. Power is held by one party, unless individuals have the technical ability to overcome the restrictions, for example by using a numerical address.

Virtue theory considers the character of the individual who acts. A virtuous person is one who classically possesses characteristics of justice, wisdom, temperance and courage. Modern-day virtues include co-operation, loyalty, friendliness and trustworthiness. However, there is no definitive list of virtues, and they may be culturally distinctive.

In the realms of e-Business, many of the issues are still finding legal precedent. Most of the ethical theories incorporate reference to legal perspectives, for example Kantians will on the whole follow the law, as will ethical egoists, since it is likely to be in their own self-interest so to do. In the global context of e-Commerce, the law simply does not provide sufficient, worldwide guidance on how e-Business managers should behave. Ethics can help fill that gap.

ARE THERE DISTINCT ETHICAL ISSUES IN E-BUSINESS?

e-Business enthusiasts will be well aware of the technical

and financial advantages of e-Commerce. There are also ethical benefits. These include the potential to remove prejudice and barriers, as transactions are carried out via disembodied computer screens.

The lack of need for a physical presence in a particular place, as long as computer access is available, opens up all kinds of possibilities for freedom of mobility and inclusion of those with physical needs which make working in an office environment difficult (ranging from physical disability to a distinct preference for working on a beach!).

Internet-based business activities are opening up markets, improving information provision about different products, including non-corporate information. (For example, typing 'Nike' into a search engine finds company pages as well as sites about Nike products alleging human rights abuses by the company.)

The Internet allows consumers much greater access to information, opening up the market and undermining monopolies. Such impacts are highly ethical according to a utilitarian perspective.

Freedom of speech is often cited as one of the benefits of cyberspace. Freedom of speech is a fundamental human right, yet it is not enjoyed by all. The Internet can be a means of increasing freedom of speech.

Technology and law have been unsuccessful as a means of controlling what is on the Web. This means, at one extreme, that abhorrent pornography is available and that inaccurate claims made in relation to e-Business products or services are equally difficult to control.

We generally become aware of ethical issues through dilemmas, conflicts and discomfort with situations, behaviours and acts. The more challenging aspects of e-Business, particularly the implications for workplaces reliant on ICTs and the new issues prevalent to cyberspace.

COMPUTERS IN THE WORKPLACE

The expansion of e-Business goes hand in hand with reliance on computers in the workplace. Organizations have become information technology-intensive in their operations, and this in itself has significant implications for employees.

Advantages and Changes

Anyone who works in an office will have noticed some of the great advantages of workplace computerization. Among other advantages, the new communication medium eases the sharing of information. For instance, UK customers of www. Amazon.co.uk will find that they are 'known' to the German www. Amazon.de Web site when they log on there for the first time.

There is no need to re-register even though a new retail Web site has been accessed. Customer records kept on an electronic database mean that more and more data can be gathered and marketing targeted at individuals. The computerization of many activities results in at least the potential for reducing paper files and archives.

In fact the 'paperless office' turns out to be mythical, as some aspects of computerization result in an increase of paper production (for example, the ease of producing several edited versions of a report rather than one completed one), and individuals do not have sufficient confidence that an electronic file can be held with the same security as a paper one. Despite the evident advantages of computers, the fallibility of computers and computer systems and the fragility of electronic data do not lend credibility to reliance on strictly electronic records.

Disadvantages

Prolonged computer use without a break can result in eyestrain and serious problems from repetitive strain injury (RSI), for example from constant use of the same muscles in manipulating the mouse. Back problems are increasingly common in the workplace as individuals maintain constant, inappropriate positions while sitting at a desk to use a computer. Ergonomic solutions to these problems are available but not widely used.

Damage to the environment as a result of computer use

is unknown, but the speed of technological updates results in a very short life cycle of computers as two- or three-year-old' machines are discarded as being out of date.

In addition of course, computers require constant electricity supply. Some suggest that teleworking and the reduced need for face-to-face interaction may have negative psychological effects on individuals, who experience isolation and the loss of 'social glue'. Others argue that computerization enables social freedom for the shy and the removal of potential prejudice, as race, age and disability cannot be seen through a computer screen of text.

COMPUTER-MEDIATED COMMUNICATION

One of the key questions confronted by business ethicists is whether computer-mediated communication (CMC) requires fundamentally different ethical considerations than have gone before. Those who argue that there is a difference cite areas such as the following for their reasoning: the changed relationship between humans, the fragility and ownership of electronic data, use and abuse of workplace facilities, and monitoring and privacy.

While none of these factors is in itself unique, the combination of new perspectives, and the rapidity with which new technologies are becoming the norm in the workplace, do establish a heightening of certain issues in a unique combination in relation to ethical use. Here the focus is particularly on electronic mail and Internet technology and use.

The Changing Nature of Human Relationships

A key characteristic of the computerized workplace is the changing nature of relationships between humans that ICTs have enabled. There can be a lack of 'social glue' in a highly computerized world, where there is no natural space for casual conversation.

The extent to which e-mails are really different from previous technologies such as communication by fax machine or disembodied telephone is unclear. There *is* a difference: we say things in e-mail that we might never say in hard copy or verbally, and different rules of grammar, punctuation, and even honest representation and use of crude language, seem to apply.In a UK context, personal relationships are an important bond in managing business and organizations.

This is achieved even where communication technologies enable increased personal distance between those communicating. Just as a 'business' telephone call may begin with some social conversation, an e-mail too can combine the social and strictly functional business for which it is composed.

Electronic communication may even support 'social glue' by enabling naturally shy people to take part in communication fully without the psychological pressure of face-to-face contact.

The removal of the immediate proximity of sender and receiver of messages may have Equal Opportunity implications. While telephone helps prevent some prejudicial judgements such as those based on skin colour, age or dress, dialect and manner of speaking may still be discerned. The typewritten script of an e-mail, although not guaranteeing grammatical accuracy, offers everyone the opportunity of an equally professional status.

Interestingly some interpret this as 'coldness' and use symbols to convey emotions such as happiness (), thereby personalizing their message. CMC also allows the leaving of messages for respondents to pick up as and when is convenient for the respondent, and potentially avoids the need for individuals to waste time chasing up absent colleagues.

Telephone answer machines can operate on the same principle, but an e-mail can cope with a rather more complex message. This sophistication does not prevent individuals ignoring their messages, but that is a human rather than electronic frailty! CMC commonly allows asynchronous 'discussion', where there is a time gap between normally text-based messages being sent and responses received.

Finally, a key point here must be the combination of communication media. Where a sensitive point is being made about which the response of the receiver cannot be predicted, the messenger may choose face-to-face or telephone communication in order that the response can be read *as the message is delivered,* and the tone of delivery adjusted simultaneously.

In fact, just as with other communications methods, there is still a need for 'interpersonal skills' in choosing the medium and the mode of delivery. CMC can be seen as a liberating social force, offering an additional means of communication, and empowering those who are less comfortable with other methods. While it might be a mistake to consider it as a replacement for other means of communication, it can certainly act as a complement and, used sensibly, enables communication rather than disabling it.

Fragility and Ownership of Electronic Data

The apparent fragility of electronic data, for example the fact that important data tables can be altered with almost no trace, adds additional responsibility to the conveyors of electronic information. Issues of responsibility for accuracy and the protection of information become paramount.

This, it could be argued, is one of the distinctive features of electronic communication, since systems of protection for intellectual works (such as patenting and copyright) were designed for tangible products.

At the moment there is neither clear protection for electronic data nor understanding of the limits of ownership and responsibility for accuracy. Such issues are compounded by the potential for mass dissemination via the Internet and by means of electronic mail.

Given that even accidental inaccuracy by experienced keyboard operators occurs at a rate of one inaccurate keystroke per 100, the potential for incorrect information dissemination is great. Similarly the ownership of electronic data, accurate or otherwise, is unclear and could have critical implications for the user and subject of information.

Even if we accept that employers own the data that is sent on their systems (that is, e-mail content sent by employees), interpretation of the data may be incorrectly handled by employers, particularly since e-mails are commonly written in shorthand and abbreviated form.

Use, Dual use and Abuse

The increasing prevalence of computer-mediated communication in the work-place has focused the minds of employers on the use of organizational equipment for non-organizational tasks. This is not of course a new phenomenon. The blurred lines between work and personal life are to be found in the use of work stationery for personal tasks, the use of private telephones for 'work' calls, the use of work telephones for 'private' calls, the reading of newspapers in work time, unpaid overtime, and so on.

Such issues are particularly relevant in office environments. Some occupations, such as factory production line work and call centre operators, are indeed more strictly controlled and delineated in the timing of their activities. There are no clear lines to be drawn in any of these cases. The introduction of widely available ICTs has again broadened the spectrum of possibilities by offering a powerful tool of information access and distribution to many employees.

A distinction can be made here between use, dual use and abuse of ICTs in the workplace. Brown (1996) distinguishes between the realms of business necessity and of individual personhood and suggests that their intersection covers the domain of workplace privacy. A link has been made between Brown's notions of 'business necessity', 'workplace privacy' and 'individual personhood' and the employment of ICTs for 'business use', 'dual use' and 'abuse'.

The associations in the diagram are not absolute but they may provide a useful framework for considering the issues of the use of workplace CMC, such as e-mail and Internet access, common to any e-business.Using the available CMC resources for business necessity is the easiest to identify. Where e-mail or the Internet are employed for purposes directly related to the functional role of the individual in the organization, there is no immediate problem.

Where e-mail or the Internet is used for purposes which

have nothing whatsoever to do with the organizational business, or the well-being of the individual in doing his or her task, it might be said that there has been an abuse of the access to CMC facilities. 'Abuse' of a firm's resources can be defined as the use of e-mail by the employee to further personal rather than organizational objectives.

This might include illegal activities such as hacking into national security databases, but is not restricted to them. Examples might be the circulation of offensive materials, the setting up of a personal private business on work equipment or the accessing of indecent Web sites. With few exceptions such actions amount to abuse of the organization's resources.

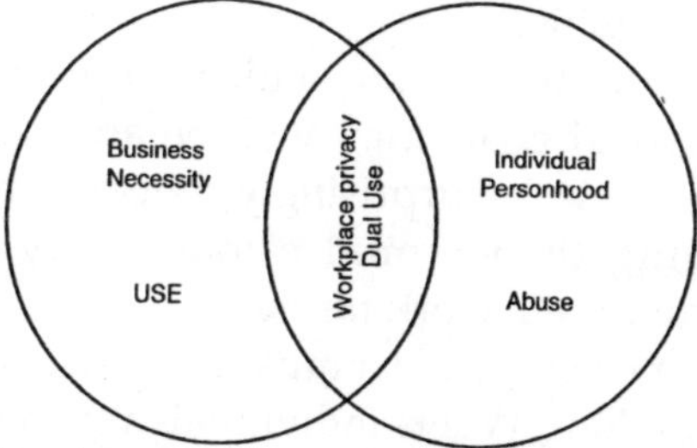

Fig. Locating the use and Abuse of ICTs in the Workplace

The most difficult area to discern is the intersection between use and abuse, the area where personal use may have some positive workplace implications, and work use may benefit the individual personally. Internet surfing for hobby interests will hone the IT skills of employees who use those same skills for work tasks. Non-work friends may enable problem solving that would otherwise cost time and resources in-house, whether they be through the resolving of ICT queries or personal counselling.

The ability of employees to resolve individual issues such as the renewal of car insurance over the Internet allows them to concentrate on work tasks. Furthermore it is natural, even desirable, that employees become friendly with colleagues, and the combining of social and work discussions within e-mails is a clear example of 'dual use'. Individuals do not leave their personal lives at home entirely, and employers should not expect them to do so. Employers might keep in mind that employees will often take work home with them, either literally or mentally. It seems a fair reciprocal exchange to be tolerant of home life making an appearance in the workplace.

Accepting employees as whole human beings, with all the benefits and some of the drawbacks this may bring, is likely to be beneficial to all in the longer term. No differentiation has been made in the discussion so far between use of workplace CMC and use of work time. This, again, is a difficult distinction.

On the one hand utilization of organizational software and hardware may not in itself be considered problematic by employers. The equipment has been purchased for work reasons and once installed the incremental costs of its use are likely to be negligible.

However, the work time which employees use in the pursuit of personal goals may well be an issue. Surfing the Internet proves to be a surprisingly time-consuming activity, and responding to personal e-mails may well distract individuals from their work tasks.

The relevance of time lost must to some extent depend on the type of work done. Where individuals are doing tasks strictly limited to particular hours, or even paid by the hour, time lost during the working day will be of significance. On the other hand, for professionals who are measured by their output rather than their (intellectual or actual) presence nine to five, time lost might be considered as merely a reallocation of time use.

The management of household matters in work time is inevitable in a social environment in which workdays are longer and household management responsibilities are shared between multiple earners with careers. Important in the consideration of the use and abuse of work time is the fact that the technology is readily available to monitor Internet and e-mail use of networked employees remotely.

Monitoring and Privacy

In the context of ICT development, electronic monitoring of employees - in and outside the workplace - has enormous potential for infringing the privacy of employees and customers. ICT archiving and particularly computer-mediated communication mean that employees in the workplace can be monitored to unprecedented levels. Electronic monitoring can be defined as the capture and analysis of 'data' to measure the work (not) performed by employees. These data may show Web sites accessed, e-mail traffic, e-mail content or the use of video and audio facilities. Electronic monitoring is sometimes seen as a sinister 'Big Brother is watching you' perspective on our lives. Reasons put forward to defend the use of electronic monitoring in the workplace include the following:

- *Security*. Closed Circuit Television (CCTV) can protect against theft and violence.
- Employers pay employees to do a particular job. It could be argued that employers have a *contractual right* to check that employees are doing what they are paid to do.
- Monitoring of employees stops abuse of work time and *increases productivity*.
- Electronic monitoring is simply an electronic version of *'managing by walking about'*, which saves management time.
- Electronic means of measurement mean that performance appraisal of employees is backed up by precise statistics and is *unbiased*.
- Electronic monitoring provides data *quickly and frequently*.
- It ensures *realistic targets* are set.

Electronic monitoring may be used as a deterrent to stop inappropriate work-place behaviour, rather than being used to penalize those caught not working 100 per cent of the time. This can be likened to Jeremy Bentham's Panopticon. The Panopticon was a circular prison with no bars. All the cells were arranged around a tower with a single guard in it. From the tower the guard could see into all the cells. However, the prisoners could not see whether they were being observed.

Their behaviour was thus controlled by the fact that they *might* be being monitored. In the same way that a speed camera without a film in it can still influence motorists to keep to the legal speed limit, the fact that employees or customers know that they may be being watched means that they act as they would if they *were* being watched.On the other hand, like watching rats in a cage, constant monitoring can have uneasy effects on individuals. Those against electronic monitoring argue that:

- It constitutes an *invasion of privacy*. Being paid by an organization does not mean that it owns you.
- Monitoring implies suspicion of misbehaviour. This *undermines the trust, goodwill and loyalty* of employees toward the employer.
- Monitoring results in the setting of *unrealistic targets*, because employees cannot keep up the fastest rate constantly. The result is increasing stress, absenteeism and ultimately employee turnover.
- In a climate of increasing empowerment, monitoring erodes the independence of the individual to work in a way which suits him or her (e.g. chat to a friend between 9:30 and 10:00 but work over lunchtime) and *disempowers* the individual's control.
- Electronic monitoring is more suited to *measuring quantitative* factors than qualitative ones, hence number of phone calls rather than relationship building with potential clients is most likely to be measured in a call centre.

In most countries, legally there is generally no reason why employers should not monitor employee e-mails, yet it is unlikely to be in the employer's self-interest to exercise the right. Monitoring employees to check whether they are abusing company resources may be justified if the system is being overloaded, although setting limits would achieve the same ends. Being an employer does not mean having the right to monitor private conversations.

ETHICS IN CYBERSPACE

Cyberspace as comprising all forms of computer-mediated communication which take place in a 'geographically unlimited, non-physical space, in which - independent of time, distance and location - transactions take place between people, between computers and between people and computers'. In the workplace, common journeys into cyberspace would include sending an e-mail, looking at a Web site, using a search engine and making bookings or purchases over the Internet. Cyberspace communications have some distinctive characteristics that are important in relation to ethics. These include:

- The ease of communicating to many *anonymous* people simultaneously. For example, by sending an e-mail to a group. Communication can be *spontaneous*.
- The *disembodied* nature of electronic communication - communication is in text, and hence does not convey tone of voice or other non-textual clues, although 'symbols' are increasingly used to convey for example a joke or happiness:) =, or sadness:(=.
- Where a common language is understood, images, documents and *complex ideas* can be communicated across the world as long as the technology is available.
- Cyberspace is *not secure*. This means that transactions on the Web can be accessed by those not party to the transaction. Security is improving, however, and of course terrestrial transactions are not 100 per cent secure either.
- The *borderless* nature of the Internet makes control extremely difficult. Attempts at national controls, such as prohibiting the purchase of Adolf Hitler's *Mein Kampf* over the Internet in Germany, have failed.
- Communication in cyberspace has extraordinary *archiving* capabilities. Internet sites accessed are recorded (hence Gary Glitter's conviction for accessing child pornography). Companies can also track the cyberspace activities of those who have visited their Web site, if they have the right technology.
- Those who control the technology become very *powerful,* for example Microsoft Corporation and Netscape.

All these factors open up a whole range of possibilities for communicating quickly and easily to people across the world. A new resulting phenomenon of some of these factors is the advent of 'flaming', a kind of electronic road rage in which individuals send rude or offensive, even libellous messages to individuals or sometimes groups, often with no clear understanding of who has access to reading it (for example to a bulletin board or chat room).

THE DIGITAL DIVIDE?

As the reach of the information superhighway extends, assumptions about equal access to its benefits are increasingly made. These range from the expectation that all those reading this text will have used e-mail and surfed the Internet to claims that the Internet overcomes global disparities between more and less economically developed countries.

Companies from all over the world can compete for the same business via the Internet, with Web pages that don't necessarily convey company size, longevity or financial success.In fact, at a local as well as a global level, access to the Internet is far from universal. In 1999 it was estimated that 170 million people had Internet access.

This is a minute 4 per cent of the world's population. The figure is more meaningful still when it is considered that over 80 per cent of those with Internet access are in North America and Europe. So, rather than being a social leveller, the Internet is yet another divide between rich and poor, the haves and have-nots, the networked and the non-networked.

PROFESSIONAL BEHAVIOUR

The increasing power of information systems professionals, and correspondingly e-Business professionals, requires a high degree of integrity. Codes of conduct, such as that of the British Computer Society, begin to acknowledge some of the difficult decisions faced by computer professionals. Such codes are, however, often too broad to give meaningful advice. Some take a more focused approach. Rosenberg (1999) reports on the 1996 Computer Professionals for Social

Responsibility 'Electronic Privacy Principles' which suggest that 'Each employer should provide and act on clear policies regarding the privacy implications of the computing resources used in the workplace. ' The policies should explicitly describe:

- Acceptable use of electronic mail and computer resources, including personal use.
- Practices that may be used to enforce these policies, such as the interception and reading of electronic mail or scanning of hard disks.
- Penalties for non-compliance with these policies.

Many argue that employees should at least be informed of any electronic monitoring systems that might be used on workplace computers. These principles suggest a basic position of transparency of any monitoring policy.

Codes of conduct are widely criticized for many reasons, for example that they are only for public relations purposes and just add to bureaucracy, that they ignore context and deny individual responsibility and moral diversity. Codes do have the advantage of offering some guidance, however, and this is desperately needed in an e-Environment which so far lacks any common understanding of appropriate use.Recommended features of a useful code of conduct are as follows. A good code of conduct:

- Is negotiated with stakeholders and acceptable to them.
- Consists of clear and well founded ethical rules.
- Is internally consistent and coherent with other policies and strategies.
- Should balance: (1) rights and duties, (2) the interests of internal and external stakeholders.
- Allows for exceptions (and shows how to deal with them).
- Anticipates conflicts (and shows how to deal with them).
- Respects individual freedom.
- Would not be used to indoctrinate.
- Is easy and inexpensive to apply.
- Is part of a process with regular review.

Chapter 4

Design and Payoffs

CHARACTERISTICS OF E-COMMERCE

LEADERSHIP

To move forward with e-commerce, the CEO and other senior managers must pursue several initial activities. Leadership comprises words and deeds, explicit and implicit behaviour, control of purse-strings, and leadership by example. Successful e-commerce leadership has four main characteristics, which can be implemented as follows.

- *Commitment at the Top: The CEO and Other Senior Managers Must Embrace E-Commerce.* Implementing an e-commerce plan requires strong leadership at the top of the organization. The CEO and other senior managers must understand the issues surrounding e-commerce well enough to evaluate the organization's strengths and weaknesses and make appropriate decisions on strategy, structure, and systems. The CEO must view IT and its applications as a vital component of the company's strategy and publicly demonstrate this belief through words and actions. The CEO must also adopt the attitude that e-commerce is not optional. The company may decide to have a larger or smaller role for e-commerce and may develop that role quickly or slowly, and it may sell directly to customers or limit its major initiative to the back-end systems, but it cannot ignore e-commerce entirely.

— Commitment at the top
— Thorough competitive analysis
— Significant financial investment
— Cultural transformation

Many CEOs have become e-commerce believers by discussing the topic with more experienced executives at other companies. For example, a conversation with Michael Dell of Dell Computer led Jack Welch at GE to hasten his company's movement into large scale e-commerce activities. Others, such as Howard Lester at Williams-Sonoma, have been convinced by believers within their own firm through some positive pilot e-commerce projects. In any case, the CEO should begin an earnest dialogue with people who understand e-commerce to learn about its successes and failures in relevant industries.

Other leadership roles are also important. The CIO must be a proactive member of the senior management team who communicates well with the CEO about the usefulness of IT applications. Rather than serving strictly as a technologist, the CIO must also be a strategist. The CIO should serve in a leadership role in cross-functional teams that combine business units, IT, and e-commerce.

The CFO needs to understand the strategic role of IT in the business and consider its ramifications in funding decisions. Other members of the senior management team should have an active role in e-commerce, in a direct advisory role when it relates to specific relevant areas of responsibility and in a support role for other areas of the company. If possible, senior management should include persons who have prior e-commerce experience.

- *Thorough Competitive Analysis: Determine Company's E-Commerce Position.* In crafting an appropriate e-commerce strategy, it is vital for the company first to understand its e-commerce position relative to competitors. At this point, there are few industries where there has not been a first mover in the use of e-commerce.

  Even in industries where traditional companies have been laggards, pure-play companies have stepped into the void with varying levels of success. In fact, in most industries, a pure-play of some type was the first mover.

This existence of a first-mover competitor does not mean that other companies in an industry cannot gain competitive advantage over their traditional competitors by making significant e-commerce investments and efforts. CEOs who find themselves in an early-mover position should continue to invest and innovate to maintain their advantage. Charles Schwab built a significant advantage over competitor Merrill Lynch, despite having been preceded online by pure-play competitors such as E*Trade.

If a company is a late mover into e-commerce, it can still desire to be the first to provide a particular service, combination of services, or other unique value proposition. Catching up, however, often requires a very high level of investment and a willingness to explore new business models and processes. Regardless of position, a CEO must adopt a broader mode of thinking about competitors because in e-commerce, industry boundaries are more blurred and competition can come from unlikely sources.

- *Significant Financial Investment: Determine Appropriate Role of E-Commerce.* Once the CEO has evaluated the company's e-commerce position relative to other industry members and specific competitors, a decision must be made as to the appropriate role of e-commerce within the company.

  Given the increased usage of the Internet by leading companies in most industries, the senior managers will typically need to move forward with expanding or at least maintaining the company's current e-commerce position relative to its competitors.

The relevant decisions include whether the company is going to sell online and, if so, how its offerings will compare with its traditional offerings. It should also consider the geographic scope of its e-commerce sales, since the Internet permits unlimited worldwide access, which can introduce a myriad of complications and challenges. The extent to which e-commerce will be utilized in procurement and distribution must also be considered, as well as internal functions such as human resources, accounting, and marketing.

Of primary importance is that the company determine appropriate levels of IT activities and provide for appropriate levels of IT funding. This approach requires taking all necessary steps, including acquisitions or strategic alliances, to ensure that the company's IT capabilities are sufficient for a successful e-commerce venture.

The CEO must then work with other executives to ascertain the amount of investment necessary to fully implement the chosen e-commerce strategy. Investment decisions should be primarily strategic, and returns should be viewed, including the measurement of both short-term and long-term value creation, with a broad view of potential impacts.

- *Cultural Transformation: Determine Implementation Needs.* Since structure and systems can be used to implement strategy, most systems decisions are made after an e-commerce strategy has been formulated. But at an attitudinal level, cultural transformation will usually begin even earlier.

  Senior managers have a responsibility to establish a minimum level of IT acceptance and competence throughout the company by demonstrating and communicating commitment and creating appropriate training programs. Some companies will be better prepared for this transition than others; senior managers must carefully consider the required preparation and the implications for implementation speed.

To rapidly implement an e-commerce strategy, IT and e-commerce basics and the purpose of e-commerce must be understood. Communicating purpose is one of the most important actions of a CEO. Employees must realize that e-commerce represents an important challenge and opportunity rather than a threat.

Whether the e-commerce strategy is to be implemented

within a month or a year, a sense of urgency is required. The CEO must present e-commerce as having the power to transform the organization in a positive way. Equivocation at every level, from the CFO's hesitation to fund technology to the salesperson's fear that e-commerce will decrease personal commissions, must be avoided. That does not mean reckless risk-taking to move forward, but it does mean a committed acceptance of e-commerce throughout the organization.

STRATEGY

In designing an e-commerce strategy, it is critical to recognize what the Internet changes. Not every value proposition in traditional commerce can attract customers in e-commerce, and not every traditional strategy is a viable source of increased profitability. The best strategies do not ignore the fundamental properties of the Internet and the behaviour of its users.

The organization must develop strategies for e-commerce operations that are consistent with overall corporate strategy. (Since this is a dynamic model, the order of appearance of these elements may be different. Strategy may precede leadership and resource commitments and structure and systems already in place may constrain the strategy decision.) The goals should include an increase in customer acquisition, enhanced channel optimization, improved customer loyalty and retention, and capturing value for the organization.

- Well-positioned online brand
- Online-friendly offerings
- Reliable customer service
- Cross-channel coordination

Four strategic moves are :

- *Well-Positioned Online Brand: Acquiring Customers and Building Trust.* The simplest way for companies to initiate e-commerce operations is to transfer the brand name to the Internet, using the company's name as the domain name so that existing customers and potential new customers can easily find the company's Web site.

The company can then advertise the Web site in various physical locations and in all print publicity materials. All letterheads, business cards, other types of business publications, and traditional advertising media should include the Web site address.

In-store signage, kiosks, advertising on bags, and other materials have also been successful in drawing customers to the online channel. Large online marketing campaigns are likely to produce click-throughs and hits, but not customers, and have typically proved to have poor payoffs.

A brand name will draw customers to the company's site and can help assure customers about the quality of the offerings, the accuracy of the information, and the security of the Web transactions on that site. The brand name can also promote customer loyalty. The company must continue to provide the level of service and security that the brand name implies, or it will fail to attract repeat online customers and may even damage the traditional brand.

If the company's traditional brand is centered on price competition, it must reevaluate this strategy for e-commerce. Price competition is rarely a viable source of profitability in e-commerce. Search costs for comparing prices are negligible online, and price wars have typically led to prices decreasing to just at or above cost.

The Internet also offers easy access to stores that offer price differentials, because customers do not need to travel any physical distance to get to any given store. Only in limited contexts should companies expect to achieve long-term competitive advantage based on price.

- *Online-Friendly Offerings: Product Selection and Differentiation.* The company must decide what products to offer on the Web site. Companies such as Office Depot have found that they are able to provide more total products to customers through Web sites. Physical store space limits the number of inventory items available in stores, while the Web enables the company to provide a larger product offering. Even when integrating their offline and online brand management, a company should not feel compelled to offer precisely the same products online as in its physical stores. The ability to offer a large quantity of products, especially in retail industries, is a major inducement to acquiring an online channel.

Further, it is fully appropriate for a company to eliminate online offerings that are simply unprofitable or otherwise inappropriate. General retailers such as Wal-Mart and grocers have used price minimums, margin requirements, and category restrictions to limit their online offerings. Some companies also require a minimum total purchase on their Web site.

Companies should also consider peripheral offerings in addition to those provided by the company's physical facilities. Such additions are especially appropriate for companies in service industries and companies with large business-to-business (B2B) components. For example, Office Depot's business services offerings are a strong complement to its office supplies business.

Another differentiator is offering customers the ability to obtain unique or uniquely tailored products or information. Customization can be a powerful differentiator because it allows customers to control the product or service choices, and loyalty can be built partly due to high switching costs. Personalization gives customers their very own version of the site that can include information and recommendations based on the customers' prior purchases and demographics.

- *Reliable Customer Service: Inspiring Loyalty among Customers.* Building trust online requires more than a strong brand; it requires strong customer service practices that emphasize the convenience of the online channel. The customer must trust the company and its Web site. Trust can be built through assurances of privacy and transaction security and by providing accurate information.

  Trust in the transaction's completion is built through prompt and accurate fulfillment of orders. Many people purchase at Amazon rather than other Web sites because of its consistently highly rated fulfillment and customer service operations.

Web site design also contributes to satisfying customers. Basic characteristics of the site, such as simplicity, legibility, clarity, and a professional look, are necessities for all Web sites. Strong search engines are especially important for companies with a large number of product offerings. Information about physical stores, customer service, and delivery and return policies should be easily accessible from the home page.

Technology should be a facilitator and not an end in itself, however, and the company should not invest too heavily in design features without being confident of their appeal. Neiman Marcus found that its customers were not interested in viewing luxury products on a high-technology platform. Barnes and Noble discovered that they could not create interest in online parallels to their in-store coffee bars and author visits.

The site should also provide a number of services for customers who need information about the site, the offerings, or products they have purchased. These include comprehensive FAQ (frequently asked questions) sections, easily accessible information on delivery and returns, and rapid email response and technical support, where appropriate.

Numerous delivery options should be available to the customer to allow for both speed and low-cost preferences. Companies such as Nordstrom's, which offers products that need to be examined in person before the sale is complete, have provided particularly generous return policies to overcome the hesitation to purchase online inherent in their product line.

Physical stores can also be used for pick-up of items that are needed immediately in industries such as pharmacies. Customers should also be offered convenient opportunities to return defective or unsatisfactory products, including returning such products to the physical stores.

- *Cross-Channel Coordination: Convenience and Revenue Stimulation.* The Web site and physical stores should not be seen as two separate entities that happen to share a brand name. Cross-marketing is an important component, but ultimately, the online and traditional stores must have complementary roles in the overall corporate strategy. Exploiting the advantages of integration means more than drawing customers to the Web site through promotion in the physical store.

Allowing online customers to pick up and return orders to physical stores provides customers with choices and convenience, bringing more traffic to the physical stores. Initially many traditional companies did not allow online customers to return purchased products to their stores.

Today, virtually everyone allows customers to return undesired items to physical store locations. Numerous studies have shown the propensity of customers to make additional purchases when drawn to the store by online-generated functions. Therefore, the Web site should include an easily accessible store locator function that includes a map to the location, a phone number, and store hours.

The physical store and online operations can each be used to stimulate sales in the other channel. Some products that require high levels of interaction with the product can be introduced to the online customer but sold in the physical locations.

Kiosks that provide a computerized access to the online site, on the other hand, have been a successful mechanism in physical stores to stimulate online traffic. Many retailers have encouraged the use of kiosks to order online products not available in the physical store or when delivery of the products is more convenient. Kiosks are also effective in overcoming concerns about online shopping for less computer literate customers.

The Web site can also provide more convenience for customers who wish to purchase specific items immediately rather than wait for delivery. For example, Office Depot can now direct customers to local stores that currently have the product in inventory. Customers need not call all the local stores and tolerate taped messages and long waits to find a product. Even Internet pure-play companies like Amazon, through its alliance with Borders, for which it provides Web site operations, can direct customers to the nearest Borders store that has a desired product. Customers need only provide a zip code.

Integration of physical stores and online operations can also lead to greater efficiencies. Supply chain advantages that lead to more effective purchasing, inventory control, and logistics management may enhance the company's overall cost structure and result in greater profitability.

STRUCTURE

After formulating an e-commerce strategy, senior managers must develop a plan for implementation. The company's organizational structure may at times conflict with the goals of e-commerce, and senior managers must anticipate these conflicts and act accordingly, whether by changing the structure of the traditional organization or by creating new structures specific to e-commerce. These considerations span the areas of financing, management teams, and operations. A final consideration is the use of strategic alliances .

- *Internal Investment: Maintain Full-Equity Interest in E-Commerce.* The company faces a decision about equity for the e-commerce venture, whether to retain complete ownership in the e-commerce venture or to spin it off as an independent company.

  The lessons are clear. Many high-profile failures occurred in traditional companies that tried to imitate the pure-play model by spinning off. Investment in the venture should be made from within the firm, and reliance on outside capital typically seems like an indicator of trepidation about e-commerce on the part of senior management.

Spinning off e-commerce was popular in the early period of e-commerce, and the results have generally been disastrous. Building up large market capitalizations through IPOs was a popular trend, but it has become less desirable in a weaker and more skeptical stock market. The vast majority of these companies, including Wal-Mart, Kmart, Barnes and Noble, and

Staples, have bought back the stock from equity partners and folded the e-commerce spin-offs back into the company.

- Internal investment
- Integrated management teams
- IT know-how from within
- Strategic partnerships

The other main justification for spinning off was that the company lacked the experience needed to pursue e-commerce or that additional investment capital was necessary. While it may be true that stand-alone firms sometimes find it easier to quickly develop e-commerce expertise, integrated e-commerce ventures in large organizations can also do this. Since e-commerce capabilities are becoming an increasingly important core competency, companies should develop the expertise and control the e-commerce operation inside the company through a full integration into business units and functions.

- *Integrated Management Teams: Innovate without Spinning Off.* From the distribution side, e-commerce should often be seen as simply another sales channel and thus changes in the management structure are kept to a minimum.

  In industries that already have multiple channels such as banks (i.e., physical branches, ATM) and catalog businesses (e.g., Nordstrom), an integrated structure is particularly relevant. With full integration, business functions such as marketing are easy to coordinate and organizational territorial conflicts are reduced. A less ideal but still viable alternative is to create a separate business unit for e-commerce. Many companies that began with spin-offs and then brought e-commerce back within the company chose to adopt separate strategic business units (SBUs).

Many companies have started their e-commerce operations with entirely separate management teams, often proposed to increase the focus on innovation and e-commerce, under the premise that e-commerce will not be given enough attention or independence by senior management at the parent organization. These management teams have often been established far from company headquarters, have had loose organizational cultures, and have been led by independent leadership often drawn from pure-play or other entrepreneurial companies.

Certainly innovation, flexibility, and creativity are needed to drive a successful e-commerce operation. But we have seen that this can occur successfully within traditional organizational boundaries. A formal set of management control structures and systems is necessary to balance the desired empowerment. When separate business units are established, they should function primarily to coordinate the full integration of e-commerce throughout the business units.

As with other organizational functions, it is sometimes desirable initially to establish a central organization both to drive and to coordinate these new activities. But, as the function matures, it should generally be more fully integrated into the business units. The separate functional units and the integrated functions within the business units may need unique structures and systems including unique performance measures and compensation and reward systems, but this customization of the organizational structure can be accomplished within existing organizational boundaries. There is no need to spin off core capabilities and detach valuable corporate assets.

- *IT Know-How from Within: Building Future Capabilities.* Not every company, especially those late to e-commerce, will have invested well enough in IT to develop e-commerce independently. Many e-commerce companies, even those with strong IT departments, have chosen to outsource e-commerce because of the necessity of speed.

  Speed is indeed a powerful motivation for outsourcing, but outsourcing should be used to catch up, not to give up. Although outsourcing may be used initially to create e-commerce solutions, the company can reassume control over e-commerce and IT and eventually can use the e-commerce systems for traditional commerce as well. Staples followed this approach in attempting to catch its IT-leader rival, Office Depot. Staples invested heavily in IT to build technology close to its core capabilities, but also created a sole-sourcing partnership to avoid delays in more peripheral areas of the business.

Another alternative is to acquire IT capabilities by purchasing a small IT firm and integrating the firm while the e-commerce solution is being implemented. UPS has followed this approach several times in its attempt to hold its IT leadership position over rival Federal Express, and UPS has been able to continually roll out new services while integrating its acquisitions.

Other companies, however, have made the mistake of selling equity to venture capitalists and then relied on these partners for all of their IT needs. Barnes and Noble made this mistake and then was hamstrung further when Amazon sued them for a patent violation related to their Web platform. Borders and Toys 'R' Us have taken the dramatic approach of having a competitor, Amazon, run their Web site for them. Companies must learn from these mistakes and not place themselves in such a precarious position with respect to IT.

- *Strategic Alliances: Moving beyond Core Competencies.* Although companies are advised to maintain equity interest, management control, and IT integration, traditional businesses can benefit from alliances with online companies in other ways. These relationships are most beneficial when the arrangement gives the traditional company access to supply-chain management, peripheral offerings, and customer bases.

Supply-chain management is a particularly useful area for partnership when the company cannot simply supply online customers from the same distribution channels as physical stores. Wal-Mart, Kmart, and Target have all made such arrangements to deal with their general merchandising businesses. CVS also simplified its procurement process for its Web site by entering into a partnership with Merck.com.

To provide peripheral offerings that will be available only online, alliances have also proven to be a successful approach. Neiman Marcus partnered with several luxury retailers to create a limited-scope "luxury portal" of high-end goods within its Web site. CVS partnered with WebMD to provide medical advice to complement pharmacy services.

Finally, traditional companies can gain access to large online customer bases by making strategic alliances with portal and ISP companies. Wal-Mart and Kmart entered agreements with AOL and Yahoo respectively to co-brand Internet service packages that would bring their customers online and to their site in particular.

Traditional companies may also profit from providing a physical presence to online companies that are realizing the inevitable trend toward integrated channels. Target has agreed to house E*Trade kiosks and customer representatives in its stores, in what has been a beneficial relationship for both parties. For E*Trade, the Target deal was just one aspect of a bricks-and-clicks strategy that culminated with the building of a New York super-centre.

SYSTEMS

Senior managers must finally ensure that organizational processes are capable of implementing the e-commerce strategy. Information practices, human resources, performance measures, and customer management are all areas in which traditional systems may require adaptation to implement an e-commerce strategy.

- *Modernized Internal Processes: Using Information Effectively.* The cultural transformation described earlier may be enough to make e-commerce possible, but more must be done to maximize its benefits. Information practices must be adapted to promote transparency and availability.

  Changes must ensure that information flows freely throughout the company and is not hampered by artificial organizational boundaries or personal ambitions.

— Modernized internal processes
— Incentive-laden HR practices
— Aligned performance measures
— Improved customer management

In addition to information sharing, the decision-making processes of the company should be reconsidered. Cross-functional teams and remotely located teams should be assembled with greater frequency, with less emphasis on hierarchical reporting. Decision makers should also have greater self-governance and flexibility.

An important internal process is value chain management. Every company should identify ways to leverage the Internet in each part of the value chain, from procurement to distribution to delivery. In fact, failure to adopt e-commerce-specific cost savings will likely put a company at a serious competitive disadvantage. Strong supply chain management is often the basis for providing superior service.

In the area of procurement, a company can reduce the cost of goods sold by obtaining products through the Internet. Distribution strategies must not only cut costs but also provide the fastest and most convenient customer service. Delivery strategies should maximize convenience and speed for customers, using both the Internet and the company's existing infrastructure to provide these benefits. The best supply-chain practices, however, depend on the type of offering.

- *Incentive-Laden HR Practices: Bringing Your People on Board.* Compensation systems must be aligned with strategy and structure for the e-commerce venture to be a success. The CIO must be compensated as a member of the senior management team to signal the importance and respect shown for the IT function and the centrality and commitment to improved IT and e-commerce.

  At lower organizational levels, compensation systems have additional consequences on alignment. By compensating e-commerce managers the same as managers in traditional commerce, the company sometimes fails to create the necessary incentives for e-commerce success. Though parallel compensation systems can often work, both market forces and the need for speed, creativity, flexibility, innovation, and extra diligence often requires additional incentives and rewards.

Differential compensation, often through stock options, can create an incentive to cannibalize from the company's traditional channels. Such practices can cause conflicts with traditional business units but are often necessary to optimize the use of each channel, especially during the formative years of the e-commerce initiative.

Typically, e-commerce compensation should be tied to the overall success of the venture rather than rewarding individual units or channels for performance. This is particularly relevant when the company is seeking full integration, because it helps ensure cooperation and seamlessness between departments.

The Internet also provides opportunities to improve the hiring process. Cisco is just one company that has found great benefits from hiring online, including lowered costs, faster filling of positions, and higher competence. Companies may also want to consider specialized HR practices for their IT departments.

- *Aligned Performance Measures: Planning for the Long-Term.* Strong measurement practices are among the cornerstones of all good systems. Performance measures for e-commerce must overcome the uncertainty and unique dynamics associated with the Internet, and they may be more frequently adjusted in response to real-time information.

  With these considerations, it is clear that no company should simply extend its existing performance measures to the e-commerce venture without extensive customization. Still, long-term cost differentials, balanced with a variety of financial, nonfinancial, and leading and lagging indicators, are particularly useful for successful e-commerce implementations.

Some skeptical companies have made unreasonable

demands with respect to e-commerce performance. Because they misconceived e-commerce risks and rewards, they had unrealistic expectations of immediate growth and ROI that would not be demanded of any traditional long-term investment. Worse yet, they tied further investment to achievement of these goals, dooming e-commerce before it even could get off the ground.

In most companies, new projects and ventures require short-term ROI, and revenue projections, many of which an e-commerce venture and its related projects may not meet. If the company decides to enter or expand e-commerce, it cannot hamstring the venture by insisting on such short-term requirements throughout.

E-commerce has also led many companies to create performance measures other than revenue, ROI, and traditional financial indicators. Some of the new, poorly designed performance measures have had a disastrous effect on strategy implementation.

For example, indiscriminate customer acquisition and attempting to maximize revenue through online advertising often have negative implications for long-term profitability. Single-purchase customers and advertising revenue independent of the company's value proposition are not sustainable strategies. Worse still are nonfinancial measures such as Web page hits and registered users, which may not even be tied to a short-term revenue stream.

In addition to measuring the performance of the business, e-commerce brings added importance to measuring the value and functionality of operations. Most e-commerce strategies will have a strong operational component, including cost savings from value chain management and cuts in labour costs for the online channel. Operational measures should be tracked by some dedicated resource and balanced between financial and nonfinancial assessments of operational performance.

Moreover, companies must create a value capture process to evaluate the success of IT projects associated with the e-commerce venture. Looking at nonfinancial performance measures, the value capture process can help convince skeptical employees of the importance of IT. Even with the value capture process, however, the full benefits of IT investment are often underestimated.

- *Improved Customer Management: Better Service and Better Data.* Companies must also reconsider the internal processes required to provide the high levels of customer service necessary in e-commerce. Online customers need access to some level of customer service at all times.

  There is a trade-off between service that entails a high level of human input and service that is automated and more cost-efficient. Finding the proper balance is a function of the company's offerings, its customer base, and customer feedback.

Customer data is a significant benefit in e-commerce, because of the vast amount that can be learned about customers during a Web site visit in contrast to an in-store visit. Many Web sites, however, have mistakenly focused only on counting hits and visits, while ignoring the more valuable information that can be gathered.

Tracking of customers' interaction with the Web site can be used to identify customers' price sensitivity and information preferences and to gauge satisfaction with the Web site design and accessibility. Gathering and using customer information is important to refine the value proposition and better allocate internal resources. Marketing strategies for the Web site can also be continually refined, using real-time information gathered from customers during their visits, a practice that Staples has used well.

Once a company has established an e-commerce strategy, organizational structure becomes a primary concern in the process of implementing that strategy. In many cases, e-commerce will not initially fit neatly into the existing organizational structure of a traditional company. E-commerce, even to the most technologically savvy company, represents a new channel for procurement, distribution, and sales. E-commerce ventures also put new demands on individuals and business units at every level of the company.

A dynamic model in which strong and supportive leadership and a well-formulated strategy provide the basis for transforming a company through e-commerce. To implement that strategy, structure and systems must be adapted for e-commerce.

Corporate strategy, structure, systems, resources and the external environment are all both inputs and constraints to the determination of e-commerce strategy, structure, and systems. Planning for an e-commerce venture should use the existing structure to determine what existing company strengths can be utilized or enhanced with e-commerce. Implicitly, even some companies that have been unsuccessful in e-commerce have grasped this fact.

But instead of treating existing structure as an input, companies have often treated it as an impediment to e-commerce, deciding to create an entirely new structure outside the organization. They believed that they could not create a new e-commerce structure inside the organization that could effectively implement the e-commerce strategy. They also did not believe they could integrate an e-commerce operation into the corporate strategy, structures, or systems. Sometimes e-commerce was split off as a separate company, sometimes it was separated as a separate functional or business unit, and in a few cases it was fully integrated.

These concerns have been at the core in the debate over structure in e-commerce. Through the late 1990s, companies feared the disruptive nature of e-commerce and were unwilling to make changes in existing company structures and systems. Many companies chose to separate e-commerce from the main company structure.

These separate-structure decisions included establishing separate business units far from company headquarters, creating separate management teams, outsourcing of the entire e-commerce platform, and selling large equity ownership of the e-commerce business to venture capitalists and other outside interests.

Many of these companies have belatedly realized the value of an integrated structure for e-commerce. High-profile failures may have served to convince uncommitted leaders, but the rationale for integration runs much deeper than an analysis of past outcomes. The application of fundamental business principles should also make the benefits of an integrated organizational structure abundantly clear.

Some previous discussions on e-commerce have divided the debate of e-commerce structure into a number of separate decision dimensions. Some have encouraged executives to consider integration or separation of equity, brand, management, and operations, while others focused on leveraging two dimensions, the financial and the operational. Although these dimensions are relevant in terms of developing an e-commerce structure, careful choices must be made.

Companies must rely on a well-developed and coordinated implementation of an e-commerce strategy, with aligned e-commerce structure and systems. It would have made little sense, for example, if Wells Fargo had integrated its management structure and operations and then followed in the footsteps of competitors, such as Bank One, by creating a new brand for e-com-merce. Likewise, Office Depot would likely have destroyed most of the benefits of its operational integration if it had sold equity in OfficeDepot.com to a venture capitalist.

In the final analysis, the most fundamental analysis is whether or not to integrate e-commerce, and this choice should direct all the subsequent financial, management, and operational decisions. The implementation of an e-commerce strategy can take different forms, and the structure and speed of implementation are part of the strategic choices. However, companies should make a commitment to long-term full integration. It is the path to that full corporate integration that is an issue. A lack of commitment to e-commerce integration can cause wavering dedication on the part of the company. While Bank of America is currently a leader in online banking, it faced early obstacles because it initially pursued an integrated e-commerce approach. It later moved on to a separate strategic business unit to foster creativity, and then had to switch back to an integrated approach.

Solutions are also described for problems faced when companies lack the internal capabily to fully implement the e-commerce strategies. Finally, the contexts in which external strategic alliances can be a desirable solution are presented.

MOVING TOWARD AN INTEGRATED COMPANY

It's clear that, while looking at integration as the ideal solution is a useful mantra, implementing a full integration strategy is challenging. Systems and strategy must be aligned to both the corporate and the e-commerce structures for success. There should be a commitment to stay within the organization for the financing, management, and operational capabilities that e-commerce requires, where possible.

At times, this commitment is difficult. Challenging financial decisions may make venture capital and the prospect of an initial public offering of a separate e-commerce entity look desirable, as it did to many in the late 1990s. In addition, managers may need to take on new responsibilities, implement new policies, and deal with conflicts that could be more easily handled by a separate management team.

Systems will likely need to change. Speed may be sacrificed to develop a Web platform internally, when outsourcing could put the platform online weeks or months earlier. None of this, however, justifies the inconsistency that occurs between a viable internally constructed e-commerce strategy and a separated e-commerce structure.

At its most basic level, integration means viewing e-commerce as an integral part of an existing business. Many companies have demonstrated a commitment to integration by refusing to break out e-commerce profit, revenue, or other financial figures to the public. Rather, it is an additional important channel for procurement and distribution in addition to other important uses.

Financing E-Commerce and E-Commerce Structure

An integrated company should not spin off its e-commerce operation, because this new aspect of a company's business is essential to the future of the organization and creates significant future corporate value. Unfortunately, this lesson has been a painful experience for many companies in e-commerce's brief history.

Companies have turned to venture capitalists to sell stock in their e-commerce venture for several reasons, which have not always been about money. E-commerce expertise was one of the main capabilities sought by companies such as Wal-Mart, Staples, and Nordstrom.

Other reasons for turning to venture capitalists have included access to managerial talent, back-end technological capabilities, speed of implementation, and fulfillment services. Unfortunately, a major contributing factor to the decision of many companies to spin off their e-commerce venture has been the need to respond to a perceived competitive threat.

But the venture capital model of e-commerce has been exposed as doing significant damage to integration strategies. In most cases, selling equity to venture capitalists was followed by setting up a new management structure with reduced input from the parent company and more input from those interested in bidding up the stock price of the dot.com. At the same time, the technical side was almost entirely outsourced, often to the consulting arm of the venture capitalist, with little or no input from IT professionals who knew the industry. Under these conditions, nearly every benefit of e-commerce, including cross-promotion, economies of scale, and supply-chain efficiencies, was wasted or rendered impossible.

This system also created a cycle of dependency, wherein companies were rendered incapable of further advances in e-commerce without the support of this new management structure or a second outside source of e-commerce experience. The examples are numerous, and the experiences of companies across industries have been remarkably similar:

Why Companies Spin Off E-Commerce

E-Commerce Management and Separate E-Commerce Business Units

While the spin-offs were failing, companies looked for

other creative ways of achieving "separation" without spinning the e-commerce venture off entirely. One method has been to create a separate business unit so divorced from company headquarters as to seem to be its own organization.

This separation may be achieved by physical distance, radically different business unit structure, systems, rewards, and culture, or the selection of leadership to run the unit. Some companies have elected to have entirely separate management structures. One concern is whether these structures can aid in the implementation of an effective e-commerce strategy that is focused on ultimate company-wide integration of e-commerce. For many companies, the preferred approach is to establish an e-commerce unit flexible enough to foster innovation but integrated enough to be consistent with a well-formulated e-commerce strategy.

This type of unit should largely resemble the company's other business units, serving as a profit centre and reporting through normal channels and the existing hierarchy on issues ranging from the effectiveness of e-commerce initiatives to the integration of those initiatives within the overall structure of the company. It may, however, have different management control systems from the rest of the company, especially in the areas of performance measures and incentive systems. It is these differences, not pretenses of geographic distance or office design, that can truly foster innovation.A successful separate business unit for e-commerce displays numerous attributes.

- The SBU should be well integrated into the traditional business management structure so that the goals of the SBU are aligned with those of the company.
- A primary function of the SBU should be to lead the company's integration effort to the point where the e-commerce initiative becomes a part of every level of the company, not just the original SBU, to both increase revenues and decrease costs.
- The SBU should be given enough freedom to utilize e-commerce in ways that were not possible for the traditional business of the company.

- The SBU should be charged with specific goals regarding the company's e-commerce strategy and integration efforts.

The e-commerce unit, however, may also take on some characteristics of a traditional functional unit. Depending on their breadth, these units are sometimes treated instead as cost centers to serve the business units rather than external customers. In addition to integrating the Web channel with other channels and business units, the unit (whether functional or business unit) may also provide e-commerce solutions to other parts of the company and integrate the company's back-end systems. Some examples of separate business units and the forms they have taken include the following.

- UPS formed a wholly-owned subsidiary, e-Ventures, in 2000 to provide services for small and medium e-commerce companies. The unit operated semi-autonomously but used the same trucks and warehouses as the rest of the company. The unit boosted its capabilities by acquiring a number of smaller logistics firms.
- Tesco built its grocery internet unit out of Tesco Direct, a small unit that began direct retailing in the mid 1990s, and opened a Web site in 1996. Tesco.com was also a 100 percent-owned subsidiary, although at one point there was discussion of a possible spin-off. Internal investment in the unit was cautious, with an eye on gradual geographical expansion.

  The unit chose not to build inhouse warehouses, instead supplying customer orders directly from the physical stores' shelves. The Web site did, however, offer more heterogeneous product offerings, including music, small electronics, and dishware.
- Wells Fargo runs e-commerce from a very tightly integrated "total business unit" that treats the Internet as another delivery channel. There is strong integration on both the front end and back end, with offline customers automatically signed up for an online account, and aggressive cross-promotion. The

unit does not separately track profitability for e-commerce, but it points to lower attrition rates and higher purchase rates as measures of success.

Some successful companies have chosen not to create a separate business unit for e-commerce, instead treating the Web as a co-equal with other sales channels and integrating it throughout the organization. Still others have created a hybrid business unit that combines e-commerce and other parts of the business, such as catalog sales, in a much more limited fashion than full integration.

The rationale is that catalog sales and Web sales have much in common, especially in contrast with a physical store channel. Moreover, because of the expenses associated with mailing catalogs and maintaining catalog call centers, an effort to shift catalog customers to the Internet is highly cost-effective. Nordstrom Direct, which evolved after Nordstrom.com was folded back into the parent company, is an example of this structure.

Keeping e-commerce management internal is vital to implementing e-commerce strategy, but the successful implementation of e-commerce must also allow for flexibility in the management structure. The IT backbone that implements back-end systems for e-commerce should also provide the basis for a highly networked organizational structure. As such, the company can reap the benefits of decentralization without incurring the high costs or loss of the advantages of a more centralized and integrated structure.

OUTSOURCING

Though typically not desirable, outsourcing of IT as a part of e-commerce is not always a harmful decision. In limited contexts, the benefits of outsourcing can outweigh the costs of contradicting the integration paradigm. Back-end capabilities should, however, be developed internally in cases where they are related to a core competence, represent a source of competitive advantage, or involve unique or idiosyncratic activities. To understand those proper contexts, one must examine the range of IT capabilities relevant to e-commerce.

- IT infrastructure is a first priority for a company seeking an integrated e-commerce effort, and speed is a strong consideration. Although a company's legacy systems may have their unique characteristics, the software and hardware in this area is highly imitable and does not represent a likely source of competitive advantage. Therefore, a company should feel equally comfortable outsourcing this task or acquiring the capabilities and handling it internally.
- In functional areas such as payroll and human resources, e-commerce can also provide ample opportunities for cost savings. Software packages in these areas are also commodities and an unlikely source of competitive advantage.

  If upgrading capabilities in these areas is a part of the overall integration of e-commerce and it is not a core organizational competency, outsourcing may be an acceptable approach. For smaller firms, these commoditized solutions can provide relatively similar, if not superior, capabilities in areas such as payroll and human resources at a fraction of the cost of an in-house approach.
- Logistics is a third area in which a company has a reasonable choice between internal fulfillment and outsourcing. If logistics has been a core competency in traditional commerce, such as was the case with Wal-Mart, it should continue to be handled internally for e-commerce.

  If, however, fulfillment capabilities cannot be quickly and cost-effectively developed from within, outsourcing may be an acceptable alternative, in that it is unlikely to matter to customers by whom the order is fulfilled.

Despite its spin-off model of e-commerce, Staples showed an understanding of this contrast through its model of IT development. Its IT department focused on solutions that directly impacted the customer, while it outsourced back-end operations to a single vendor. This single-vendor form of outsourcing sometimes increases costs in the short term, but it often saves costs related to future vendor competition and is a good alternative to internal development because of uniformity and clear lines of responsibility.

It also facilitates a much easier integration if the company decides to bring the capabilities inside at a later date. When operational capabilities involve direct interaction with the customer, outsourcing becomes a generally undesirable choice. Web site design and customer service related to the Web site must be core competencies for any large company seeking success in e-commerce.

Failure to develop core competencies in these areas is an indication that a company has not made enough of a commitment or investment in e-commerce. Proceeding without developing these competencies is likely to do considerable damage to the brand name and future customer acquisition and retention efforts.

WEB SITE DESIGN AND INTERNET PLATFORM

Building a Web platform is an activity that should typically be handled internally. Web site design expertise is widely available and may be acquired if necessary. Though utilizing consultants and Web site design firms can provide some valuable needed guidance and experience, handing the task off completely to a consulting firm often prevents the company from imparting vital business-specific knowledge into building the site.

It also lengthens the learning period for employees who will need to understand the site's design, while at the same time handicapping the company's future e-commerce development by not cultivating this knowledge internally.The design of the site is closely tied to the customer service and support capabilities of the site, which are among the most vital capabilities to develop from within.

Many companies that have gone outside the company for Web site design have done so because of the service capabilities provided by their partner. The highest profile examples have been alliances between Amazon and Toys'R'Us, Borders, and

Target, among others. No one story describes the relationships with the companies that have partnered with Amazon.

- Toys 'R' Us partnered with Amazon because of its failure to develop internal e-commerce capabilities, especially in the area of fulfillment. Even as a venture capital-funded spinoff, the e-commerce venture of Toys 'R' Us was running out of money and had created too much damage to the company's reputation to grow revenue.
- Borders joined Amazon because they realized that Amazon's first-mover advantage within the bookstore industry prevented Borders from becoming an industry leader in e-commerce capabilities. This union permitted Borders to have a relatively easy-to-maintain digital "storefront" for its traditional brick-and-mortar operations, without competing against Amazon on the electronic front.
- Target's agreement sought to capitalize on Amazon's unique customer-care capabilities while eliminating the need for separate fulfillment partners. Target had rejected the spin-off model of e-commerce initially attempted by competitors Wal-Mart and Kmart but determined that its brand-driven integration strategy would not work without stronger fulfillment capabilities.

These alliances notwithstanding, a company often sacrifices a substantial amount by turning its customer service capabilities over to a third party. Amazon's reputation and capabilities are unique online, and since not every company can hope to strike a similar alliance with Amazon, its example should not be viewed as a generalizable model for e-commerce success. The more reliable approach is to build and acquire the necessary resources to handle customer service from within and integrate both online and physical channels for maximum customer convenience.

PARTICULARS OF E-COMMERCE ALLIANCES

A strong rationale for funding, managing, and providing

IT solutions for e-commerce from within the organization. Selling part of the e-commerce venture or outsourcing operations to IT firms simply does not usually permit a company to reap the maximum benefits of e-commerce.

At times, however, it may be in a company's interest to go outside the firm and form strategic alliances with companies in the same or complementary industries.As is the case with outsourcing operations, such as the relationships with Amazon, alliances should not generally relate to the company's core competencies. They also should not typically relate to customer interaction activities such as customer service and fulfillment, unless there are clear advantages related to a company's capabilities.

In two areas, however, alliances have been very successful in e-commerce: procurement and customer acquisition.For procurement, alliances can help overcome some of the unresolved issues on the B2B side of e-commerce. Although e-commerce clearly provides a potential for vast savings in purchasing, not all industries have been able to realise these savings. Industry leaders such as Dell, GE, and Wal-Mart have been able to realise these savings, while at the same time sending their competitors scrambling to catch up, as detailed in the following.

- The union of HP and Compaq has provided many challenges and opportunities. However, a major obstacle in the company's competition with Dell has been its attempt to meet Dell's level of productivity by cultivating the type of supplier alliances that have given Dell such an advantage over others. The merged company is hoping that the union of the two companies will allow it to overcome its entrenched supplier methods and improve performance.
- Omnexus is an alliance of many of GE's competitors in the plastics industry. Facing competition from both GE's well-established

Polymerland and pure-play public market PlasticsNet, the founders of Omnexus tried to carve out a position by offering scale (founders included BASF, DuPont, Bayer, and Celanese) while maintaining GE's more private format and hosting value-added services. Omnexus' alliance partners, many of whom have their core competencies in chemicals rather than plastics, maintain some internal control over the venture while having the advantages of a collaboration that may lead to a less costly and more successful strategy.

- The Worldwide Retail Exchange (WWRE) is a large partnership that includes discount retailers Kmart and Target, pharmacies, and a host of specialty retailers. The WWRE allowed Kmart and Target to compete with Wal-Mart on the procurement side because of the sheer scale of the WWRE's buyers. Because the WWRE is integrated with each company's systems, these benefits are achieved without damaging the overall integration for the company, which is especially relevant for Target, which was one of the earliest advocates of full e-commerce integration.

Alliances have also been used to gain access to new customer bases through some of the sites that serve as portals for the Internet. Viewed broadly, this category includes Internet service providers such as AOL, portals such as Yahoo, browser operators like Microsoft, and the increasingly ubiquitous Amazon.com and eBay. Companies in a variety of industries have attempted to draw customers from these central locations to their businesses.

- Office Depot struck a deal with Amazon that allowed it access to the bookstore giant's huge customer base. Unlike deals with Toys 'R' Us and Borders, this deal did not entail Amazon taking over operations for Office Depot. Rather, it is only a complement to the originally successful OfficeDepot.com. The Amazon component of Office Depot is more targeted to the individual consumer than the B2B-friendly OfficeDepot.com.
- Bank One was the first company to partner with Microsoft and its new line of.NET services in 2002. The partnership allows BankOne's online customers

easier access to a variety of online services, but it also calls for Microsoft to sell BankOne products through the widely used MSN.com and Hotmail.

- UPS entered a partnership with eBay to allow customers in the consumer to consumer (C2C) transactions easier access to shipping options. The deal was more than simply a link to UPS.com; a special shipping function was integrated directly into eBay's site. UPS was able to access a new customer base in an industry that does not typically lend itself to online marketing.

In each of these deals, the company was able to benefit from an outside alliance without threatening an overall integration strategy. Some of the characteristics of successful e-commerce alliances are:

- Alliances should not be used to substitute for deficiencies in aspects of a company that are core competencies.
- Typically, alliances should not be used in ways directly related to customer interaction.
- Alliances can be used to reinforce B2B relationships for needs such as procurement and support systems.
- Sharing of information, ranging from customer information to production data, is essential in successful alliances.

MANAGEMENT SYSTEMS FOR E-COMMERCE SUCCESS

Over the past five years, e-commerce has rapidly evolved from an experiment for trend-conscious businesses to a vital channel in the business world that no company can afford to ignore. In response to this change, there has been a plethora of studies on the subject of e-commerce, most of which have focused on the formulation of e-commerce strategies. More recently, the importance of structure has come to the forefront, as the dot.com bust caused a reexamination of failed e-commerce structures and as a trend toward integration has spread throughout business.

The importance of management control systems in e-commerce, however, has often been overlooked by both managers and observers of managerial practices. Although studies of traditional business readily acknowledge the importance of various systems, studies of e-commerce have given rather scant attention to systems, in part because the early e-commerce environment embraced two opposing positions on systems.

One view was that e-commerce changes everything and that traditional systems were obsolete. Many e-commerce startups reveled in their rejection of traditional business systems, embraced creativity as the ultimate virtue, and ran companies that barely resembled traditional businesses. At the most trivial level, this meant behavioral changes, such as the rejection of dress codes and cubicles in the work environment.

More important, it comprised the rejection of traditional business models and operating procedures and traditional measures of success. In the stock market, these changes were reflected in huge market capitalizations that had no relation to company profitability. Many traditional companies strived to imitate the startup model and gave their spin-offs similar operating rules.

The second position, held by many traditional companies less convinced of the validity of the e-commerce model, was that e-commerce changed nothing. To many corporate boards, e-commerce was derided as "just technology, " and this condescension was reflected in the type of systems that were set up for e-commerce ventures.

Spending was tightly controlled from above, budgeting had to conform to outdated corporate standards, innovation was discouraged, and few incentives were created for employees working in e-commerce. Often, e-commerce would be a part-time project or diversion for both employees and the executives charged with overseeing it.

We now know that neither of these visions is appropriate for the creation of an e-commerce business or for e-commerce systems. The values that underlie those two visions are certain to doom any e-commerce venture, regardless of the specific strategy or structure. With our new understanding of the proper role of e-commerce, it is necessary to articulate how proper management control systems are critical for a successful e-commerce venture.

As with strategy and structure, the relationship between e-commerce systems and the traditional business is dynamic. There is an ever-changing dynamic relationship between corporate strategy, structure, and systems and e-commerce strategy, structure, and systems.

The systems used to implement an e-commerce strategy will have implications throughout the company and its traditional business, and the effects of changed policies and regulations will not be limited to e-commerce. Our general e-commerce business model highlights the importance of e-commerce systems and the relation of these systems to corporate and e-commerce strategy and structure and to organizational systems.

Owing to this dynamism, commenting on e-commerce systems requires two separate but equally important perspectives. One is the extent to which traditional systems must be altered, augmented, or eliminated to create a business environment in which e-commerce success is possible. The second perspective examines how a focus on the success of e-commerce can bring greater effectiveness to the governance of the traditional business.

These e-commerce systems decisions fall into four broad areas: information practices, human resources, measurement processes, and customer service. First, a company's information practices can become the bridge from appropriate corporate culture to successful individual and organizational behaviour. Though strong leadership and resource commitment can help to create a culture in which IT knowledge and stature are sufficient for starting e-commerce, long-term e-commerce success requires more.

The company must categorically promote information sharing and information transparency, instill a sense of urgency, and enable real-time and flexible decision-making processes. The company can also benefit from e-commerce by putting these information practices to use throughout the value chain. E-commerce provides opportunities for cost savings and speed improvements at every stage of the value chain.

Human resources policy and practices is the second area of systems that needs to be carefully managed for e-commerce success. Because e-commerce is characterized by speed, risk-taking, and new business models, a company must create the proper incentives for those overseeing e-commerce. For the CIO and for all IT and e-commerce personnel, employees must sometimes be rewarded outside the traditional compensation structure.

Managing incentives and rewards to give organizations equity and the appropriate incentives for creativity, flexibility, and innovation is often a significant challenge. E-commerce can benefit the traditional business in the hiring practices of HR. Using the Internet to stimulate job applications can bring both efficiency and a more IT-knowledgeable applicant base.

Measurement is another area in which the nature of e-commerce demands rethinking traditional systems. E-commerce facilitates improvement in measurement systems throughout the organization, allowing a better flow of timely information to decision makers and an aggregation and disaggregation of data never before possible. It permits an analysis of causal relationships and the business model to better understand the payoffs of various corporate actions.

Finally, the systems that govern customer relationships must adjust to implement the important customer service aspects of an e-commerce strategy. Providing service at all times and across channels makes unique demands on the parts of the company closest to the customer. But e-commerce also provides unprecedented capabilities to learn about customers, their behaviour, and their interaction with offerings. Mining this customer data is an area that is still maturing and offers new competitive advantages.

INFORMATION PRACTICES

For e-commerce to be successful, it is necessary but not sufficient that members of the organization are competent and confident in their use of IT. Strong leadership and investment can bring an organization to that stage, but systems must be created to harness the power of IT for organizational integration. It has recently been emphasized that interactive control systems in traditional business must focus on constantly changing information.

These systems provide the sensing and monitoring that is necessary whenever strategic uncertainties are high. In most businesses today, more interactive control systems are needed as strategic uncertainties have been increasing. In e-commerce, these systems become increasingly central to the successful implementation of strategy.

A new policy on information practices must become a central component of the company's systems. Information should be transparent and the sharing of information facilitated. Organizational boundaries must not impede the flow of information. An integration strategy cannot be properly implemented if information about e-commerce stalls within the e-commerce unit and is not disseminated widely.

Ideally, internal processes are developed in-house with substantial consultation and communication; obstacles are easily recognized, understood, and dealt with, internally and quickly. Companies such as Amazon and Office Depot not only have garnered more efficient business practices because of their internal development, but also have been able to expand into other markets such as technology consulting and Web design because of their in-house expertise.

Companies can also use the implementation of an e-commerce strategy as a starting point for proper information practices. Prior to moving online, 3M had a fragmented information system that made it difficult to cross-sell to existing customers. Even having the same customer listed in different systems had additional costs. After moving online, the company created a $20 million data warehouse to store all information, as part of a larger restructuring of information systems.

Senior management must set the example of open information practices and transparency, even when the information is bad news for the company or reflects negatively on an individual or business unit. Problems should be discussed openly, without fear of repercussions. As appropriate, information on the company's goals, measures, and progress should be made available to all employees and the public through the company's Web site.

This information is increasingly available to interested parties, and by making it transparent, a company may build trust with its constituent groups. In addition, it is often beneficial to increase the information flow to the public to ensure that accurate information is communicated, rather than to risk inaccurate information being made public by a third party.Further, many organizational processes should be restructured to fully take advantage of e-commerce.

In particular, e-commerce should encourage and facilitate companies to move away from strict hierarchical reporting in some areas and move toward the use of cross-functional remote teams. By collaborating with other business functions and units, the e-commerce initiative is likely to encounter less resistance in the traditional business. Processes should also be adaptable and flexible enough to respond to changes in real-time information. Numerous virtual organization techniques serve these purposes, including:

- Cross-functional teams that form themselves
- Teams that may go into and out of existence regularly
- Use of both in-person and remote meetings
- Teams that span organizational boundaries
- Encouragement of innovation through mutual trust
- Self-governance
- Harnessing global resources to solve local problems

An organization that utilizes these processes should then be able to assemble teams to innovate or to resolve challenges associated with e-commerce. Most important, all these techniques should be fully consistent with an integration strategy, eliminating any need for moving e-commerce outside the organization.

By upgrading these information practices, a company positions itself to make significant improvements throughout the value chain. For many companies, value chain management is an integral part of the e-commerce strategy. But even for those companies that focus primarily on selling online, subtle improvements can be made with minimal extra cost and effort. Thus, improving information practices can create significant benefits for sales, distribution, and procurement, along with various other processes throughout the organization.

Cisco has used its real-time capabilities to create supplier-side processes that vastly improve its supply-chain management. Cisco and its suppliers and manufacturers share extensive information on product quality. This allows Cisco to measure the number of defective products while they are still in the supplier's possession, rather than after they have been delivered. In turn, the supplier can make faster adjustments in its manufacturing process to minimize future quality problems.

Dell has mastered the use of e-commerce in limiting the amount of inventory kept on hand. Many component parts such as monitors and peripherals are never kept in inventory by Dell, and their movement and distribution is entirely handled by email communication. But even for parts retained by Dell, real-time ordering forecasts are sent to suppliers to minimize the inventory and buffer stocks on a cycle as short as two hours. This relationship with suppliers, coupled with its information practices, also permits a *negative* cash conversion cycle.

At the delivery end of the supply chain, Tesco spanned traditional organizational boundaries to create the most efficient delivery process. While many in the grocery industry mimicked the Amazon model by attempting to deliver from large, high-tech warehouses, Tesco chose to deliver directly from stock at local physical locations. While this limited the potential delivery zone, it also saved Tesco the effort and resources of building expensive warehouses with uncertain profitability. Delivering from the store meant no separate inventories and no need for entirely new processes.

Nike, Inc. recently implemented a supply-chain system

linking the company with its manufacturing partners. Before these system changes, 30 percent of Nike's total volume of shoe orders were based on estimates; now, only 3 percent of the orders are guesswork, because of better forecasting and planning.

Whirlpool Corporation has linked every Whirlpool factory and sales site worldwide through e-business software, allowing factories and sales sites to coordinate with suppliers and key retail partners. This has reduced inventories and increased vital communication.

Krispy Kreme Doughnut is another company that has used e-commerce to its advantage by devising an intranet network linking its stores. The Web system tracks doughnut mix, doles out the right colors of sprinkles, monitors managers' decisions, and permits users to fix errors such as damaged goods, by allowing replacements to be sent. The system allows employees to focus more on customer service, reduce problem orders, and increase productivity.

For proper information practices to improve the success of e-commerce implementations:

- Organizational boundaries should not represent an impediment to the free flow of information in a company.
- Company leadership must set the example of open information practices.
- Companies must be willing to move away from strict hierarchical reporting systems.

HUMAN RESOURCES

Management of personnel is also central to the implementation of e-commerce strategy. Even in the aftermath of the fallout of the dot.com bust in the stock market, e-commerce is still inexorably linked to the notions of large performance bonuses, stock options, Silicon Valley whiz kids, and new-wave office environments.

It is still necessary to find ways to develop and retain employees who are creative, flexible, and innovative—in addition to competent and diligent. In this light, a company must endeavor to put systems in place that retain key personnel and make strategic new hires throughout the course of an e-commerce venture.

Designing appropriate compensation systems is instrumental both in attaining initial e-commerce success and in retaining the leaders and employees who made that success possible. Above all, compensation systems must be properly aligned with strategy and structure.

Symbolically, the CIO's compensation is one of the more important decisions a company dedicated to implementing e-commerce will encounter. CIO compensation should be in line with that of other members of senior management to signal respect for the IT function as a creator of value. Failure to fully and explicitly acknowledge the value of IT and e-commerce contradicts the other messages that must be communicated for e-commerce to succeed.

At lower levels of the company, compensation systems have more practical consequences for alignment. Some companies believe that compensating e-commerce managers the same as managers in traditional commerce fails to create proper incentives for e-commerce and value creation. Differential compensation sometimes creates an incentive to cannibalize from the company's traditional channels as well as more effectively and more quickly to execute an e-commerce strategy.

But, e-commerce compensation should be tied to the overall success of the venture company-wide, rather than rewarding performance within an individual unit. This is particularly true when the company is seeking full integration, because it helps ensure cooperation between departments.

Companies must be prepared to manage the channel conflict that often arises when e-commerce begins to cannibalize the traditional business. Cannibalization is necessary to optimize the use of each channel, and an integration strategy cannot succeed if traditional business units do not accept it. Companies must design compensation systems that gradually shift compensation toward the creation of value, particularly in businesses heavily dependent on salespersons who work on a commission basis. Traditional business units must be placated not by compensating inefficiencies, but by carving out new roles that optimize the use of each channel and produce a successfully integrated and profitable multi-channel coordinated effort.

At aviation parts distributor Aviall Inc., a few weeks after an upper-management shakeup brought in a new CEO in 1996, a new Web-based order-entry system was introduced. In response, Aviall's 300 sales reps feared their jobs were at stake and told customers not to use it. Despite the benefits to the consumer that were realized through the Web-based system, the role of the sales reps had not been modified to permit them to survive such a drastic change in company strategy.

As companies develop and implement e-commerce strategies, the Internet must be examined and the pre-existing channels must be modified in a way that complements the e-commerce initiative. While compensation systems must often be reevaluated and reconstructed in e-commerce implementations, hiring practices can be improved simply by using the same Web site that showcases other e-commerce activities. Hiring online can significantly reduce advertising costs associated with print and other listings.

It can also ensure that potential applicants possess at least some skills in using the Internet and implies a confidence and understanding of the importance of e-commerce. Cisco is one company that greatly improved its hiring process by advertising openings online. Further, special attention should be paid to HR policies covering to those who work in e-commerce and IT.

Companies should recognize the fluidity of the IT labour market and must often create more flexible labour policies than for other employees. To ensure that proper human resources practices are employed in an e-commerce implementation;

- Compensation systems for traditional and e-commerce personnel should be properly aligned with the company's new e-commerce strategy.
- Companies must be prepared for channel conflict due

to cannibalization of traditional company segments into an e-commerce venture.

- Hiring practices must fully take advantage of the exposure opportunity and cost savings made available by Internet hiring.

MEASUREMENT

Strong measurement practices form one of the cornerstones of good systems, particularly in e-commerce. Performance measures for e-commerce must overcome the uncertainty and unique dynamics associated with the Internet and must be more frequently adjusted in response to real-time information.

With these considerations, no company should simply extend its existing performance measures to an e-commerce venture. Still, long-term cost differentials must be balanced with other financial and nonfinancial measures and leading and lagging indicators that are particularly useful for successful e-commerce implementations.

The information systems of the 1990s gave CEOs a new method of accessing, analyzing, and reporting on the accountability of their organization. The systems developed during this time of advancement in information technology helped to create a more streamlined capability for centralized accountability. The variety of data made available to a company at that time ranged from corporate-level results to the small-scale measurements of performance that enabled management to recognize advantages and potential problems in real-time. E-Commerce transforms these capabilities.

Like the root system of a massive tree, IT accountability systems helped management reach and observe every aspect of their business. With the addition of e-commerce to a pre-existing IT accountability system, companies can simplify access to previously collected information for those within the company and for external stakeholders, including partners, customers, and investors. New information could be created and both financial and nonfinancial measures could be integrated into the decision-making process.

The information could also be easily and quickly aggregated and disaggregated to facilitate various decisions. Managers could now measure inputs, processes, outputs, and outcomes in ways never before possible. Cisco's new systems permit outsiders to view on its Web site not only its general business plan but also the company's performance statistics at any given moment.

Seamlessness between internal IT systems and e-commerce gives Cisco the ability to provide such information with relatively little effort. This transparency between internal and external systems also helped Cisco endure many of the pitfalls associated with the technology bust by expanding the role of e-commerce to replace human positions throughout the company.

But e-commerce can be used for more than simply replacing employees. Instead, the information made available through a well-developed e-commerce initiative can empower employees at every level of business. Improved measurement is a key component. Management receives information in a timely manner, which lets it act on up-to-date measures of performance, while lower-level employees can access information at any time and take the initiative based on that information, with or without direct managerial direction.

Among the most important aspects of e-commerce as it applies to system management and measurement is maintaining consistency across all company lines. A company implementing a new e-commerce solution should ensure consistency among accounting systems, information technology systems, and e-commerce systems and related measures. However, the implementation of an e-commerce solution also necessitates working to ensure compatibility between the systems of business partners using unified e-commerce solutions.

The uniquely advantageous relationship between Dell and its suppliers would not be possible without seamless internal and external systems that enable a free flow of information and measures between companies. E-com-merce can facilitate consistency of information and measurements by cascading information throughout the organization and then externally to other stakeholders.

In addition to measuring the performance of the business, e-commerce brings added importance to measuring the value and functionality of operations. Most e-commerce strategies will have a strong operational component, including cost savings from value chain management and cuts in labour costs for the online channel. Operational measures should be tracked by some dedicated resource and balanced between financial and nonfinancial assessments of operational performance. This analysis can lead to a better understanding of the payoffs of investment in e-commerce initiatives.

CUSTOMER RELATIONSHIPS

Under traditional business models, it may be sufficient to offer customer service during normal business hours, either at physical locations or over the phone. E-commerce dramatically changes those expectations both in terms of company strategy and the customer's perspective.

Near-universal and constant customer service availability is expected for almost any viable e-commerce strategy. Companies must re-examine their customer service practices and make numerous key decisions in moving toward universal availability. Two of the main considerations are the distribution of response tasks between human and automated systems and the operating hours for human responses. Each of these include trade-offs among speed, cost, convenience, and efficiency.

Most e-commerce ventures have developed some FAQ (frequently asked questions) function on their Web sites. This function may consist of rudimentary inquiries only or a highly sophisticated taxonomy of nearly every conceivable question. The nature of the offering and the Web site dictates how sophisticated the FAQs should be, but no company can exhaust the list of possible questions.

The challenge then becomes how to provide service to customers who are dissatisfied with the FAQs. A company may choose to provide immediate or delayed email support to customers or may offer a phone line for further inquiries. The company must weigh the value of instant response and satisfaction to the customer against the added costs associated with phone banks or with rapid and 24/7 email response.

Some pure-play companies like Half.com chose to keep the process entirely online and not offer phone service. For traditional companies, however, this strategy is more difficult, as it can inundate the traditional business phone lines with Internet inquiries. Delta Airlines, on the other hand, was able to reduce its phone volume and increase its status among elite customers by moving reservation information online while simultaneously implementing a wireless initiative.

Delta first identified such a programme as "nice to have" but not a necessity, but the company quickly recognized the appeal of wireless capabilities to its elite customers by providing quick access to vast amounts of information. Implementing this programme was not only a cost-saving move, but also a successful effort to appeal to customers who desired this level of functionality.

For companies that do provide phone service in addition to their FAQs and Internet support, a decision must be made on availability. Limiting phone support to normal business hours reduces some of the value added associated with the Web site. On the other hand, labour costs may not justify 24/7 phone service for industries that offer commodity goods. More technical industries, B2B companies, and companies with customized and personalized Internet-related offerings should carefully consider offering a 24/7 service.

Another aspect of customer service practices is the development and implementation of policies on shipping, delivery, and returns. In particular, companies that use physical branches as part of a bricks-and-clicks strategy must not neglect proper training on the traditional commerce side necessary to facilitate e-commerce developments and service. Customer service representatives in physical branches must be thoroughly familiar with the Web site, its function, and its policies.

While e-commerce requires changes and enhancement to

customer service policies, it also affords most companies excellent opportunities to refine marketing strategies, selling practices, pricing, and Web site design by observing customer behaviour. Physical branches have more limited opportunities to collect customer data, particularly data from sites where customers can impart complaints or grievances.

When customers shop online, however, their every mouse click is potentially revealing and useful for future improvements in e-commerce service.Although these methods require substantial analysis, companies can draw strong implications and direction about customer behaviour from this data. Unused search results may indicate a problem with the search engine.

Aborted purchases may indicate that the checkout procedure is unclear or too time-consuming. Consistent nonpurchase of a product may indicate that more precise information is needed to inspire consumer confidence. Corporations must be willing and able to redesign their Web sites and refine customer processes based on the gathered information as well as direct feedback from the customers. Since convenience is a prime source of competitive advantage, problems with customer service systems must be addressed immediately.

Although shutting down the Web site is undesirable, important changes should be made by closing the site for a few hours in nonpeak time and by warning the customers in advance of this downtime. Thus, to effectively manage and enhance customer service attributes,

- Companies with an Internet presence should provide any information that a customer might need while online.
- Corporate Web sites should incorporate some form of direct contact mechanism, whether it is as simple as a service phone number or as advanced as online chat capabilities.
- Companies should ensure that the Web site easily connects to any other aspect of the company service that a customer might need information about,

ranging from traditional brick-and-mortar locations to shipping policies.

PAYOFFS OF E-COMMERCE

We have examined how various organizational inputs and processes can impact the outputs of e-commerce. We have examined leadership, strategy, structure, and systems both in the corporation generally and related specifically to e-commerce. We have also seen how these key factors of success can be successfully managed in a formal process to improve customer acquisitions, customer loyalty, cost savings, channel optimization, and value creation.

Although these outputs are important, the resource allocation decision should rely on understanding the impact of e-commerce decisions and actions on the outcome of improved corporate profitability.

Many researchers and managers have recognized the need to identify and measure the impacts of corporate actions and to provide a better analysis of the return on investment (ROI) of e-commerce expenditures. However, the appropriate metrics have not been well developed. The framework presented here provides the necessary specificity to identify both the causal relationships that lead to e-commerce success, and related measures. In this way, both general managers and IT and e-commerce professionals can more effectively evaluate the success of e-commerce and the potential and actual payoffs of e-commerce investments.

Managers now can also examine the interrelationships among the characteristics of e-commerce success discussed here. The causal linkage analysis illustrates the importance of leadership, strategy, structure, and systems and highlights the specific managerial actions that lead to success.

Some writers have suggested the need for more measurements of the effectiveness of IT. They note that corporations have overlooked economic rationality in justifying IT expenditures and instead have leaned toward a strategy that resembled an arms race, where firms acquire the best and most recent technologies to outpace others, regardless of the results. To assess the payoffs of e-commerce investments, companies must implement systems that evaluate the impact of e-commerce initiatives on financial performance and the trade-offs that must be made among competing organizational constraints and barriers to implementation.

These systems assist senior executives as they develop an e-commerce strategy and allocate corporate resources to support that strategy. The systems also assist e-commerce managers to evaluate the trade-offs and decide which projects provide the largest net benefit to both short-term financial performance and the long-term success of the firm. The careful identification and measurement of the payoffs also permits e-commerce and IT managers to demonstrate the impact on corporate profitability and value creation.

It also provides information for better corporate resource allocation decisions in the CEO's and CFO's offices, based on a better understanding of the ROI—including a fuller understanding of the benefits and costs of e-commerce. Hence, to implement their e-commerce strategy, companies are faced with a significant challenge: to quantify the link between corporate actions in e-commerce and corporate financial performance.

Indeed, only by making the "business case" for e-commerce expenditures can managers truly integrate potential e-commerce impacts into their business strategies. Yet, many companies have failed to make a case for e-commerce initiatives. Instead, they have often acted because they had a feeling that it was the right thing to do or because their competitors were making the leap into e-commerce ventures. However, projects put into place for these reasons alone are vulnerable to cost overruns and poor ROI, changes in senior management, or shifting corporate or consumer priorities.

To present a clear business case for e-commerce initiatives, senior managers need to identify the metrics of e-commerce performance and how that performance impacts overall long-term corporate profitability. This increased attention to the thorough identification and measurement of the metrics of e-commerce is echoed in popular measurement frameworks such as the popular strategic management system "balanced scorecard."

Frameworks such as balanced scorecard and shareholder value analysis focus on the causal relationships and linkages within organizations and the actions managers can implement to improve both customer and corporate profitability and drive increased value. However, substantial work is required to establish the relationships that relate specifically to e-commerce strategies.

Undeniably, the identification and measurement of the impact of e-commerce strategies is particularly difficult as they are usually linked to long time horizons, a high level of uncertainty, and impacts that are often difficult to quantify. But this analysis is important to improve resource allocation, decision making, and profitability.

In recent years, companies have placed increasing importance on the development of performance metrics to better measure and manage e-commerce performance. Software programs and information systems have been developed to provide a broader set of measurement tools to incorporate into new strategic management systems.

Although the need for performance measures for e-commerce has been identified, a large number of specific metrics have not been proposed. E-commerce analysis has typically been operating without measures that permit an effective evaluation of e-commerce benefits, success, or value. This lack of performance metrics has meant a lack of both actual and perceived accountability for firm e-commerce operations to various stakeholders.

It also examines how companies can make a compelling business case for e-commerce programs. Senior managers understand how to measure the value of e-commerce and understand the payoffs of e-commerce investments. Its purpose is to answer the question, "Is it worth it?" for companies deciding to start or expand e-commerce projects. This quandary is compounded as senior managers consider the high costs typically associated with e-commerce and the seemingly small percentage of e-commerce or IT projects that succeed. Sometimes the projects are flawed, but often the measures of success are flawed.

Examples abound where companies have attempted e-commerce initiatives and have either failed dramatically or have incurred costs that far outweighed the gains. Though some would suggest that those failures occurred when companies were not so well centered on ensuring that IT-related funds were well spent, companies today face similar questions about the value of their e-commerce initiatives.

For most companies, it is not a question of whether or not to invest in e-commerce, but when and how: Should it be a large amount up front, or perhaps a smaller expenditure at a later date? Such decisions are critical and difficult. Key to making these decisions is understanding the causal relationships and identifying and measuring the success of the specific actions that managers can take to drive e-commerce success.

ENSURING E-COMMERCE SUCCESS

Many decisions related to the operations of the company significantly affect the success of all e-commerce initiatives, including decisions related to leadership, strategy, structure, and systems. In this section, determinants of e-commerce success are identified. As they are essential to superior e-commerce performance, these success factors become the foundation for rigorous performance evaluation systems for e-commerce.

The main model describes the inputs, processes, outputs, and outcomes of e-commerce activities. These are further articulated as e-commerce objectives within the e-commerce causal model of performance. Corporations must make important choices regarding the formulation and implementation of e-commerce strategies in relation to the overall external environment and corporate resources, strategy, structure, and systems (inputs).

Other factors, such as leadership and e-commerce strategy, e-commerce structure, and e-commerce systems (processes) also significantly affect the performance and success of e-commerce initiatives. The consequences and success of the company's actions on these inputs and processes impact various outputs, including improvement in customer acquisition and loyalty, in cost reduction, in channel optimization, and in overall value capture.

If the strategy formulation and implementation is successful, these outputs should ultimately be seen in improved overall corporate profitability (outcome).

E-Commerce Causal Model of Performance: E-Commerce Objectives

Outcomes	Long-term Corporate Profitability
Outputs	Customer Acquisition Customer Loyalty and Retention Cost Savings: Related to customer and supplier interactions Channel Optimization: Increased site traffic and sales Value Capture: Increased e-commerce profits
Processes	Leadership: Commitment and focus on e-commerce initiatives E-Commerce Structure: Integration into business unit structure E-Commerce Strategy: Coherent and aligned strategy E-Commerce Systems: Appropriate processes for effective implementation
Inputs	Resources: Adequate capital and people Corporate Structure: Appropriate organizational structure Corporate Strategy: Alignment with type of products offered, customers served, and competitive positioning Corporate Systems: Suitable training, information, and processes External Environment: Adapted to external forces

After carefully identifying the specific e-commerce objectives, the drivers of success must be defined. These help specify more precisely the keys to e-commerce success and the actions that managers must take to improve corporate profitability.

Managers must make many choices. The uses of management control levers and performance measurement and management systems typically affect the implementation of e-commerce strategies. The objectives, the drivers, and the metrics related to e-commerce success should be part of a clear articulation of the causal relationships leading from the inputs to the processes and then flowing to the desired outputs and outcomes.

It is important to identify and communicate these causal links throughout the organization to guide the formulation and implementation of e-commerce strategies.

The causal linkage map of drivers is useful to ensure that all necessary actions are taken to achieve success, that unnecessary actions are not taken, and that all employees understand their critical roles.

INPUTS: EXTERNAL ENVIRONMENT, CORPORATE RESOURCES, STRATEGIES, STRUCTURES, AND SYSTEMS

In the past many companies made decisions related to e-commerce with an arms-race mentality, where the focus was on the competition rather than the potential benefits of the new technology.

In the current business climate, with increased focus on corporate accountability and efficiency, it has become increasingly important to estimate and monitor the costs of an e-commerce project in comparison to the benefits likely to accrue.

When considering e-commerce ventures, it is crucial that senior managers fully evaluate the external environment and the resources, strategies, structures, and systems already present in the company to determine an initiative's fit and its likelihood of success.

EXTERNAL ENVIRONMENT

Though many inputs to e-commerce success are controllable by corporate managers, some inputs constrain many corporate activities, require significant corporate adaptation, and influence success. The external environment may include changes in the business environment, the economy, technological developments, competitors, suppliers, and customer needs. Even though companies may have coherent strategies, structures, and systems and adequate corporate capital and labour resources for e-commerce success, changes in the external environment can be an important input that will significantly impact corporate decisions.

CORPORATE RESOURCES

The most important corporate resources within an organization are its people and its capital. In determining whether a corporation has the capabilities and resources to support new or expanded e-commerce operations, it is necessary to look at the people and capital that currently exist in the corporation. Are the company's employees highly motivated and trained? Do they have the skills necessary for success?

Such questions convey the conduciveness of a company's employees and organization to the changes and challenges that accompany an escalation in focus on e-commerce. From a capital perspective, if a firm is already overextended and short on funding, it may have trouble allocating sufficient funds for a major e-commerce initiative. The availability of financial resources is also dependent on the commitment of the senior management to new or expanded e-commerce initiatives.

Without adequate financial resources, these ventures cannot succeed. Thus, corporate resources are a critical input for e-commerce success.

CORPORATE STRATEGIES

The development of e-commerce strategies must fit within an overall corporate strategy. Thus, though the model is dynamic and corporate strategy may be altered by the development of e-commerce, the corporate strategy remains an important input to the formulation and implementation of an e-commerce strategy.

Companies make very different choices as to geographical diversity, product type, product mix, customer type, level of service, and pricing. These choices not only impact corporate strategy but also, significantly affect e-commerce strategy.

CORPORATE STRUCTURES

An organization's corporate structure plays a big part in determining the organization of e-commerce operations within it. Whether a company has a large number of strategic business units or networks across a wide geographical area with many different languages will influence many e-commerce decisions.

Whether the company is more or less decentralized with independent business units and whether the organizational structure is arranged by geography, by product type, by customer type, by channel, or with a matrix will influence the choice of e-commerce strategy and implementation. These structures become inputs to the e-commerce strategy, structure, systems, and leadership necessary for e-commerce success.

CORPORATE SYSTEMS

A company's corporate systems are highly relevant in weighing the appropriateness of a new or expanded e-commerce venture.

The corporate systems related to information flow, human resources, compensation, management control, measurement, and others will affect the choice of e-commerce strategy, structure, and systems.

PROCESSES: LEADERSHIP, E-COMMERCE STRATEGIES, STRUCTURES, AND SYSTEMS

Once the viability of e-commerce initiatives is determined, by evaluating the inputs available in an organization, senior managers who are planning and developing e-commerce programs can focus on the processes that drive superior e-commerce performance and connect the inputs to e-commerce success.

Four main processes are critical for e-commerce success: leadership, e-commerce strategy, e-commerce structure, and e-commerce systems. The managers' effective use of these processes will determine the outputs and outcomes.

LEADERSHIP

A company's leadership must be both knowledgeable about e-commerce and committed to the e-commerce venture for it to succeed. Senior managers must provide full support to all e-commerce initiatives and communicate that support throughout the company. If a company cannot secure strong public support of e-commerce programs at the senior management level, then even though an e-commerce programme may be installed effectively by technical staff or consultants, it is unlikely to reach its potential.

E-COMMERCE STRATEGY

E-commerce success is dependent on a well-formulated and well-executed e-commerce strategy. The strategy must be consistent with both corporate strategy, structure, and systems, and e-commerce structure and systems. Its alignment with these other inputs and processes is critical to success.The company's choice of the number of products and services that it wants to provide online, the costs and prices related to its online offerings, the customer profile, and the product and service capabilities the firm already has are just some of the factors that will affect the e-commerce strategy.

E-COMMERCE STRUCTURE

Choices about how a company decides to design and implement its e-commerce structure are key process issues that companies must address in relation to their e-commerce initiatives. Factors critical for this decision, such as the level of outsourcing appropriate for the company, the relationships the company wants to develop with partners, the existing organizational structure, and the level of desired e-commerce integration, affect the ultimate outcome of the e-commerce initiative on overall corporate profitability.

E-COMMERCE SYSTEMS

To ensure that highly qualified employees and proper

processes are in place to meet a company's stakeholders' needs, senior managers must develop and implement appropriate systems for e-commerce.

E-commerce system issues such as employee e-commerce literacy, measurement, and data collection are part of the processes pertinent to e-commerce. The effects of senior managers putting systems in place to best meet their employee, customer, partner, and other stakeholders' needs extend far beyond items such as lower costs and more timely customer service systems, to heightened productivity and greater sales. The systems move the company toward decreasing overall organizational costs and increasing company revenues, with an ultimate goal of increased corporate profitability.

MEASURING E-COMMERCE SUCCESS

CIOs often suggest that better measures of the payoffs of e-commerce operational and capital investments are necessary to demonstrate the value creation of e-commerce initiatives and to obtain additional resources for critical e-commerce projects. The measures are essential to monitor the key performance drivers (inputs and processes) and assess whether the e-commerce initiative is achieving its stated objectives (outputs) and thus contributing to the long-term success of the corporation (outcomes).

Companies often waste resources on e-commerce initiatives or do not invest when they should because they cannot effectively evaluate the potential payoffs of e-commerce investments.Measuring returns on e-commerce projects can be a daunting challenge. Predicting customer behaviour is difficult, because using the Web to do business is still relatively new to many businesses and thus forecasting sales and profits is typically imprecise. There is not much historical data and experience for managers to draw upon when developing or applying metrics, and many economic benefits of e-commerce projects are seen as difficult to measure.

Further, the pace of change in e-business and Web-based technologies has been so rapid that precise measurements are often difficult.Many senior managers have come to believe that further investment in new technology and e-commerce is an imperative that is required to maintain or develop a competitive position. They often make expenditures without completing a rigorous analysis.

However, today's more stringent economic environment and the widely publicized negative impacts of many e-commerce initiatives has caused many senior managers to question the payoffs of e-commerce investments. As companies assess the choice of appropriate measures to evaluate e-commerce initiatives, numerous potential issues arise.

Since the choices are different for each company, because the strategies, structures, and systems are different, substantial customization is necessary. Senior managers should consider six initial questions that can lead to the development of appropriate measures for e-commerce operations:

- What measurement systems are currently in place and being utilized within the organization?
- What are the important criteria to the company and its constituencies and stakeholders?
- What does the company desire to accomplish with the e-commerce initiative?
- What is the anticipated time frame associated with the e-commerce programme?
- Who are the parties involved in implementing the e-commerce project, and who will be affected by the results?
- What critical processes are associated with the successful execution of the e-commerce project?

To address these questions, it is imperative that companies not only specifically tailor their e-commerce measurement approach but also utilize multiple measures to fully analyse their situations. Different measurement criteria are important for companies that have different strategies or may be in a different stage of their life cycle or their e-commerce development. The multiple measures will typically include both financial and nonfinancial measures that are leading and lagging indicators of performance.

They may be used in a balanced-scorecard, shareholder-value-added, or other approach and can be developed specificallyf or IT or e-commerce or as a part of an overall corporate performance measurement system. Companies can also use a weighted scoring system to evaluate investments related to overall IT, e-commerce, or business strategy.

There are many obstacles to implementing a successful measurement system, whether a lack of focus, a low priority, or just difficulty. It is the responsibility of senior managers to evaluate the e-commerce initiatives and decide on the right measures for their organization and ensure that the measures are captured and responded to properly.

To obtain adequate resources for e-commerce and to effectively manage e-commerce initiatives, the payoffs of e-commerce investments must be calculated and integrated into management decision-making systems.

DEVELOPING APPROPRIATE METRICS

To closely monitor the cause and effect relationships evidenced in the e-commerce causal linkage model, appropriate metrics must be developed. These metrics must be consistent with and support the objectives and drivers and key success factors already defined. The selected metrics will likely include a combination of input, processes, output, and outcome metrics to effectively measure performance.

Senior managers involved in the e-commerce decision-making process should develop metrics appropriate to the strategy and objectives of the e-commerce initiative, the company, and its stakeholders. During the measure selection process, it is useful for the involved individuals to choose just a few measures, to focus those senior managers involved in the e-commerce initiative on the critical performance indicators.

The list of metrics presented here is not meant to be a comprehensive set of e-commerce performance measures. Rather, it is a selection and example of some metrics that may be appropriate. Managers must select those that most closely fit their strategy and adapt or develop others. There is no rule for the right number of metrics to include in a measurement system; however, including too many tends to distract managers from pursuing a focused strategy. Generally, a complete measurement system includes perhaps three to six measures for each element being evaluated and no more than twenty measures in total.

For each key success factor, a specific target should be identified and results should be measured against these targets. These results should be widely communicated among not only those senior managers directly involved in the e-commerce initiative, but also other individuals within the organization upon whom the initiative will have an impact.

One of the important contributions that e-commerce can make to an organization is an expanded communication and informational capability. Any e-commerce measurement system will have little impact if the results are not fully discussed. Results should be monitored regularly and used to identify areas of weakness, address the plans and systems in place, and establish new initiatives to improve deficiencies.

The measures chosen should be quantifiable, in either absolute or percentage terms, as well as complete and controllable. They should be complete in that the measure sums up in one number the contribution of all elements of performance that matter; for example, profitability is a summary measure of revenue generation and cost control. They should be controllable in that employees in the organization can actually influence improvement in the factor measured.

Some of the metrics shown here are evaluations of overall firm performance. Others are indicators of e-commerce performance that are derived through an aggregation of measures of individual business units and functions. It is important to evaluate the performance of both overall e-commerce performance and the specific aspects of e-commerce that lead to revenue enhancement or cost savings to determine the success of various operations and corrective action that can be taken to make improvements.

The measures should be of use to both senior and middle managers in the business units and functions. Thus, they must be disaggregated so each unit can examine its contribution to the achievement of the company's e-commerce strategy.

These analyses ensure that each unit is making a contribution to the e-commerce initiative and improving corporate profitability. Additionally, these metrics can be used to provide a gap analysis that permits managers to determine what other inputs or processes are required to meet the company's e-commerce project objectives. Different tools and techniques are available to measure the different aspects of e-commerce performance.

For example, online surveys and polls are powerful tools to help e-commerce enabled companies to better understand the benefit of Internet usage for increasing revenue or decreasing costs related to their customers, thus providing valuable information regarding opportunities to improve overall profitability. Internally, surveys, focus groups, and other techniques are increasingly being used to measure and monitor employee, personnel, and stakeholder reactions and provide valuable feedback.

Once metrics have been developed, data on these indicators must be collected and statistical analysis, such as multiple regression, should be performed to analyse and test the validity of the customized e-commerce measurement system and causal relationships hypothesized by the company.

As companies evaluate the initial measurement system's performance, they will typically add some metrics and drop others because of a lack of evidence of a strong relationship. It is here that a final measurement system emerges, and the focus then shifts to applying the model to support improved decision making.

Outputs and outcomes: Overall-firm and e-commerce-specific performance. If the e-commerce initiatives are well designed and executed and the model of causal relationships properly specified, the identified inputs and processes should lead to improved performance. This should include increasing the success of the e-commerce initiative (outputs) and ultimately to improve corporate performance either through increased revenues or decreased costs (outcomes). To properly evaluate e-commerce performance, input, process, output, and outcome measures are all necessary and should be clearly linked in a causal relationship.

These performance indicators empower senior managers with the information to evaluate whether the e-commerce programme is achieving its stated objectives and contributing to overall corporate profitability.

For example, metrics such as the percentage of customer attrition are indicators of the e-commerce customer service provided by the company and the related level of customer satisfaction. Since the goals relate to increasing corporate profits, not just improving customer satisfaction, both output and outcome measures are necessary.

A weak performance on the output metrics should signal a need to examine the inputs and processes and determine whether they have been misspecified or just poorly executed. It also can provide an opportunity to identify potential benefits to organizational effectiveness and profitability from e-commerce that may have been overlooked.

This is an opportunity to examine how well e-commerce programs are contributing to corporate profits and should unveil specific opportunities, directions for improvements, and standards of performance. The e-commerce measurement system should highlight the specific contributions of the e-commerce activities, in addition to providing valuable feedback that can lead to future e-commerce programme and corporate improvements.

Results from the e-commerce evaluation and measurement process should be widely communicated throughout the organization. In a well-executed e-commerce venture, all units of the company will have some involvement in the e-commerce initiative.

The evaluation and measurement of the e-commerce programme will have little impact if the results are not disseminated throughout the organization to the many disparate areas that both affect and are affected by it. Results should be monitored regularly and used to identify areas of weakness, challenge the plans and systems in place, and present new initiatives to improve deficiencies.

OUTPUTS: CHANNEL OPTIMIZATION, COST SAVINGS, CUSTOMER ACQUISITION, CUSTOMER LOYALTY, AND VALUE CAPTURE

CHANNEL OPTIMIZATION

Achievement of channel optimization is accomplished and exhibited through an array of items that vary from increased site traffic to informational gains and improvements in demand and supply chain relationships. As consumers become more aware and partial to a company's Web site, traffic typically increases. Managers are able to evaluate increases in metrics such as site hits, page views, and stickiness.

While additional analysis is necessary to properly assess the impact of these gains, some of the frequent outputs of these items are greater sales and an expanded market base. It also encourages cannibalization and provides opportunities to increase revenues through the use of an additional or alternate channel and reduce costs through the use of this lower-cost channel of distribution.

By encouraging customers and suppliers to use the channels that provide the highest revenues and lowest costs, the e-commerce initiative's outputs are evident and the impact on the ultimate outcome of corporate profitable becomes achievable.

E-commerce also permits the gathering of increased information on customers, partners, and competitors to improve the accuracy of business forecasting techniques and improve relationships in both the acquisition and distribution of goods. Information can be more widely disseminated in a more timely and consistent manner.

This permits companies to communicate with remote, mobile, and distant parties in a way never before possible. The electronic information also tends to be more accurate due to fewer transcription errors and lower costs related to printing, distribution, and updates.

It is through improvements in data handling that e-commerce endows the greatest gains to demand and supply chain relationships. Studies have shown that when companies establish demand and supply chain relationships that are facilitated by online means, they can markedly decrease their costs of doing business.

The benefits to doing business in this way can be shared among customers, suppliers, and others. These benefits can take many forms, including increased partner collaboration on products and services, reduction in time and cost associated with product acquisition, delivery, and development, freeing up employees to complete other tasks, as well as reducing inventory shortages and costs of procurement.

COST SAVINGS

Though much of the early focus of e-commerce initiatives was on increasing revenue, the potential for cost savings is at least as large. This could include savings in administrative, customer service, material acquisition, distribution, and sales costs. E-commerce can support improvements through online processes that assist in activities such as ordering, invoicing, tracking, payment, and delivery. Superior cash flow can be accomplished with e-commerce-facilitated better management of inventory levels. Also, critical business processes such as procurement, sales, and customer relationship management can be increasingly automated.

These create cost savings through reduced paper handling and requirements for human intervention in administration. IBM recently realized significant cost savings by creating an online intranet for employees to Web conference, collaborate on ideas, and improve skills. In the process, IBM realized $375 million in annual savings from the training budget and another $20 million from reduced travel expenses due to the high-volume use of Web conferencing. General Motors Corporation now uses online auctions to sell used cars to auto dealers at the end of the cars' leases, saving about $180 million yearly.

CUSTOMER ACQUISITION

Providing company products and services over the Internet creates a new channel for a company's existing and potential customers. Further, though many potential customers were previously able to access a company's products or services through other channels before e-commerce was available, providing a business channel on the Web allows customers to reach companies beyond their local areas in a manner never previously available at the same scale. Companies that move more commerce to the Web can accomplish significantly expanded global coverage and exposure with a relatively minimal investment.

This wider coverage encompasses new products, new markets, new distribution channels, new partners, and so forth. Through online activities, companies can offer products or services directly to their consumers. The e-commerce initiatives and the e-commerce leadership, strategy, structure, and system should permit an increase in new customer acquisition as a powerful potential output.

CUSTOMER LOYALTY

Customer loyalty can be seen through both repeat customers and increased overall customer satisfaction levels. The common business truism that it is less costly to make additional sales to existing customers than to develop sales through new customers is certainly applicable in an e-commerce environment. The Internet permits companies to connect with their customers, partners, and suppliers in a virtual environment. This permits increased communication and a greater ability to intertwine the company's operations with the external stakeholders' needs and requirements.

The intertwining of interests not only allows the company to provide better customer service to these external stakeholders, but also links the two groups in a manner that facilitates recurring purchases. E-commerce activities can provide an important opportunity to improve customer service levels and relationships leading to increased customer loyalty and repeat purchases.

VALUE CAPTURE

Capturing additional value is at the core of company objectives. As customers are better able to compare the products and services offered to them through e-commerce, they can more easily compare alternatives and competitor offerings in an expedient manner. Thus, it is critical for each company to be able to differentiate itself from its competitors, for the benefit of its customers as well as itself.

Companies also capture additional value through improvements in both costs and prices. As the cost of sales is reduced, the opportunity to offer lower prices to the customer is greatly increased, leading to the ability to be more competitive and drive increased revenues.

Companies can also create and capture additional value by providing additional services to their customers such as customization and personalization. These services are far reaching, and the opportunities for the creation and capturing of value for the company and its various stakeholders are significant.

OUTCOMES: INCREASED REVENUES AND DECREASED COSTS LEAD TO IMPROVED PROFITABILITY

One important lesson from the development of e-commerce is that improving customer traffic and other outputs of e-commerce activity is not enough. For e-commerce initiatives to be of value, the intermediate outputs must eventually pay off in increased corporate profits. Viewed simply, increased profitability can only be achieved through improving revenue or decreasing costs.

To evaluate the payoffs of e-commerce investments and better allocate corporate resources, senior managers must be clear about the ultimate goal and develop ways to measure success. Further, if IT and e-commerce managers want to obtain additional resources for e-commerce investments, the ultimate effect on corporate profitability must be measured and the payoffs and ROI be clearly calculated.

Chapter 5

E-Business Environment

Access to on-line information resources and the use of electronic transactions increasingly augment the operation of modern colleges and universities. These resources and functions are important both internally and in collaboration with external partners. To reap the full benefits that these resources and processes can offer, all members of the campus community must be able to function easily and securely throughout this rapidly growing electronic information environment.

Although campuses have made great strides toward developing robust and ubiquitous communications network infrastructures, the rich information environment envisioned in Sustaining Excellence in the 21st Century will not be realized unless equally robust and ubiquitous enabling services are developed within the infrastructure of our campuses and throughout the higher education community.

The electronic information environment as that set of electronic information services, on-line resources, communications services, applications software, and workstations that enable us to teach and learn and work more effectively and without the M.

Stuart Lynn, a colleague and friend to most of us in the information technology community, provided ideas, advice, counsel, and constraints of time or place. Within this environment, we need directories and other finding aids, credentials that can establish identity and roles for both consumer and supplier, and a myriad of other supporting services.

Infrastructure support services will enable easy and secure access to information resources, support authorized and verifiable transactions over the network, and make possible appropriate management of licensed materials and other intellectual property. With a coordinated approach, we will be able to leverage investments being made already in new applications on our campuses as well as across the higher education community.

As the electronic information environment grows and expands, it becomes necessary to acknowledge and implement certain constraints on users of these resources—the "network citizens" who navigate that environment. We must develop analogues of the administrative controls with which we are familiar in the traditional environment. These controls should be supported by generalized infrastructure services put in place and managed by the institution.

Existing access control and authentication mechanisms are largely a legacy of older centralized technology. Traditional institutional applications have been developed from the ground up, providing for all aspects of the process in an idiosyncratic way. Today we understand that many of the components of these applications have a great deal of commonality.

These include a secure and reliable way to affirm that users of our resources are who they purport to be and that they are authorized to use the resources to which they seek access. There must be a source of definitive information regarding their affiliation with the campus as well as other business-related data. There must be directory services to help them find the resources they need.

There must be standards and supporting services for encryption to secure data transmission and to create the digital equivalent of a personal signature. There must be efficient mechanisms to support accounting for the use of a wide variety of networkbased resources as well as services that can be supported by network communications.

Lack of common general solutions for authentication, authorization, directory services, and encryption will impede the development of a broad range of information resources, from client-server financial systems to digital libraries.

If properly designed, these technical building blocks can be combined and extended to form a set of common services, or "middleware, " that will enable a wide variety of complex capabilities that are available almost transparently to the end user. These new and critical middleware services will enable members of the academic community to become true universal network citizens and roam freely and securely, without undue let or hindrance, throughout the emerging electronic information environment.

The availability and use of these and other building blocks also can form the basis for more robust and efficient management of institutional resources. Rule-based authorization processes can support distributed operation and responsibility. Well-designed and reliable support services can help the campus protect intellectual property.

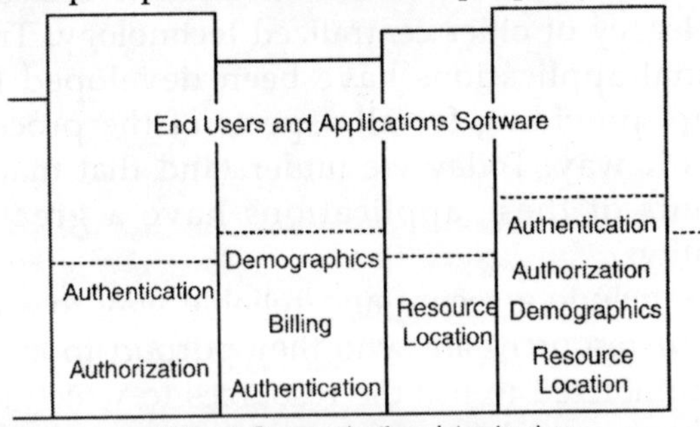

Fig. Existing Applications with Independent Solutions to the Same Set of Problems

Differences among campuses in their information environment middleware services tend to inhibit sharing of resources, a tendency that will become exacerbated as critical new shared resources such as virtual digital libraries begin to emerge. Currently a faculty member or student at one campus who is visiting another campus must make special arrangements in order to make use of many of the services at the second campus.

If the services require access control, the individual must

acquire yet another password and account name. Coordinated middleware services can allow the identity and affiliations of any member of the higher education community to serve them wherever they may be working at the moment.

The metaphor of a network citizen traveling throughout the electronic information environment to illustrate the basic middleware building blocks. It is with the goal of catalyzing the development and implementation of the best technologies to implement these services within the higher education community that we begin this management tour of the electronic information environment.

THE TERRAIN: THE ELECTRONIC INFORMATION ENVIRONMENT

The electronic information environment is an increasingly complex territory in which valuable resources can be found, but it is foreign to our usual senses. Many of the familiar problems and processes are found here but take a different form. What is our identity? What can we do here? How do we find resources? How do we traverse the environment with safety? How do we account for what we use? Do we share a common reference for time or place?

The foundation of the electronic information environment is the complex of interconnected networks (including our campus networks) known as the global Internet. Accessible from desktops both within our campuses and via the Internet are an ever growing variety of databases, information servers, vendors doing business via e-commerce, computational servers, and a panoply of applications programs from e-mail to collaborative systems based on interactive virtual reality. E-commerce is developing rapidly in many forms and will enable reliable transaction of institutional business as well as new opportunities for individuals.

Our helpers in traveling the information environment are client software and programs that interact with other electronic entities by means of well-defined protocols. Just as in the analogue world, these protocols provide for successful interoperation among widely differing entities. The World

Wide Web is an excellent example of this concept: the same set of complex text, graphics, audio, and video can be found and viewed on almost any modern computer regardless of what kind of computer might hold them.

One significant advantage of this layered approach to complex systems is that individual pieces of the environment can be built or replaced without affecting the rest of the infrastructure. Another advantage is that end-user platforms can be tailored to different user communities and application needs. This layered approach must guide us in the development of essential information environment support services.

Passports: The Authentication Service. The fundamental support service that will empower the network citizen is a universal, distributed, reliable, and robust digital credential system. Just as travelers must carry their passport when entering a different country, network citizens should carry a recognized credential when entering the electronic information environment. This credential, which can be validated by any service encountered, will ensure the authentic identity of the individual holding it.

Passports are recognized as authoritative around the world because the issuing authority is recognized by international treaty. So too should the network credential be recognized as authoritative so that network citizens can visit various sites and resources without having to resort to site-specific identification. Instead of an international treaty, there must be agreements among cooperating administrative domains to trust each other's credentials. Such agreements are based on understanding the methodology and management of the process for issuing the credentials.

The concept of a digital credential that refers to a single electronic identity is powerful because it can enable easy access to resources for the traveler. The credential itself may not carry much information about the individual, much as the traditional passport carries not much more than a picture, an address, and a passport number.

However, that passport number can be the key to

determining additional attributes about the holder. In an analogous way, the digital credential should have an identifier (e-ID) that is unique to the credential holder and can be used as a key to discovering further identity information.

Relying on a single credential is fraught with the potential for abuse if it is mishandled. Since e-IDs will let travelers into many places, they must be issued only with strong assurance that individuals are who they claim to be. Once the e-ID is issued, the holder must recognize that it is an extension of his or her personal identity, protect it carefully, and never lend it to another person.

Even with reliable credentials, it will be desirable in many cases for an individual to have several e-IDs to be used for different purposes. All individuals and their organizations must consider the potential impact of a compromise of the security of any e-ID. For example, the manager of an administrative computing system might have an e-ID that carries with it special privileges.

That e-ID should be used sparingly and only in conjunction with that system so that compromise of the more powerful e-ID would have consequences of a more limited scope and could be dealt with more readily. The system manager would use a less powerful e-ID when doing routine work, such as checking e-mail or writing reports.

An e-ID represents an assertion on the part of a registration authority that a known individual or entity is represented by that e-ID. If the registration authority is well designed and reliable, then services in cooperating administrative domains, or realms, can be comfortable accepting those externally registered e-IDs.

Thus, in the general case, the e-ID must indicate not only the individual but also the registration authority that issued the e-ID. Ultimately this concept could be extended to commercial registration authorities so that, for example, high school students registered with a local electronic notary might be able to use their own credential's e-IDs in submitting electronic applications for admission to a college or university.

Once a campus has a robust digital credential issuance

and authentication service in place with reliable operational support, all of the important campus server applications should be adapted to use this system.

Parts of this process could take a long time since many applications are vendor supported and vendors are not yet responding to this broader vision. Until there is a well-established generalized authentication service, each server or application has little choice but to implement its own idiosyncratic method of authentication, and the network citizen must deal individually with each one encountered.

TICKETS AND PASSES: ATTRIBUTE AND ELIGIBILITY DATABASES

Eligibility, as distinct from authentication (which warrants the identity of a particular user), is an equally important support service in the electronic information environment. Eligibility helps define what network citizens may do or that to which they may gain access.

It may be based on a person's e-ID or on any set of attributes associated with that e-ID, such as the person's affiliation with or within the institution, role, or current status. Often it is desirable to separate authentication service from eligibility and attribute functions, and it may be desirable to support them on different servers.

Eligibility does not necessarily imply authorization. The network citizen may be eligible to gain access to a resource, but at the time access is requested, the service might be oversubscribed or otherwise unavailable. For example, holding an airplane ticket may not result in authorization to board that flight. Authorization is a function of the service or application based on specific business rules. These rules might take into account a variety of factors in addition to the individual's identity, such as time of day, location of the individual, or the availability of resources.

In the historical model of mainframe computing, authentication (often referred to as access control) and authorization were often closely linked. Authorization usually was determined by loose association of attributes with the user account identifier (for example, "root" or "user, group, and other" in Unix systems) or by tables of authorized users.

Since each system kept its own set of authorization data, management of these data in a consistent way across a large number of servers and client platforms was problematic, although a number of projects attempted to address aspects of this dilemma. Little thought was given to generalized information environment management mechanisms until the number of different systems and services began to grow dramatically.

Today we need generalized and scalable network-based mechanisms not only for authentication but also for eligibility and attribute information. As an example of how this might be provided, suppose the network citizen requests access to a restricted database. The database server can simply query a specified attribute server, supplying the network citizen's e-ID, and receive information on the roles, affiliations, or other attributes defined for that individual. The database server then can apply a prescribed set of business rules to determine whether that particular network citizen is to be allowed access to the restricted data.

Suppose the network citizen's affiliation with the institution is "full professor and dean of the college." This might imply eligibility to view college budgetary data and approve spending plans and personnel actions, as well as to gain access to academic records and information.

The same person might also be appointed to a multicampus task force on student diversity and because of that affiliation be eligible to retrieve sensitive student ethnicity and gender data. A database server that returned roles and affiliations for any given institutional e-ID would make management of this type of generalized eligibility much easier.

Such eligibility or affiliation data might be useful in transactions external to the institution as well. Appropriate individuals in any department could be given authority to submit electronic data interchange (EDI) purchase orders over the network, for example. A different set of individuals could have authority to approve payment of EDI-based invoices electronically. Workflow systems could identify individuals who need to be informed of such transactions for possible post-transaction audit.

Whereas administration of an attribute service should be hierarchical and coordinated centrally, responsibility for actual eligibility data with respect to any given service should be distributed to conform with campus management structure. This is primarily an administrative rather than a technical issue.

Suffice it to say that developing and managing a database service that combines all important attributes, roles, and affiliations and allows them to be managed by the office of record would provide important generality while maintaining the institution's established administrative structure.

WHO'S THERE? THE DEMOGRAPHICS DATABASE SERVICE

One particularly vexing problem is the maintenance of accurate personal data, such as home address, campus office address, or preferred e-mail address. Today there are far too many different databases wherein the same data are entered, usually by different individuals, from separate forms that must be filled out repetitively by the person who actually "owns" the information.

For example, in many cases the same individual is both a student and an employee, which means that the same personal data often are maintained by entirely separate offices. Clearly it would be desirable to have a single comprehensive database of record that would hold information about all members of the campus community and in which personal data could be maintained by the relevant individual or appropriately designated staff.

With strong authentication and a well-designed attribute service, it would be possible to build such a demographics database system. It might well be combined with a basic eligibility service so that a single database system supports both. Fields within a record would have associated rules for access or updating.

All institutional applications that require use of personal data would use this comprehensive demographics database by either periodic downloading or indirect relational reference. In particular, on-line directory services for locating campus community members would use this authoritative database as their data source.

Campus network citizens could be responsible for maintaining all of their own personal data and also could check on the completeness or accuracy of other attribute data, such as payroll title or salary, status toward a degree, or the parameters of their employee benefits.

MAPS AND GUIDEBOOKS: DIRECTORY SERVICES

Information services and resources abound on campuses and beyond. The community of users changes and moves about, and the topology of the network changes periodically. How does a network citizen find anyone else or any particular service or information?

The Domain Name Service was the first widespread directory service in support of the information environment. Other common directories exist today, such as directories of people and searchable databases of information resources. Many more kinds of maps and guidebooks are needed to serve the new and complex information resources we are deploying.

For example, the network citizen might want to find an on-line copy of Van Gogh's Child with Orange and the nearest colour printer that she or he is eligible to use and that is capable of high-resolution, large-format printing. New resource location services must support more complex data and search strategies.

A well-managed set of directory servers and search engines for information objects will help the network citizen discover resources and navigate easily throughout the electronic information environment.

SAFE PASSAGE: ENCRYPTION AND DIGITAL SIGNATURES

Authentication and access control alone are not sufficient

to guarantee safe passage throughout the electronic information environment. Passwords can be guessed or stolen, data can be monitored in transit, and identities sometimes can be forged. The strongest defence against these challenges involves the use of modern encryption methods to ensure privacy of data transmission and create the digital equivalent of a pen-and-ink signature.

Our networks are truly open systems, which is one of their strengths as well as a source of many vulnerabilities. Any transmission might be intercepted, and any data received might be questionable. Attacking computers on the Internet has become a rampant obsession among certain curious and occasionally antisocial groups.

Fortunately, modern encryption technology offers potential solutions for most of these concerns. Encryption of data while in transit can protect privacy as well as the confidentiality and integrity of data. The technology required to implement data encryption has become commonplace and should be considered for all administrative or other institutional business applications.

Encryption alone may not guarantee authenticity, however. We need the equivalent of a seal or at least a recognized signature associated with the contents of the document.

A digital signature must be some set of data that cannot be forged and that binds the contents of a digital document to a specific individual, role, or other entity. It must be something that only the signing entity could have created and must be verifiable by anyone in the electronic information environment.

Standards now exist for creating this type of digital signature using public key cryptography (PKC). Clearly digital signatures of this sort would enable a wide variety of institutional business to be transacted over the network with at least as reliable verification and auditability as we have now with paper forms and manual signatures.

A public key infrastructure (PKI) is critical to enabling the use of encryption and digital signatures. Fundamental to the PKI is a unique pair of very large prime numbers, generated for each credential holder, that are keys used for encryption and decryption of information. Software on the network citizen's workstation generates this pair of encryption keys and gives one of them (the "public" key) to the PKI certificate authority (CA).

The other key (the "private" key) is closely guarded by the network citizen. The CA stores the public key in a directory along with the PKI certificate. Upon request, the CA or directory server provides any registered user's public key to any application that needs it.

In addition to support of the local community, a CA must have a way to find other trusted CAs on other campuses or anywhere else in the electronic information environment. This ability is part of an overall PKI and may be implemented in a number of different ways.

The basis for trusting a traditional signature is either direct knowledge or the ability to look it up in an archive maintained by a trusted authority, such as a bank. In the digital world, trust must be established through preestablished contracts based on mutual understanding of business practices, the basis for registering individuals with the CA, and the viability of the cooperating CAs.

The resulting so-called web of trust must be scalable to millions of users in thousands of locations. This can be achieved through a hierarchical model wherein a community-based CA registers subordinate CAs after verifying their viability.

A consortium of college and university campuses, for example, could operate such a certificate authority and the associated services on behalf of its members. This CA in turn could register under national and international CAs to allow fully general and trustworthy access to verifiable public key directory servers anywhere in the world. A campus PKI with its root certificate authority also could register subordinate CAs for departments, the library, or special-purpose requirements.

Until and unless encryption mechanisms and support

services are in use, no one should send anything of value or of a sensitive nature, such as a credit card number, over the data network.

SHARING LIMITED RESOURCES: LICENSE SERVERS

The network citizen is now equipped with the basic tools for verifying identity, invoking authority, and concluding transactions safely. These capabilities enable easy and appropriate access to a wide variety of resources within our electronic information environment. Unfortunately, not all of those resources are without significant cost to the institution.

A traditional library might hold five copies of a popular book or journal. Ideally this would be enough to meet the peak demand at any one time for this resource. It would not be economical to purchase one copy for every registered patron, yet we often provide software and other resources in this cost-inefficient way.

It is quite possible for software or other digital resources to be purchased by subscription, much like printed documents today. The cost of such a subscription would be based at least in part on the size of the simultaneous user community. For example, a physics department might purchase a subscription for twenty simultaneous "users" of a virtual physics laboratory software package.

During laboratory classes, the students make use of the software on computers located in the facility. In the evening, when doing homework, up to twenty students could make use of the same "subscription" to run the software on their own personal computer.

One way to enable this type of sharing of expensive resources is a network-based license server (NLS). The NLS serves as a clearinghouse to ensure conformance with the terms of the institution's subscription. An early implementation of the NLS concept was available with the Apollo domain computers. Macintosh and PC versions of license servers offer similar capabilities.

Standardizing on an openly available NLS technology would enable publishers to develop products that could fit readily into our electronic information environment. A single NLS could moderate access to a wide variety of licensed resources, including databases and documents as well as software.

PAYING THE BILLS: AUTOMATED DEBIT THAND UNIFIED INVOICING

Much of the electronic information environment today is accessible without direct cost to the network citizen. However, as the real costs become significant, the campus may need to find efficient ways at least to account for the usage of expensive resources and possibly allocate some of the acquisition and support costs toward the end users.

A building block that could help achieve this is an efficient network accounting server. Ultimately every member of the campus community, as defined in the campus's demographics database and corresponding eligibility servers, could have one or more "virtual accounts."

Transactions for services would be posted to a designated network accounting server using encrypted data flows. A wide variety of network citizen services, from print-on-demand syllabi to lunches and storehouse items, could be accounted for in this way. The network citizen should expect a single statement each month describing all services used and any costs incurred anywhere within the institution. This might include transactions with external partners as well. Eventually this monthly accounting could result in an automated debit against an external financial service, much like debit cards are used today.

WHAT TIME IS IT? THE NETWORK TIME SERVER

It may not seem obvious but many of the services we are developing need to have a common frame of reference for time. Billing information, for example, must show accurately the date and approximate time of the transaction. Network management information often needs time stamps to be accurate to within a few milliseconds. Electronic postmark or notary services must have an auditable date and time guaranteed to be within a known degree of accuracy. Thus, an important element in the set of enabling services within our information environment is the network time server.Technologies in support of network time services exist today and are deployed on most campuses.

However, not all of these are synchronized with each other or with a universal time standard, such as the National Institute of Standards and Technology broadcast standard time service.Even where synchronized network time servers exist, not all essential end systems can take advantage of them yet.

Campus information technology managers must understand the importance of this element of distributed systems and take appropriate steps to ensure integration of this service.Our network citizens may wish to set their own "electronic watch" from this service as well. Most modern workstations can be configured with automatic utilities to accomplish this.

WHERE TO NOW?

The building blocks are all part of a larger set of standards that comprise an information technology architecture. The basic enabling services include the following features:

- A coordinated set of authentication servers
- An attribute and demographic database server on each campus that can include a wide variety of information, including affiliation and eligibility data
- Directory and resource location servers
- PKI servers that manage certificates and public encryption keys for individual users and make possible digital signature verification
- Electronic license servers in support of site-licensed software, library materials, and databases
- Billing transaction servers that can handle a large volume of small-value debit records extremely efficiently
- Time servers and digital notary servers that form the basis for reliable and verifiable on-line content and digital institutional archives

The building blocks might relate to each other and to the communications system and applications programs. Other building blocks might include software version control servers.

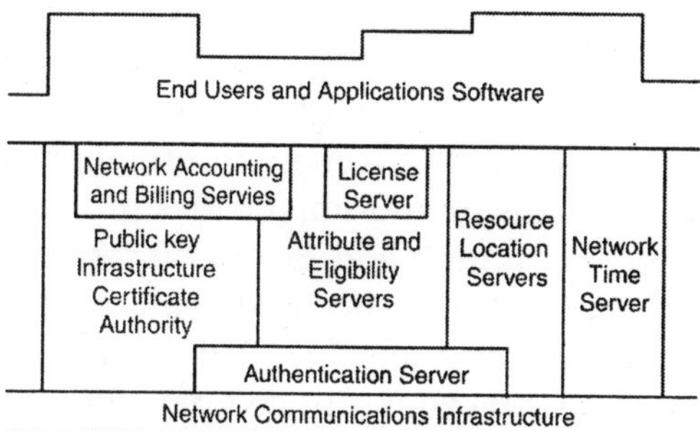

Fig. Information Environment Building Blocks with Common Interoperable Solutions for Basic Supporting Services

Campus users have access to the latest version of critical application programs, and alias servers to support consistent mapping between e-IDs and e-mail addresses or traditional identifiers such as employee number or student ID number. Current and potential technologies behind each of the building blocks described above are in different states of development and deployment.

With persistent vision and cooperative efforts, we can refine and deploy appropriate versions of all these enabling services over the next few years. If we do not start now, it may become very difficult to develop and retrofit a coordinated set of these services later. There is much to be done before network citizens are fully empowered. Information Policy to Support

CAMPUS E-BUSINESS

The unprecedented flow of information across networks and between organizations, coupled with the power of computers to extract, compile, organize, and republish information, has made e-business possible. These same capabilities are also raising significant concerns and issues related to the appropriate use of institutional information and the protection of information originating or residing in college and university information systems.

The developmental phase facing colleges and universities

today on the road to enabling e-business as one of integration. Our progress in adopting e-business in higher education will be enabled or constrained by institutions' abilities to develop, implement, enforce, and automate complex rules that authorize these consumers to partake of university services—for example:

- What rights will distant learners have regarding access to licensed university information resources?
- How can colleges and universities protect usage logs that record student and faculty library consumption activity for materials licensed from third parties?

The privacy, access, ownership, and security issues posed by e-business are extraordinarily complex and represent as much a set of cultural, behavioral, and policy issues as technical ones.Colleges and universities have long—and correctly—been described as self-governing anarchies or adhocracies.

Higher education's hallowed and well-established traditions of self-governance and shared governance are responsible for our remarkable history of achievement, service, and innovation. These traditions also make integration hard. In many ways, achieving the necessary level of technical integration to enable e-business is the least complex aspect of preparing the institution for e-business.

Many campus chief information officers (CIOs) understand what it means to reorient systems from their current functional office views to the end-user views (student, parent, alumni, inter-enterprise) that e-business will demand. In most cases, the technical tools to achieve this kind of integration exist.

In short, technical integration is a significant issue that can be addressed by vision, talent, and money. The thornier integration challenges are cultural and relate to role definitions, authority and power, and values. These issues will define the boundaries of an institution's approach to, and its likelihood of success in, implementing e-business.

THE NEED FOR A POLICY FRAMEWORK TO SUPPORT E-BUSINESS

In a farsighted article, Graves, Jenkins, and Parker at the

University of North Carolina described the development of an electronic information policy framework. As e-business drives the Internet and Web from an infrastructure for storing static information to one over which much of the institutional mission is delivered, the need for such a policy framework becomes overwhelming.

Although sound information policies will not guarantee entry into the world of e-business, lack of these policies will bar the door. Colleges and universities will need to develop a cohesive and consistent set of policies to guide the members of their community in a number of areas, including the following:

- Digital identity and the access to institutional technology and information resources
- Use of the institution's name and trademarks
- Acquisition, retention, and disposition of information resources
- Ownership of information in institutional systems and the management of intellectual property rights

Each of these issues is enormously complex, and colleges and universities worldwide have struggled with them for years. Digital Identity and Access to Institutional Technology

AND INFORMATION RESOURCES

In the technical context, colleges and universities must develop the means to authenticate an individual as himself or herself, recognize the individual as a member of the institutional community, and confer on or deny this individual different rights and authorities as a community citizen. In physical reality, these activities are transacted in a variety of complex formal or informal ways. We can demand photo ID cards, check signature files, or wave to the familiar librarian who regulates access to the closed stacks.

The regulation of access to institutional resources in the physical context is governed by a tapestry of policies, procedures, customs, norms, and historical happenstance that computers are not yet intelligent enough to deal with. Instead, computers depend on precise information that derives absolute answers to the following questions: (1) are you who you claim to be, and (2) are you allowed to ... [consume this service, enter this building, use this parking lot]?

Not only is this a technical challenge of enormous proportions, it is a policy quagmire that requires colleges and universities to make explicit and public distinctions about the rights and privileges that accrue to different members of the academy. What rights does the president's spouse really have? What rights do lecturers have, relative to career-ladder faculty? These policy issues will become more complex as colleges and universities move into distance education and implement cradle-to-grave strategies to create relationships with promising applicants, lifelong learners, and potential donors.

Of course, it is important to note that for public institutions, managing access to institutional information must be situated in the context of public records laws, which themselves are hard to reduce to simple rules that can be automated.

USE OF THE INSTITUTION'S NAME AND TRADEMARKS

The Internet and the World Wide Web are, among other things, a publishing infrastructure. Web browser technology is relatively simple to programme as well as to use, allowing "a thousand flowers to bloom." At nearly every college and university, a myriad of operational and dead Web pages make volumes of campus information and misinformation available to anyone with an Internet connection.

Many institutions provide incoming students with sufficient disk storage to encourage their development of personal Web sites. Of course, into every flower garden will come the occasional weed, snail, or other predator. From a policy perspective, the challenge posed by the Internet and the Web is the challenge of cultural integration. Colleges and universities must specify policies that regulate the appropriate use of these very public resources. At stake in this extraordinarily complex area to govern are a variety of serious legal and public relations issues, including these:

- Pornographic materials on official institutional sites
- Sale of advertising on pages containing campus trademarks
- Creation of fraudulent sites
- Commercial use of campus resources for personal gain
- Trademark infringement
- Neglect of sites that make inaccurate, anachronistic, and obsolete information available to legislators, trustees, donors, auditors, and others

All of these issues can and will emerge within the broader policy contexts that typically respect and encourage free expression by members of the institution's community. As Graves, Jenkins, and Parker advise, "Any policy will need to balance the institution's role in protecting access to sensitive or potentially objectionable information and its role in supporting an individual's right of free expression". This difficult balancing act is hardly new, but is complicated by the levels of integration anticipated by e-business applications.

ACQUISITION, RETENTION, AND DISPOSITION OF INFORMATION RESOURCES

E-business, in much of the popular literature, begins with something called "e-tailing": the marketing of the enterprise to its existing or prospective clients. In one context, higher education institutions have been doing this for years. Each year, colleges and universities acquire the files of high school students who achieve high scores on the PSAT and shower these college-bound tenth and eleventh graders with literature extolling the virtues of their campus.

In an e-business context, smart and aggressive institutions will acquire more and more information in the competition for the "best" students. These institutions will likely develop robust profiles of students to match against the target profiles of successful applicants. Similarly, the pathologies of university hospital patients will be profiled for matching against promising experimental drugs and therapies for possible targeting of such patients for clinical trials.

These practices are entrepreneurial, effective (relative to their goals), and probably beneficial; certainly college-bound students want to be discovered and patients want access to the best modes of treatment available.

However, the unprecedented ability of institutions to acquire personal information, combine this information in unique ways, and store massive amounts of this information on individuals who may, or may not, be part of the institutional community will raise significant privacy and security issues.

New policies regarding what kind of information is to be collected, how this information is to be used, and how long it is to be retained will become increasingly important. The failure to develop new standards of practice in this area will invite new regulation of this area of institutional activity. The issue of individual and institutional access to this kind of information will also rise in importance and must be dealt with explicitly in campus information policy.

In addition to developing the technologies and policies to ensure privacy and secure and protect information under institutional management, colleges and universities will need to devise and implement new policies to describe, manage, and protect related classes of information.

Such classes of information include confidential information (tenure and promotion files), proprietary information (patents, trademarks, copyrights), privileged information (attorneyclient communications, counseling files), and trade information (public and private research activities).

E-business, among other things, assumes an unprecedented level of interoperation among the systems and data resources of "trading partners." In the future, campus suppliers will have access to institutional procurement systems, as will publishers, high schools, consortium partners, and others.

This integration of systems and information will demand that policies and contracts regulate the acquisition, use, retention, and disposition by others in the newly extending community.

This has already become a complex area of policy development at research universities, where the university values of open sharing of research findings clash with desires of private clinical research sponsors to protect information as proprietary.

A final area of concern under this broad umbrella is the management of licensed software and information resources. Campus information policy must respect the rights of authors and distributors. Evolving technologies and law will likely enhance authors' and distributors' ability to track the use of their licensed property and perhaps even to implement campuswide penalties when infringements are identified.

INFORMATION AND INTELLECTUAL PROPERTY RIGHTS

Information policy must seek to distinguish the ownership status of information embodied in institutionally owned digital storage and transport media from the responsibilities for managing this information. Information policies should strive to define the standards and care with which information resources must be managed, while recognizing the inherently decentralizing tendencies of networked information and resources.

Most information policy frameworks that address networked information define and articulate a concept of information stewardship that allows the web of campus-related information to evolve in a fashion that balances the needs of individuals and local campus units with those of the institution as a whole.

Perhaps the most complex aspect of preparing the campus information policy environment for e-business is the set of policy issues surrounding the ownership and management of intellectual property generated on the campus. Colleges and universities have developed robust policies for the ownership and management of intellectual property protected by patents, but the rights to intellectual property developed by faculty and protected by copyright have traditionally remained with individual faculty.

In fact, the total economic value of published college and university intellectual property has been small historically, and the institutional investment in the creation of this property has also been small.

The application of Internet, Web, and other information technologies to the core educational mission of higher education is changing all of this. Today, pioneering faculty are investing considerable time and energy to Web-enable their courses. Institutions in many cases are partnering with these faculty by providing grants to purchase release time from other obligations and by placing a variety of technical tools at the faculty's disposal.

For the first time, faculty course materials organized in this fashion can reach beyond the confines of the classroom, hence changing simultaneously the cost structure, the investment model, and the economic value of traditional course materials.

Courses created in this fashion become courseware and begin to accrue many of the attributes of books, which also are evolving to become more interactive.As the e-learning aspect of the e-business revolution evolves, institutions, their faculty, and publishers are looking at course materials as scalable economic goods that can be modularized. New pedagogical standards are evolving in concert with new neuroscientific findings about the learning process.

Institutions such as the University of Phoenix and Great Britain's Open University are investing millions of dollars in curricula for networked delivery. Faculty course notes on the Web are being reportedly pirated and repackaged for distribution by new proprietary e-business enterprises.

Clearly the new potentials posed by the integrated technologies of e-business suggest the need for new policies regarding the ownership and management of rights to faculty course materials.

Such changes are, however, countercultural and could also lead to new divisions on the campus. e-business is likely to change the way institutions operate. It is a mission-critical undertaking that will challenge longstanding institutional policies and will therefore demand the careful application of change management techniques and processes.

ELEMENTS OF AN INTEGRATED POLICY FRAMEWORK

Although each institution will develop a policy that best reflects its priorities, strategies, values, and history, a framework should contain some common elements. The list that follows is offered as a starting point.

Critical Assumptions

The institution will balance the rights of individuals with the institution's responsibility to make information available to support the mission. The role of the central campus is to articulate the standards of data access and integrity and to differentiate user rights and privileges so as to achieve such balance. The following key assumption will need to be articulated:

- Under what conditions (responsibilities of resource users) and for what members of the community are access to the network, network-based services, and networked information a basic right of the campus community?

OPERATING PRINCIPLES

Policies are by definition value laden. Institutions can be well served by considering bounding the framework by principles. At the University of North Carolina (UNC), information policy is bounded by principles that do the following:

- Identify the responsibility for making information available
- Limit the institution's regulatory responsibility for information for which it is not responsible
- Assume institutional responsibility for defining access privileges to its information for classes of users

The UNC policy framework and those of other leading institutions also outline in broad terms legal, ethical, technical, governance, and economic issues for the purpose of acculturating the policy reader to the complexity of the issues and the basic values of the institution.

Information Access and Security

It will be important to establish the notion that institutional electronic information resources—including data, applications, systems,

"We don't want just anyone coming in here and making toast. Type in your password." hardware, software, and networks—are valuable. Institutional assets, including electronic information resources, must be protected according to the nature of the risk and to the sensitivity and criticality of the resource being protected.

Information policy should endeavor to identify major classes of information assets requiring protection and assigning to them differential levels of protection. Information classes might include privileged information, personal information, personnel information, and public records.Areas in which security-related policies need to be addressed include the following, paraphrased from the University of California's "Business and Finance Bulletin IS-3: Electronic Information Security":

- Logical security. The policy should identify security measures to be enforced through software, network, or procedural controls (version management, and so forth), as well as communications security and reduction of risk from intrusive computer software. Various measures include end-user access controls, system administration access controls, applications software development and change control, and controls on data backup, retention, data privacy, and data transfers and downloads. Encryption policies will also need to be developed as these capabilities become ubiquitous, as will policies that specify which applications and resources must be protected by firewalls.
- Physical security. Even in an e-business environment,

there are physical disaster controls and access controls (for example, check stock and other financial instruments) that must be covered by institutional policy.

- Managerial security. Although there are unique risks inherent in the management of electronic and particularly networked information resources, many of the risks remain people related. An information policy framework should attempt to integrate institutional policy related to bonding and background checking for personnel with access to sensitive and critical information. Procedures to implement such policies should also identify the processes for altering authorities when changes in duties or employment status occur.
- Responsibilities. An information policy framework must identify both those responsible for maintaining the policy and those responsible for its implementation. Ideally, policy compliance escalation procedures should be specified.
- Definitions and authorities. A policy framework should define key terms such as authorized user, disaster, and security. Information management roles such as stewardship and proprietorship should also be defined. Regulations and laws that govern an institution's access and security policies should be referenced, including public records law.
- Digital certificates. An emerging technology to meet the needs of electronic security in the networked context is the use of public key infrastructure and digital certificates. Institutions that implement certificate authorities and digital certificates also will need to develop congruent policies that identify processes for approving authorities, standards for certificates, and identification of certificates. Policies will have to be enacted that govern whether certificates are issued to individuals, servers, or certificate authorities; what the responsibilities of these authorities

- Are; and what the expiry dates of these certificates will be. Finally, policy in this evolving arena will need to describe the processes for registering and issuing certificates, maintaining a repository of certificates and public keys, revoking or renewing certificates, and managing the certificate authority's private key.

Disaster Protection

The information policy framework should describe the institution's plans, policies, and procedures for ensuring business continuity, including plans for testing critical systems periodically.The disaster recovery plan should identify emergency response procedures and specify teams of personnel responsible for responding to emergency situations.

E-MAIL

Although e-mail is not specifically a tool of e-business, its governance as a critical element of the overall campus information policy framework is critical. Institutions are advised to develop specific policies related to e-mail that establish the following elements:

- E-mail accounts as institutional property
- The institution's service commitments regarding e-mail
- The ownership of information produced and received using institutional mail accounts
- Institutional access to information in mail accounts under normal or extraordinary (emergency, investigative, and so forth) conditions
- Allowable use, including use for individual commercial gain, representations, and false identity
- Security and confidentiality of information in institutional mail accounts
- Individual and institutional responsibilities and authorities for ensuring compliance with policy

INTELLECTUAL PROPERTY

Policy related to the management and ownership of

intellectual property is highly complex. For intellectual property not developed on campus and covered by copyrights, patents, licenses, or other contracts, the policy parameters tend to be straightforward:

- Software resident on institutional hardware must be used according to the terms specified under the appropriate software license agreement.
- The institution is responsible for compliance with licenses entered into by the institution on behalf of members of its community. It should maintain the right to revoke licensed privileges in cases where violations have been identified. Substantial violations of license conditions should be specified under policy, as should the process for investigating alleged misuse and for implementing remedial action.
- Information resources such as databases, books, and journal articles are governed by copyright law or by license agreements with their publisher. Institutional policy should affirm the rights of authors, publishers, and distributors to their intellectual property; define what constitutes fair use in the context of law and licenses; and identify the processes for investigating alleged misuse and for implementing remedial action.

For intellectual property developed on campus, the institution must distinguish between so-called works for hire and other works produced in the discharge of an employee's work-related roles:

- The ownership of a work for hire is generally assumed to be the property of the institution. The information policy framework should make explicit reference to the institution's assumptions about what works are considered to be works for hire and what ownership rights the institution wishes to assert. This policy should also specify what rights individuals who are creating works for hire may have (publication of a work report in a professional journal) and what the process is for securing individual access to such works.

- The ownership of other intellectual property produced by members of the campus community is more likely to fall under an institution's faculty handbook, or in policy covering patents, or even conflict of interest and commitment. As the boundaries between course materials and published materials begin to blur, institutions will need to revisit the ownership issues as part of an integrated information policy framework.

Policy by its nature is soft, squishy, and difficult. Policy development and the policy environment are inherently value laden, and therefore there are no detailed instructions for policy formulation. Policies are for the most part context specific. A Bible college's definition of appropriate use of technology will likely differ from that of a public research university.

Policy can be integrative, and integration is the mandate that looms ahead for institutions seeking to implement e-business solutions. Colleges and universities anticipating the move to e-business must recall that e-business in many areas is not merely the application of new technology to old processes.

E-business applications will open new vistas and create new risks. Extending the name and reach of your college and university can and will swell the ranks of members of your communities. As communities grow, opportunities grow. And along with opportunities come fraud, abuse, and misuse. An integrated information policy framework will be hard to institute. On the other hand, an integrated, e-business environment without a supporting policy framework will be nearly impossible to manage.

Chapter 6

Electronic Retailing

MAIN E-RETAIL PRODUCT CATEGORIES

The top categories that account for three-quarters of all European sales comprise: books, music and DVD movies, groceries, sex products, games and software, electronic and computer equipment, travel and clothes. In addition, although perhaps not a category, auctions are among the most popular UK e-retailing sites.

BOOKS

Books are by far the largest e-retailing category in the UK. Research carried out by Ernst & Young illustrates that 65 per cent of the purchases made by Web shoppers in the UK consisted of books. This is understandable in the light of books scoring highest in de Kare-Silver's (2001) ES (electronic shopping) test. In de Kare-Silver's sample table, books score a total of 38 points out of a maximum of 50, ten points ahead of the next category (hotels).

Books score highly on *product characteristics,* being low-touch products that are simple to deliver by post, and *familiarity and confidence,* as customers usually know exactly what they are ordering. Finally, the higher-weighted *consumer attributes* parameter is particularly favourable to books: typical book buyers and the e-shopping early majority tend to be younger, better educated and of a higher socio-economic group than the general population.

Amazon is the outstanding leader of the books e-retail category, with a market share of over 50 per cent (and is also market leader for CDs/DVDs). When readers of the *Sunday Times* were asked for their experiences of e-shopping, Amazon 'streaked ahead' of all others as the country's favourite e-retailer. This means that Amazon is the undisputed favourite on considerations such as convenience, reliability and customer service.

Amazon has achieved worldwide success and brand recognition by attention to these considerations and heavy (offline) advertising, becoming one of only three dot.com brands in the Interbrand world league table. It is an illustration of the power of branding that Amazon is the world's top e-retailer and head-to-head with Barnes and Noble for the title of the world's biggest bookstore.

Other dot.coms such as Easy Value have attempted to exploit the Web's facility for quick and easy price comparisons, claiming that 'people know the products and price is driving them'. Indeed, a price comparison site such as Book Brain can often find prices for identical books significantly cheaper than Amazon.

These cheaper prices often come from suppliers such as Swotbooks that do not have Amazon's heavy marketing costs. Nevertheless, even competitors such as Tesco, with offers like 'the top 100 books 10 per cent cheaper than Amazon' have failed to make a substantial impact on the online books market. As Brynjolfsson and Smith (2000) put it, 'the most expensive is not always the least patronised', pointing out that Amazon.com maintained a US market share of 80 per cent while charging 10 per cent more than the cheapest.

MINI CASE STUDY 2.1: BOOKBRAIN.CO.UK AND SWOTBOOKS.COM

BookBrain does not sell books, but is a shopbot that claims to provide 'the most accurate and comprehensive price search of UK online bookshops on the Web'. Fourteen sites were searched at the time of our site test.

Once you've found your ideal read, a quick search reveals prices of postage and packing, often with significant differences.... The site lets you know the availability of each title, how long it takes to be delivered, and it has smart editorial reviews too. Bravo.

For our site test we chose a book that might be useful for various disciplines, *Discovering SPSS for Windows: Advanced Techniques for Beginners* by Andy Field, published by Sage. The search took 13 seconds, returning a table of the cheapest eight suppliers, with links to the book on the suppliers' sites, details of how delivery charges are calculated, stock availability, base price, delivery charge and total price. The pricing information is particularly helpful, as, when going directly to many of the suppliers' sites, it is difficult to find the delivery costs until the very last stage at the checkout.

MUSIC

From the suppliers' point of view, the music industry is largely not a happy story. According to Lehman Brothers figures, music as a percentage of consumer

	Lower cost	Differentiation
Broad target	Cost leadership Swotbooks	Differentiation Amazon
Narrow target		Focus Abebooks

Fig. Exemplar Strategic Positioning of Books E-retailers

Expenditure is falling and music sales in the UK dropped by 8.1 per cent in 2002.

The biggest drop was in compact disc (CD) singles, which, according to British Phonographic Industry (BPI) figures, slumped by 25 per cent.

Consumers have often complained about what are alleged to be unfairly high prices for CDs. On the other hand, the major companies tend to blame piracy and illegal Internet downloads for the slump (single tracks are obviously quicker and easier to download than albums), claiming to have lost

US$1 billion in revenue worldwide in 2002. In the US, the Recording Industry Association of America (RIAA) has taken legal action against hundreds of 'major offenders' alleged to have illegally distributed an average of more than 1,000 copyrighted music files.

It was widely reported that a 12-year-old girl, a university professor and an elderly man who rarely uses his computer were included in the first wave of actions, resulting in negative publicity for the RIAA. E-Retailing of music can be considered under two categories: CDs and online.

CDs :There are many different formats which are used to listen to music such as tapes, CDs, records, mini discs, etc., but since the 1980s the most popular form has been CDs. According to the BPI, music buyers spend on average over £80 per year on albums, of which 92 per cent are CDs. The BPI estimates that market penetration of CD albums is 50 per cent of UK households.

Many leading retailers of music products such as HMV and Tower Records have now begun selling CDs on the Internet but are facing huge competition from pureplays such as CD WOW and CDNOW - now owned and run in conjunction with Amazon).

Indeed, CDWOW has grown hugely in the competitive CD market and was recently voted by *Net* magazine readers as number two in the world's 20 best online stores, second only to Amazon. Similarly, in the UK, *Sunday Times* Doors readers voted CDWOW the country's second-favourite e-retailer, again behind only Amazon.

PRICES OF CDs

It is usually said that the Internet enables consumers to find cheaper products. This is an important consideration for CDs, as there has long been a consumer perception that CDs are overpriced in the high street.

One of the main advantages of e-shopping vs. bricks shopping for consumers was found to be 'prices favourable'. Table reports our comparison test, indicating a wide range of prices. The cheapest overall was CDNOW, e.g. for U2's album

Best of 1980-1990 CDNOW's price was £8, compared to CD WOW in second place selling the same CD for £13.99.

E-RETAILING CDS - THE ES TEST

The Electronic Shopping (ES) test was developed by de Kare-Silver (2001) and is used to assess a product to evaluate the likelihood that it will be purchased online. According to de Kare-Silver, a product's potential for e-retailing can be judged by assessing three factors: 'Product characteristics', 'Familiarity and confidence' and 'Consumer attributes'. Consumer attributes are considered to carry more weight than the other two and are therefore loaded three times as highly in the model. The example of CDs follows below.

Table: Price Test Results for CDs

HMV	*Tower Records*	*CD WOW*	*CDNOW*	
U2 Best of 1980-90	£18.99	£23.65	£13.99	£8.00
Justin Timberlake	£13.99	£12.78	£8.99	£8.50
Big Brovaz	£10.99	£13.42	n/a	£18.70
Best of David Bowie	£15.99	£15.66	£12.99	£8.00

Product Characteristics

A CD is a product that a consumer either wants or doesn't and is down to personal preference. The consumer gets the same product whether they buy from HMV or Tower Records. A CD does not need to be tried on, smelt or touched before it is bought. The only thing that the customer may want to do is listen to it, and they will probably have heard the music already on the radio or TV.

Familiarity and Confidence

A consumer will usually be familiar and confident when choosing a CD. They will buy a CD of their own taste, whether rock, soul, hip hop, etc. Furthermore, leading brands such as HMV sell online and CDNOW uses Amazon as a channel to sell their CDs at cheaper prices. They are well-known brands so consumers are likely to feel confident buying from them.

Consumer Attributes

The typical music buyer is younger, better educated and of a higher socioeconomic group than the general population, i.e. closely fitting the profile of the typical Internet user. *Score: 22 out of 30.*

Table. Evaluation of the E-shopping Potential of CDs Using the ES Test

Product	Product characteristics (10)	Familiarity and confidence (10)	Consumer attributes (30)	Total
CDs	8	8	22	38

The total score for selling a CD online was 38 out of 50. De Kare-Silver stated that if a score is above 20 then the product has good potential of being bought by consumers online. The total score therefore indicates that CDs have a high potential to be purchased on the Internet, which justifies the reason why CDs have high sales online. This can be compared to basic clothing that de Kare-Silver scored at only 19 in the ES test. This means that clothing has a lower potential for e-retailing compared with CDs.

Online music

Industry insiders estimate that three times as much music is downloaded on the Internet (largely for free) as is being sold on CD. A Forrester research study found that 45 per cent of European broadband users download music and half of them saw no problem in not paying for it. Nevertheless, following a settlement between AOL Time Warner and Microsoft, legal, paid for online music now seems to be taking off.

ONLINE PAID CONTENT

Online paid content from the US grew by a massive 22 per cent in 2003. According to eMarketer (2003), music is the biggest category. For example, over 17 million tracks have already been downloaded from Apple's iTunes, despite competition from free file-sharing services such as Kazaa.

Paid content is not new. Financial news and pornography (now mainly downloaded videos and 'live' webcams) have been around since the early days of the Web. What is new is the fast rate of growth of many other categories.

There are two ways of receiving music online: downloading or *streaming*. In the US one of the leaders, iTunes, launched by Apple Computers, has been successful in persuading consumers to pay 99 cents per download - 6.5 million times in the first three months. The biggest sellers included The Eagles and U2 - perhaps appealing to a more mature and affluent market than the typical pop music buyer. iTunes is also popular in Europe, with each track costing around £0.60, even though it is still only available to Apple Mac users.

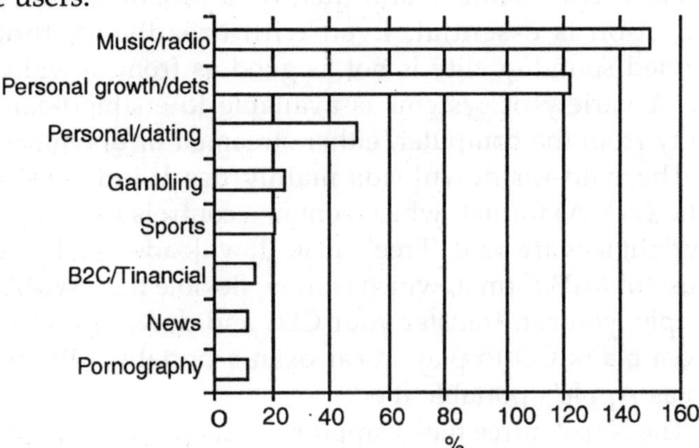

Fig. Paid Online Spending Growth Rates for the US for 2003 Percentage Increases on 2002

Streaming means playing the track live through a computer, rather like broadcast radio. In fact, the most frequently used type of streaming is digital radio.

Interactive services where you choose your listening are gaining ground. For ex-ample, in the UK, On Demand Distribution provides a 'music club' service for HMV and Internet service providers such as Freeserve and BT, charging a fixed monthly fee for streaming and limited downloads.

But if you stop your subscription the downloads stop playing. OD2 has deals with all the big five music companies, managing the transfers to ensure that artists and record companies get paid the royalties. The company has more than 200,000 tracks by 8,500 artists. OD2's success may be partly due to the personal influence of founder Peter Gabriel (former singer with the 1970s' band Genesis). 'I have helped open doors' says Gabriel. 'We are pretty much the only player left in town'.

OD2 music is also available as downloads from MSN and from Virgin, costing from around £0.60 to £0.99 per track. One incentive that OD2 uses to lure consumers to pay is offering music up to six weeks before release on CD (i.e. less likely to be available as illegal downloads). OD2 also includes exclusive versions and extra songs not available in the CD format.

For a reasonable sound quality, a broadband Internet connection is essential. Even with broadband, though, streamed sound quality is not as good as from downloaded files. A variety of systems is available to enable near hi-fi quality from the computer, either streamed or downloaded.

The paid-for downloads mainly use Windows Media Audio (WMA) format, which contains controls to ensure that copyright fees are paid. 'Free' music downloads usually utilize the useful MP3 format, which is more flexible than WMA. For example, you can transfer your CDs and downloaded tracks on to a blank CD to play in-car or in a portable MP3 player such as Apple's portable iPod.

The Napster free file-swapping site has been closed down, but there are many other websites dedicated to helping users download music for free. For example, Kazaa, probably the leading site of this type, claims that its software has been downloaded 200 million times, with 2.8 million copies of its software downloaded per week. According to the *Sunday Times*, when all *P2P* services are taken into account, approximately 2.6 billion files are copied per month.

MINI CASE STUDY 2.2: THE IPOD - AN ICON FOR THE 00S

The iPod MP3 player weighs less than two CDs but fits 10,000 songs into your pocket. Top fashion houses have designed accessories for it, TV directors have included it in plotlines and word of mouth has made it one of the coolest gadgets.

The iPod may be little more than a storage device, but it has revolutionized the way we listen to music and has become a cultural icon at the same time. Small, light and easy to use, it has helped non-technical audiences to catch on to the benefits of the personalized music library that can be enjoyed on the move.

Annual sales of 1.5 million iPods have made this one of Apple's most popular products. Its success comes from not just a stylish design, but also the ultra-fast FireWire connection for transferring music from the computer. It is also an alarm clock, games console and, with optional attachments, a voice recorder and radio.

MINI CASE STUDY 2.3: KAZAA

According to www.download.com, by February 2003, Kazaa had been downloaded 192, 921, 732 times! Obviously, consumers like free products. Kazaa offers searching for music, video (e.g. episodes of soaps or movies) and image files. The process is relatively simple: download the free software, agree to the terms and conditions and launch the Kazaa Media Desktop.

Click 'Search', type in an artist or track title and the results are then displayed. To download, click on one of the files listed. At the time of our test, there were 4,130,879 users online sharing 810,495,758 files! Once the file has been downloaded, the user has obtained the music, initially for free, although it is the users' responsibility to pay the copyright royalties.

The operators of the site state explicitly that they do not condone activities and actions that breach the rights of copyright owners: 'As a Kazaa Media Desktop user you have agreed to abide by the end user agreement and it is your responsibility to obey all laws governing copyright in each country.'

The software is free, with the costs covered through

advertising revenue. Kazaa and Morpheus (a similar service) have been reported to earn US$400,000 per month from advertising. During the 20 minutes or so of download time, the user is subjected to many pop-up advertising windows. In addition, users' personal details may be used for marketing purposes (any users who have not read the terms and conditions may be unaware of this).

Apart from the advertising and the requirement to pay royalties to the copyright owner, there are other potential problems. For example, any file that is downloaded may contain a computer virus or worm. Because of the operation of the P2P system, only the owner of an infected system can delete it and stop its circulation, not Kazaa.

In order to share music with other users, the software creates a shared folder where all files can be uploaded or downloaded. The setting can be changed so that no one can obtain files from your computer, but on the default the settings can be changed by another user in such a way that your entire computer's files can be shared with everyone.

In a test by HP Laboratories, a dummy file called 'creditcards.xls' was added and the computer left online for 24 hours. The file was downloaded four times. The same report drew attention to another problem that may be worrying to parents: pornography. For example, over 70 per cent of the results obtained while searching for Britney Spears' videos on Kazaa were of pornographic content.

In our survey of 765 young people carried out in 2003, 65 per cent said that they used the Internet to download music. Eighty-eight per cent of these said that they used Kazaa or similar software, but only 12 per cent said that they used 'legal' sites (artist's web page or legal distributor). The 'legal' users also tend to be infrequent users.

Respondents to our survey (of a single, West London, UK, school) have downloaded an estimated 92,000 'free' files, representing 6,600 albums. By comparison, the 'legal' downloads were only 1,000 files, equivalent to 75 albums. Worryingly, 32 per cent of the respondents were unaware of the security risks of file sharing.

DVD movies and Videos

DVD movies and videos are mainly available from the same suppliers as are CDs (Amazon is market leader) and carry the same advantages for e-retailing. High street retailers have, of course, long supplied videos. Happily for e-retailers, the expansion in popularity of DVDs over the last couple of years has coincided with a period of rapid growth in consumers' willingness to e-shop.

MINI CASE STUDY 2.4: BLACKSTAR

Blackstar was founded in February 1998 and operates from Belfast in Northern Ireland. It began by selling a comprehensive library of 50,000 video titles. With widespread consumer support for the new DVD format that has built up over the past two years, Blackstar logically moved into the DVD movies market and now also sells games console titles as well. Blackstar has enjoyed newsworthy successes in its short history. It has managed to attract and retain customers through its commendable level of customer service.

Typical high street video/DVD shops typically stock up to 3,000 titles, but Blackstar offers a much wider range with many otherwise-rare titles. Blackstar also offers a video/DVD hunt facility for rare or deleted titles. This service has proved to be very popular and a key factor in the company's success. However, Blackstar, like most other British e-retailers, has yet to achieve profitability. Blackstar was awarded Retail Online Success of the Year at the BVA Awards 2000.

GROCERIES

e-Grocery shopping in the UK is only around 1 per cent of total grocery shopping, but that small percentage adds up to around a billion pounds per year. The nature of groceries as non-durable necessitates delivery quickly and in such a way that quality is not lost in the delivery process. Perishable grocery deliveries can also be difficult if the recipient is not there to receive them - unlike other goods that may be popped through the letterbox or left in a lockable delivery drop.

In addition, many grocery items tend to be variable in

characteristics and quality and are often selected by look, feel and smell. Compared to typical shoppers for products such as CDs, grocery shoppers tend on average to be older and less educated, and therefore less susceptible to new technology such as e-shopping. Indeed, de Kare-Silver's ES test rates groceries at 27 (out of 50), well behind Books (38) and DVD movies.

When US bookstore magnate Louis Borders founded e-grocer Webvan in 1997, he believed he could revolutionize the grocery business. The idea was deceptively simple. It was to take orders for groceries over the Internet and use highly automated centralized warehouses and computerized logistics systems controlling a local fleet of trucks to efficiently deliver groceries to a customer at a cost no greater than if the customer had gone to the supermarket themselves. The scheme was launched in San.

Francisco, followed by another 26 cities at an investment cost of US$35 million per city. Including marketing costs, the total investment US$1.2 billion was second only to Amazon in the history of e-retail startups. With marketing costs of 30 per cent of sales and only 50 per cent capacity utilization of the distribution centres, Webvan struggled for cash. The company folded in 2001, laying off its 2,000 employees and announcing losses of close to US$0.5 billion - the largest single e-commerce loss ever.

Tesco, the leading UK grocery supermarket, is a very different story. Tesco's online shopping service has been one of very few grocery e-retailing successes worldwide, with 1 million users, 85,000 orders per week and profit since 2001. Tesco is the world's biggest e-grocer, and is the UK's number one by a considerable margin, with a 53 per cent share of the world's biggest online grocery market. The key has been twofold.

First, Tesco had first-mover advantage, rapidly increasing its operation to cover 95 per cent of the population. By contrast, the main rival, Sainsbury's, reaches 71 per cent of UK households. Second, the initial operation (still true for most food items) employed pickers to select the goods from the shelves of local stores.

This simple approach enabled Tesco to get the operation off the ground quickly and cheaply. In a warehouse, fresh food that was unsold would have to be thrown away. In addition, when e-orders are quiet, Tesco's pickers can do other work. Meanwhile, competitors have struggled. Somerfield attempted the purpose-built distribution centre approach, and retired hurt.

Safeway (formerly one of the 'big three' UK supermarkets) never launched a home delivery service and has now closed down its e-retail business completely. Sainsbury's uses a combination of warehouses and in-store picking, but is still not in profit at the time of writing. Wal-Mart Asda's two dedicated warehouses have been closed. Both Sainsbury's and Wal-Mart Asda offer delivery to less than half of households across the country at the time of writing. Iceland claims 97 per cent coverage, but is reticent about its trading results.

The Tesco e-retailing model has now been introduced into the US through a deal with Safeway Inc. Customers in Portland, Oregon, were the first to try the service, followed by San Francisco (where Webvan tried and failed). Tesco.com is also growing rapidly in the Republic of Ireland, where the service covers 70 per cent of the population, and in South Korea through a joint venture with Homeplus.

The main challenge to Tesco.com's approach in the UK may come from Ocado. Ocado operates in conjunction with Waitrose, one of the UK's top six supermarkets with stores mainly in the south of England. Ocado is 40 per cent owned by department store group John Lewis Partnership, owners of Waitrose. Ocado are committed to the warehouse model with central warehouses to the north of London and in Birmingham that can each process the same amount of groceries as 20 superstores.

From a pilot in Hertfordshire, the e-retailing service has been rolled out to the London area. Ocado's managing director pointed out that the company bases marketing on a low level of substitutions (claimed to be 2 per cent vs. an 'industry standard' of 15 per cent) and one-hour rather than two-hour delivery time slots. The operation has a long way to go to catch Tesco, though, and even Waitrose's managing director estimated that it would take three to five years to reach profitability.

EIGHT WAYS TO CUSTOMER VALUE AND PROFITABILITY IN GROCERY E-RETAILING

- Customer density
- Loyalty
- Buying power
- Ordering efficiency and customer information
- Operational efficiency and customer service level
- Large range of products
- Price level
- Shopping convenience

Tanskanen *et al.* (2002) reported on 'six lessons learned' for profitable grocery e-retailing and Anckar *et al.* (2002) identified 'four sources of customer value'. As the UK's leading supermarket, Tesco has the advantage in loyalty, buying power and range of products. Economies of scale should also give the market-leader a potential advantage in good-value selling prices.

In theory, therefore, the other players need to try to gain their competitive advantage from the remaining factors: shopping convenience, operational efficiency, customer service, the ordering interface and product information. These can be addressed by, for example, making the website informative, quick and easy to use, supplying exactly (or with a minimum of substitutes) what is ordered and providing accurately timed delivery slots.

CLOTHING AND FOOTWEAR

Clothing is not an obvious product for e-retailing. First, of course, clothing is normally bought by look, feel and fit, all of which are difficult for the e-shopper to evaluate on the Web. Second, clothing is bought not just for warmth and modesty, but also to express our self-image. Any purchase errors in (e.g.) style, therefore, carry a particularly high perceived risk.

Indeed, de Kare-Silver's ES test rates basic clothing at 19 (out of 50), well behind books (38), DVD movies and groceries (27). (For a product to be suitable for e-retailing, de Kare-Silver recommends a minimum score of 20.) Nevertheless, clothing represents one of the major categories in UK e-retail (although worldwide it is one of the slowest-growing categories).

One reason may be that clothing has historically been one of the major mail-order categories in the UK. Both shoppers and suppliers are used to home delivery channels for clothing. The clothing e-retail market leader Next has been supplying fashion clothing by mail order since 1988.

Surprisingly, lingerie and hosiery is one of the most popular product categories for e-retailing, perhaps driven by the success of the leader, Fig Leaves (www.figleaves.com), in the same way that Tesco has driven the expansion of grocery e-retailing. Fig Leaves has a winning approach both in the creative permission-based marketing and the novel online bra measuring system. In particular e-shopping for lingerie appeals to men, who may often be embarrassed to buy these products in-store.

Look and feel' goods tend to be compared and evaluated before buying - i.e. they are high involvement purchases. For example, a survey reported in the *New Straits Times* in 2001 found that 85 per cent of respondents would not buy clothes online because they prefer to try them on before purchase. Enjoyment is often a motivation for in-store clothes shopping (and other comparison shopping). In the bricks retail store, 'atmospherics' are often used to increase enjoyment and hence sales. The effectiveness of such techniques is well known in-store, we argue that equivalent considerations are also important for the e-retailer.

Emotional aspects such as enjoyment strongly predict shoppers' attitudes towards e-shopping. According to Chicksand and Knowles (2002), equivalent features can be identified to help in overcoming the difficulties of selling 'look and feel' goods like clothing online. The equivalent stimuli for the clicks store include: sound, personalization/ customization, usability of the website, visuals and text. *Web atmospherics* can help compensate for the lack of sensory experience in e-shopping. Nevertheless, the indications are that shoppers' needs for enjoyment (rather than just utilitarian) benefits are not being satisfied by e-retailers. Even clothing market leader Next makes little attempt at the use of web atmospherics on the e-retail site.

Personalization is a key element of web atmospherics, but most clothing e-retailers personalize very little. Developments aimed at helping to overcome this drawback include the Eddie Bauer (US clothing retailer) 'virtual closet' which allows shoppers to match up items with a 'Style Builder'. With Virtual Model (www.virtualmodel.com - one of the '100 best websites' from *Internet Magazine*) you can create a 3-D virtual model of yourself online and dress yourself with clothing from top suppliers such as Lands End - claimed to increase the likelihood of a sale by 19 per cent.

These e-retailers keep a database of sizes and items bought that is available on your next visit, personalizing the experience and saving purchase time. The potential for clothing includes the body scan.

For example, shoppers can visit selected Levi stores for the scan, which is then held on a database. In theory, this could then be used for e-shopping, incorporating the scan data into a 3-D virtual closet such as Virtual Model. Shoppers could be confident that the clothes would fit. Unfortunately, Levi does not actually offer the body scan data for e-retailing on the Virtual Model/Kohls (www.kohls.com) site.

Customization is another key element of web atmospherics for clothing. Mass customization refers to self-designed products. Shopper involvement in the design of the products adds considerably to the personal feel of the shopping experience.

Shopper satisfaction can be enhanced by more closely matching exact needs. In the case of Nike, shoppers can customise shoes, not just with colours and styles, but also, for example, with a name or message.

A potential drawback of this system, though, is concern over what happens if the customer wants to return the product for any reason? Fanbuzz e-retails clothes, allowing shoppers to decide their own styles, colours, graphics and sizes. These custom items are 10-20 per cent more expensive than non-custom ones, but many customers are prepared to pay more for customized products.

Although the market for e-retailing clothes is growing only slowly, if the mass-market e-retailers such as Next and Marks & Spencer were to improve web atmospherics, e.g. more attractive, interactive site design and layout, more personalization and customization incorporating features used by specialists such as Lands End and Nike, there should be considerable scope for further growth.

CASE STUDY: AMAZON.CO.UK

This case illustrates Amazon.co.uk's retail mix and the application of the Ansoff matrix. I buy all my books at Amazon.com because I'm busy and it's convenient. They have a big selection, and they've been reliable.

Bill Gates

Amazon has established itself worldwide as an online retail success, the world's biggest e-retailer of books and head-to-head with Barnes and Noble for the title of the world's largest bookstore, even though Amazon sells only online. From a start-up in 1995, annual sales have grown to more than US$1 billion and the company has over 2.5 million customers - but reported its first profit only in 2002.

The UK site, www.amazon.co.uk, was formed in 1998 by the takeover of Bookpages, and the UK is now Amazon's biggest market outside the US. Amazon is also the clear UK market leader for CDs, DVD movies and videos and offers many other product lines, including electronics, software, games, toys, travel and auctions.

According to a survey by Global Online Retailing, one in eight UK Internet users have made a purchase at Amazon.co.uk. Amazon is the market leader in the UK for selling online books with a market share of over 50 per cent, and its main advantage is the ability to deliver low-cost

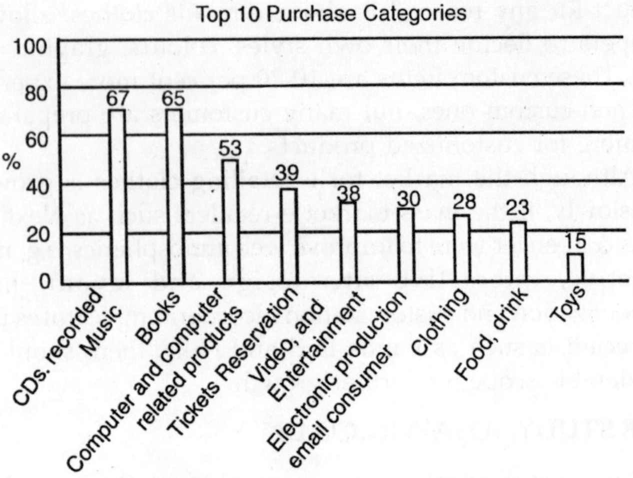

AMAZON'S E-RETAIL MIX

Convenience

Convenience plays an important role in gaining and maintaining new customers. There are several factors driving the level of customer convenience. First, the speed of downloading amazon.co.uk's website is fast, as it takes only three to five seconds although it is full of images of their products. Customers can quickly find the desired product, as the search facility is second to none.

Once the result is located it provides value-added services such as book reviews and ratings, and displays its own price and a comparison price. Comparative pricing allows customers to see the value they are receiving from Amazon, i.e. how much they are saving. Amazon makes it easy to source and buy products and track the progress of delivery.

Amazon offers industry-leading state-of-the-art online shopping technology, the '1-click' system, which streamlines the customer buying process by storing personal information such as credit card number and shipping address, saving time and hassle. According to a survey carried out by Knowledge Systems & Research, consumers become frustrated after having to click more than six times to complete a purchase and as a result they move to other websites. The website offers secure socket-layer connection, which means that sensitive credit card information is transmitted in encrypted format. In some cases it even provides a guarantee that, if unauthorized transactions are made, it will reimburse the customer. All major credit and debit cards are accepted.

One of the prime factors of convenience is based on availability. If any of the titles are unavailable, Amazon will still take your order and will let you know when the title will be available. Amazon.co.uk's main aim is to maximize customers' convenience so they do not look anywhere else for their books.

The search facility is designed in such a unique way that it provides up-selling, cross-selling and down-selling. For every result of a book title search you are given the options.

For instance, if you are looking at a book the website will also display other books in the same category. This feature allows customers to have better choice. This is e-comparison shopping as you are comparing two books while only looking at one screen. The facility increases sales as customers can always find something that they want. Customers can view their account any time, which includes information about their past orders along with shipment details. Account information is used to make recommendations about other books that customers may like.

Cost

Cost is one of the features that drive customers to shop on the Web. Nevertheless, Jeff Bezos, Amazon's CEO, believed that online customers considered selection and convenience to be more important than price. This belief is probably justified as Brynjolfsson and Smith (2000) pointed out that amazon had a market share of 80 per cent while charging 10 per cent more than the cheapest. Therefore, Amazon did not seek to compete on price alone. Customers want to get the best price with excellent customer service.

Most of the books at amazon are available at a discounted price, ranging from 1 per cent to 50 per cent off the recommended retail price. Consumers are always shown three prices: 'list price', 'our price' and 'how much you save'. Amazon has reasonable delivery charges. There are often seasonal promotions such as free delivery if the order is over a certain amount. Different options are available, including (as an optional extra) overnight delivery.

Following a similar arrangement in the US, amazon.co.uk has a deal with Toys R Us for in-store pick up, which allows customers to collect the books at their convenience. With this option, there is no delivery charge.

Communication

Amazon has established its brand name through customer intimacy and customer relationship management. From day one their aim has been to be a customer-centric company. It welcomes returning customers with their name, e.g. 'Welcome back Charles Dennis', with the help of a cookie file stored on the user's computer. This has been referred to as the Web equivalent of customizing a storefront to suit the taste of each person walking through the door.

Customers can opt in if they wish to receive more information, for example when a new novel comes out by their favourite author. Consumers can always opt out as well if they are not interested in receiving any more information. Amazon monitors the customer's ordering process through the Oracle database environment that feeds all the content to its website. It can track the speed and performance of each step in a transaction, including placement of an item in a cart, completion of an order and e-mail notification to the customer.

Amazon offers personalization by recommending similar books according to what other customers have bought. For example, the personalized screen will say: 'Customers who bought titles by this author also bought titles by these authors'. These features help users to make up their minds quickly and they can also read spotlight reviews by other readers. Amazon is to some extent a virtual community where users express their views about authors. Publishers and authors can also contribute.

Amazon uses an integrated marketing communications strategy that encompasses advertising, public relations, promotions and online marketing. Offline advertising includes TV commercials and billboards in train stations. Online activity includes the associates programme and deals with major search engines and portal pages such as Yahoo.com and MSN.

The associates programme uses other sites to promote Amazon by links that directly take users to Amazon's site. In return associates receive a small percentage commission on the total transaction value.

Computing

Amazon uses state-of-the-art technology in its back end (warehouse) and front end (website). The company has developed a customized information system and dedicated ordering system, which is linked with suppliers to automatically order books.

The search engine employs XML and Oracle database technology, which bring up results in a matter of seconds. Once the book or an item is found, users sign in using the 1-click system and the purchase is complete. The company's software processes the orders via electronic interfaces or electronic data interchange with suppliers and all the stages in the supply chain are computerized.

Customer Care

According to an internal customer research survey carried out by amazon.co.uk, 70 per cent of sales are made by repeat customers of whom 97 per cent are satisfied or very satisfied with the service-which must be one of the highest satisfaction scores among pureplay dot.coms. Its FAQs section is very informative as it explains all the main issues such as ordering process, delivery charges and returns policy.

Customer Franchise

Amazon's brand relationship is like someone who knows you, understands your preferences and tells you something new every time you make contact. This builds up a strong relationship as if dealing with assistants who have come to know customers in the course of many shopping trips.

ANSOFF MATRIX

Market Penetration

Market penetration means seeking to achieve growth with existing products in their current market segments and aiming to increase their share of the market. Amazon has increased market penetration through value-added service. It takes on the responsibility to order books that they do not have at present and let the users know as soon as they become available.

It allows users to sell used books, and prices for used books appear alongside the selling price for a new book. The extended service and options translate into greater sales. This gives the reader a chance to read the book before actually buying it. The more services offered, the more chances there are it will lead to a sale.

Product Development

Here new product offerings are developed to market to existing customers. Amazon has added second-hand books to its product range, giving its customers the opportunity to sell their used books. Amazon also now sells e-books - readable on Personal Digital Assistants (PDAs).

Product / Market	Present	New
Present	Market Development	Product Development
New	Market Development	Diversitication

Fig. Ansoff Matrix

Market Development

Market development concerns the marketing of existing products to a new audience. Amazon has extended purchasing to users of WAP or 3G mobile phones.

In addition, Amazon has signed deals with bricks and mortar bookshops such as Waterstones and Borders to sell books online for them. Customers typing in www.waterstones.co.uk will be directed to a version of the Amazon website that carries Waterstone's name (although the appearance and co-branded name are still clearly Amazon). A percentage of the profit from any books they subsequently buy will go to Waterstones in a concept similar to the associates programme.

FITURE OF E- RETAILING

CONSUMER BUYING DECISION PROCESS

A potential e-consumers buying decision process will follow the established stages of need recognition, information search, information evaluation, purchase decision and post-purchase behaviour.

Need Recognition

An e-retail website is a combination of the traditional store display window, information desk, stocked display shelving, mood lighting/sound, promotional material that shout out specials, and the time-honoured *barker/spruiker* used to stimulate shopping interest. Such an e-retail site ought to elicit a need recogni tion response from any visitor to the site.

A new or returning visitor should be treated to a combination of the four basic marketing elements - *price* (e.g. specials, discounts, interest free periods), *product* (e.g. new lines, clearance items, seasonal products, fashion and fad limited ranges), *promotion* (e.g. sales, seasonal specials, select shopper campaigns) and *distribution* (e.g. free delivery, lay-away, home installation) that accentuate the visitor's own need identification.

Technology within the website, for example cookie files, captures data about the visitor's responses and what information was accessed. Such information then enables e-retailers to improve the rapport with the online customer by tailoring the site content to consumer demand. One positive application from such data collection is the inclusion of customer loyalty programs that encourage return visitation to the e-retailer site and increased purchases.

Information Search

Improved telecommunications technology and general population access to the Internet have transformed user availability to customization of, and digestion of, large information volumes. Unlike the bricks and mortar retailer, an e-retail site has the facilities to make available such large volumes of information in a customized format to meet the immediate and potential queries of site visitors following the need recognition stage.

Without personal embarrassment or the self-consciousness of asking a stranger (e.g. a shopkeeper) what may be an obvious or foolish product-related question, the e-retail site visitor can access online product brochures, price comparisons, frequently asked questions (FAQs), suggested product applications, cleaning and repair information, and an efficient search engine technology, as well as asking for specialized information via the e-retailer's e-mail system.

Information Evaluation

When seeking to evaluate the collected information on products and services, the potential shopper will often turn to the experiences and advice of family, friends and persons who have already experienced use of such merchandise. Also, e-retailing gives the user added facilities to access evaluative experts and previous users of the merchandise in question to aid in the digestion and customization of all this information.

Many consumer groups act as such reference experts through the testing and personal evaluations of retailed products and then make these findings available to others. Experienced e-retailers encourage interactions between previous, current and future shoppers by way of:

- Online discussion groups.
- Suggesting site visitors rate the available merchandise.
- Suggesting site visitors express comments about this merchandise and the service exchange experiences.

Monitoring of the online discussions and visitor comments endows the retailer with invaluable knowledge regarding merchandise features and limitations that may be incorporated into promotional materials. To conclude, apart from all the benefits mentioned above, the e-retailer gains all this free information that would normally require expensive market research.

Purchase Decision

After a visitor to an e-retailer site has determined the merchandise to be appropriate for their needs, it is still not a certainty that this visitor will finalize a purchase. Commonly, an online customer nominates particular merchandise from an e-retail website and places those items in the online *shopping cart* (also known as a *shopping trolley*) for the checkout, but later the customer discontinues the purchase process and leaves the e-retailer's site. This action of discontinuing an online purchase is termed 'abandoned cart syndrome;

- A lower level of education.
- Higher frequency of Web purchases.
- Greater concern of online data risk and fraud.
- Greater frequency of website service problems.
- The use of shopping as a facility to see family and friends.
- High levels of concern about online retailers' tracking data.
- Younger buying groups.
- Shopping causing little arousal.
- Higher frequency of browsing for a later purchase.
- Higher fashion consciousness.
- Higher frequency of Web search for product information.

Although the e-retailer cannot yet duplicate the human

interactions possible in a physical store setting, e-retailers may still empower customers in an attempt to reduce the incidence of online cart abandonment. One positive step to improve the e-retailer's customer interactions is streamlining the order process by:

- Making improvements in the e-retailer's site navigation.
- Incorporation of help links and interactive facilities to stimulate the shopper's arousal and fashion consciousness.
- Supplying the relevant merchandise information as needed.
- Greater use of online help facilities and screen prompts.
- Establishing chat rooms and customer discussion opportunities to share experience with family, friends and new acquaintances.
- Improved guarantees (including deliveries, data security, 30-day trials).
- Offline contact details (phone number, fax number, street address).

Post-purchase Behaviour

The key to a retailer's survival and success whether offline or online is to generate repeat purchase behaviour. For a customer to return to a retailer that customer needs to have confidence in the retailer, but e-retailer confidence is often difficult to establish in light of online issues that have caused customers to make complaints and/or never return to the e-retailer. According to Cho *et al.* (2002), the online issues that often alienate customers and lead to complaints are the failure to meet customer *expectations* in relation to:

Merchandise offerings.

The e-retailer's store-front technology (this includes, but is not limited to, the website) that integrates:

- Usability of the technology;
- The technology failing to carry out a function.

The e-retailer's information sources (the policies).

Payment/settlement issues;

- Agreed conditions (including delivery timing).

To reduce the chance of customer expectations being unfulfilled, e-retailers will compensate for the lack of a face-to-face exchange by making available more information details than would otherwise be considered in a bricks and mortar environment. Dealing with each of the Cho *et al.* (2002) points, we suggest the following responses:

Merchandise offerings -

- Define all dimensions of the size options, colour variations, and accessories provided. One suggestion is to include the supply of actual colour swatches to reduce the colour errors often attributed to variations on computer colour monitors.

The e-retailer's store-front technology (this includes, but is not limited to the website) -

- Provide sufficient technology to cope with peak buying periods such as St Valentine's Day and Mother's Day.
- Keep redundant backup to take over when systems fail.
- Offer facilities to store (file) partial orders for future use should the customer be interrupted and/or wish to continue the shopping process in the near future.
- Provide improved access facilities for the disabled/ impaired computer user. Facilities may consist of:
  - Selectable larger display fonts;
  - Voice recognition commands;
  - Spoken responses embedded in the web pages;
  - Written descriptions of displayed images (these can be read out to the non-sighted user even if they can't see the picture).
- Alerts given by the e-retailer's site to advise users:
  - Pending specials;
  - Replenishment of merchandise that was out of stock;
  - Arrival of special orders.
- Such alerts can reach the user through e-mail, phone

short message service (SMS), automated faxing or other communications technologies.

The e-retailer's information sources (the policies) -

- Information is to be detailed (even exhaustive), accurate and timely (not noticeably out of date).
- Information is to be easy to find on the e-retailer site.
- Links to relevant or 'just interesting' sites shall establish the e-retail not only as an appropriate purchasing site but as a point of reference or portal for future enquiries in this area; thereby achieving a great milestone: being bookmarked as a favourite site in the user's Web browsing software.
- A continued customer relationship should be maintained after a purchase by:
  - Continued updates on the relevant and near-relevant issues by e-mail or newsgroup (for example, a customer purchases an electric grill and then receives a monthly recipe; the e-retailer keeps the contact and the customer's satisfaction in the purchase is supported);
  - Space may also be sold to sponsors seeking to promote their products.

Payment/settlement issues -

- Not all customers want to reveal their personal details and movements to online parties. To aid these potential customers, e-retailers can now provide alternatives for the customer in the shopping cycle to minimize risk.

  In Australia, a purchaser using the Wishlist retailer (www.wishlist.com.au) may opt to have their online purchases delivered to a participating BP petrol service station rather than to their home address. In this way the customer picks up the merchandise at a time that suits and conceals their personal address details while still gaining the advantages of shopping online.
- Most courier organizations (i.e. DHL and FedEx) used by e-retailers have facilities for the purchaser to trace

and track the merchandise while it is in transit. The e-retailer receives proof the item is 'on its way' and the client achieves the peace of mind of 'seeing' where the item is any time they go online.

THE HYBRID RETAILER: THE MOST LIKELY WINNER IN THE FUTURE OF RETAILING

Retailers today are not restricted to just bricks and mortar, direct and virtual categories of retailing but often opt for a hybrid business model. Hybrid retailers, sometimes referred to as 'multi-channel retailers', appear to be taking the greatest advantage of e-retailing opportunities.

In a study by Haeberle (2003) multi-channel retailers were identified as generating 72 per cent of Web-based sales in 2002, 5 per cent up from 2001, and 18 per cent up from the Web sales of 2000. Using profitability as a success measure, multi-channel retailers and particularly those established in the market as catalogue brands, made the greater impact as e-retailers.

The Haeberle (2003) study found that, in 2002, 92 per cent of those retailers for whom catalogue was the primary sales channel were profitable. That compares with 80 per cent of bricks and mortar-based retailers and 50 per cent of Web-based retailers in the study.

When John Lewis bought the UK arm of Buy.com, the takeover gave Buy.com financial credibility while Buy.com gave one of the 'Old Men' of UK retailing street credibility. Though the purchase of a virtual retailer by a bricks and mortar retailer was nothing new, it was an early example of a continuing trend as virtual retailers ran out of operating capital. These new players in the retailing arena are faced on one side by the downwards pressure on prices to stay competitive and on the other by fearful investors who remember all too clearly the dot.com crash at the end of the first millennium.

Retailer adaptation: a key to survival and growth

Long-standing bricks and mortar retailers are not only

looking at a Web presence as the means to becoming e-retailers. To improve the relationship with their customers, retailers are adopting new electronic systems that complement their physical store presence.

Sears in the US (www.sears.com) uses a system termed 'buy online, pick up at the store', where the customer places and pays for an order with a credit card at the Sears website, Sears.com, but, departing from other Web stores' procedures, picks up the merchandise from a local Sears store. An e-mail is then used to advise the customer about stock availability at the time of the order and when the merchandise is ready for store collection.

Misunderstanding or ignoring a market position of strength is a failing that leads to the demise of some retailers. The availability of a new distribution channel is not an automatic indication of future success.

Consider the US retailer Egghead (was www. egghead. com), which in the early 1990s had strong market presence with around 250 stores across the country. The retailer was well respected by its consumer market, had a solid brand image and was profitable. Long before most other retailers, Egghead created an online presence for its technology-minded customers in 1994.

Effectively, this entry into a new distribution channel made Egghead one of the first multi-channel retailers. But, as Lightfoot (2003) described, Egghead did not leverage its unique multi-channel position; rather, it decided to abandon all of its offline stores in 1998 and exclusively sell online, evolving into a virtual retailer.

Regrettably, following a series of problems, e.g. much-publicized hacking attacks on Egghead's website, technical failures in the e-commerce technology, failing customer loyalty and internal management problems, Egghead went the way of many dot.coms and exhausted its cash reserves and filed for bankruptcy in 2001 (Thornton and Marche, 2003). On the positive side for customers, the Egghead assets (including brand name and customer base) were sold to Amazon in 2001.

To Amazon's credit, the new owner honoured the privacy policy of the previous Egghead clients as noted in the statement:

Please note that if you are a returning Egghead.com customer, Egghead.com will not disclose any existing account information to Amazon.com, so you will need to re-enter all information necessary to complete a transaction. For information about how Amazon.com treats the information you give us, see Amazon.com's Privacy Notice.

WHAT CAN YOU EXPECT TO SEE AND HEAR IN E-RETAILING?

Improved customer education, availability of information and increasing legislation have given rise to a new type of customer for this new millennium. Our new customers are more demanding, have a higher expectation and are increasingly adversarial in their service exchanges with retailers. Part of the retailer response will be to empower the customer to tailor their own service exchange in the physical store and online.

Metro, an organization that already markets hardware systems to retailers, has suggested a series of scenarios in a future retail store to provide technologies that make shopping encapsulate greater individualization, reliability and convenience.

Greater Individualization

Just as Web browsing technology learns and recalls a user's preferences for colour, fonts and items for inclusion, future stores will match their offering to learned customer experiences. Once the customer is identified to the store through a loyalty card or personal *radio frequency identification* (RFID) tag, the store's 'electronic personal shopping assistant' (EPSA) technology will record the shopper's preferences for merchandise, delivery (i.e. home delivery, parcel pick-up) and method of payment.

To save the customer time, the store system would forewarn the customer of difficulties (including stock outages) and then make suggestions for alternative merchandise that is either in stock or pending (e.g. new season's stock).

Greater Reliability and Convenience

New store technology will improve reliability for both customer and retailers. When a customer selects an item and adds this to their shopping trolley, the EPSA will read the merchandise's RFID tag and present the details to the shopper via shopping trolley mounted visual display. No longer will the customer be disadvantaged by the omission of shelf pricing or getting to the checkout only to be told that the product is 'not on the system' and needs a delaying price check.

Through the use of the unique RFID tag being identified by EPSA, the customer will be advised of these details at the point of merchandise access - the shelf or bin stocking the merchandise. Once the price information absence is detected, the retailer's system can search or calculate the price before the checkout is reached.

Aiding the retailer, this technology will indicate low- or out-of-stock situations at the shelf as customers place the item into their trolley, long before the item is removed from the inventory system at the checkouts. Staff will have a perpetual inventory rather than depending upon physical stock updates.

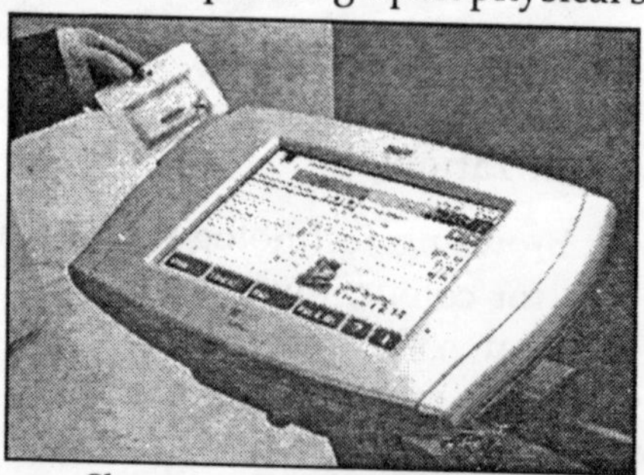

Fig. The new Shopping Trolley will Record the Selected Merchandise and Advise the Customer of the Details, Including Price and Running Total Expenditure

Retailers use a *planogram* to determine what merchandise is displayed where and in what quantities throughout a store. Shoppers become familiar with their favourite stores but what do they do when a new merchandise line is added to the store and they are unsure where it is located? What is needed is a personal guide or in the future an EPSA to direct customers through the store like a global positioning system (GPS) directs a car through traffic.

Merchandise Tracking

With delivery problems representing one of the main elements holding back the growth of e-shopping, merchandise tracking may be one of the essential development areas for the future. Early developments in bricks retailing followed research by Bernard Silver and Norman Woodland in the early 1950s. As a result, the bar code became a world standard for tracking and recording the movements of retail stock .

A standard bar code is made up of dark (predominantly black) vertical bars broken up with light (predominantly white) spaces. To read the bar code a beam of light is passed over the code where the dark bars absorb the light and the spaces reflect it. The scanner (also known as a reader or detector) then turns the reflected light into electrical pulses that may be recorded on a data file. While an excellent product identification system, bar codes have a significant and obvious limitation, that is, they need to be scanned to register stock movement.

Stock may enter or be removed from the retailer's premises and if the bar code is not scanned with a reading laser, the stock is not identified and recorded so its movement is unknown. The solution is to have the stock *speak* up and identify *itself* to the retailer's electronic inventory management system.

Fig. A Sample of a Bar Code

- RFID tags are tiny (about one quarter of a square

millimetre), carry between 64 and 96 bits of information and have a life of at least ten years. They are inexpensive (as low as one cent per unit) and can be energized and activated by radio waves from a scanner/receiver in close proximity, or can be hooked up to a battery. After being activated by the transmitter's power, the RFID tag then passes the information to the retailer's stock system.

RFID tags have already been trailed and applied in a variety of applications. McDonald's (www.mcdonalds.com) and KFC (kfc.com) are trialling RFID tags; the US Department of Defence will be incorporating RFID tags to improve the management of inventory through hands-off processing; Nokia is incorporating the tags in some of its mobile phones; theme parks are providing them on wristbands to identify the positions of children; and the European Central Bank is considering incorporating the tags on new Euro notes to reduce counterfeiting and track illicit monetary flows.

Some bricks retailers have already piloted RFID tags. Privacy concerns have since led to Wal-Mart (www.walmart.com) and Benetton (www.benetton.com) dropping trials and orders of the tags. Privacy becomes an issue when you consider that although the RFID receivers were conceived to detect the movements of the tagged merchandise, they are in effect able to track the movements of the customer carrying the tagged merchandise within a shopping district that contains multiple RFID scanners/receivers.

Consider that, if an organization has more than one member store in the company's group (e.g. a.supermarket, a bottle shop and a variety store all owned by one organization) in the same shopping mall, radio triangulation by the RFID receivers triggered by the merchandise's RFID radio signal could detect the move of merchandise and, therefore, the shopper from one store to another and so on. The data from these movements could also interpret how long the shopper spent at various spots in the mall and all this data is collected *without* the shopper having given their permission.

It is an *ethical* dilemma that will be debated for some time. Despite the debate, bricks retailers such as Tesco are pushing ahead with RFID tags for tracking supply-chain movements and for further trials in-store. The potential benefits are substantial, so we expect the development to diffuse into e-retail tracking as shoppers become more accustomed to it. As the number of applications for RFID tags increases retailers may expect to fulfil management and marketing objectives, including:

- *Reduced retail fraud and theft-* RFID tags will track products for clothing, grocery items, electrical merchandise and recorded music to reduce shrinkage.
- *Asset supply-chain control-* RFID tags will track the movement of goods from one process centre to another, e.g. delivery dock and warehouse. This is not limited to the selling inventory but includes organizational assets that have in the past left the premises without authorization or without being entered in a log book, e.g. storage pallets and shopping trolleys.
- *Inventory control-* RFID tags will transmit inventory relevant information, e.g. batch number, unit code, number of items on the property and consumer-related merchandise information such as product category, size and colour.
- *Intelligent packaging-* RFID tags can be linked to a sensor that recognizes any tampering or deterioration of the merchandise while in transit and when that damage behaviour occurred. This damage may relate to a non-deliberate deterioration error, e.g. food storage temperature being outside the recommended range.

  Equally, the sensor would detect malicious actions of third parties upon the merchandise, e.g. when a sealed lid on a container is removed and a subsequent replacement is made to disguise the tampering activity. For customers, the expected benefits from a retailer using RFID tags are:
- *Speedier checkout process-*In combination with

intelligent shopping carts/trolleys, shoppers would have all their purchases totalled automatically as the individual product RFID tags are read by the shopping cart and the totals provided at the checkout point for payment.

- *Security*- Manufacturers will introduce RFID tags into the components of final products so that if the components are removed they can be tracked. Consider the theft of car parts from a whole vehicle; in the past the panels would be almost impossible to detect and trace once removed from the original car.
- *Tracking*- 'Where are the b—y car keys?' Consumer RFID tag readers will become available to learn the tag codes of products that the consumer wishes to inventory. An immediate benefit is being able to locate the proximity of individual RFID tagged items, such as the ever-elusive car keys.
- *Preparation and care*- RFID tags provide the opportunity to include preparation and care information that will be understood by future appliances. Potential applications in this vein are:
- For allergens - home health systems that are programmed for the individual's health requirements will 'listen' to the RFID tags of grocery items. The tags may contain all the ingredients of the grocery items, even the complicated chemical codes, and notify the home health system of potential allergens that could be harmful to the customer/householder.
- For clothing - RFID tags would alert the washing machine that the fabric is not machine washable or should be dry cleaned only.
- For frozen foods - RFID tags would alert the freezer display panel that the food is near or at its expiration date.
- For frozen foods - RFID tags would pass cooking instructions to the microwave or convection oven to avoid over- or under-cooking.

In-store interactive electronic kiosks

Multi-channel e-retailers are not restricted to the sale of physical merchandise in bricks and mortar establishments, but may also market digital products and services that were previously limited to virtual retailers. Through the use of interactive kiosks, retailers will be able to offer such services as:

- Detailed product information;
- Price checks;
- Recipes and product application suggestions;
- Tickets for events;
- Reservations for events and activities;
- Self-checkout to make purchases;
- Personalized and targeted promotions;
- Photo-finishing - this is a growing segment as customers bring in their digital camera cards and have the kiosks transfer the images to final photos;
- Internet access;
- Customer loyalty programmes;
- Banking and financial services;
- Maps and direction services;
- Human resource services, e.g. recruitment.

Interactive kiosks generate extra revenue and, because the customer is self-servicing, the variety of service exchanges is increased without added staff and subsequent drains on profits.

Greater use of Electronic Payments

The advent of the cheque made it possible for consumers to make purchases for items that cost more than the cash funds they carried on their person. A cheque could only be written up to the amount of funds the customer had in, or could deposit into, the financial institution issuing the cheque prior to the cheque being cashed by the retailer. To improve on the flexibility of the cheque and to make purchases using the financial institution's funds (up to a predetermined limit) the store and bank credit card became a popular alternative to the cheque.

To make a payment by credit card necessitates the retailer obtaining a payment authorization from a financial clearance centre and the customer's identification being validated by a signature or personal identification number (PIN). All this takes time and depends upon the retailer's authorization equipment being operational. Now that consumers are carrying their own mobile technology, e.g. cellular mobile phones, there is an opportunity for the consumer to contribute to the transaction verification process.

Fig. Interactive Kiosks Come in a Variety of Styles

The consumer may pay for the goods by sending an SMS message to a specific phone number that verifies that a payment should be made to the retailer for the specific merchandise. Other mobile phones permit the transmission of an inferred (IR) transmission to the retailer's equipment to again verify that this payment is to be passed to the customer's charge or mobile phone account.

Widening the application of wireless device payments, Royal Philips Electronics and Visa announced an alliance to encourage and develop chip technology that does not require any physical contact with other devices. With this technology consumers will be able to pay for merchandise by waving the new smart card in front of a sensor in the retailer's store (Shim, 2003). For both retailer and customer it means reduced payment delays and improved customer satisfaction.

A further development in progress by the major credit card companies at the time of writing is 'pay-as-you-go', which should enable consumers who do not have access to credit to e-shop.

Audio Visual Shopping Trolley

As seen in the section Greater reliability and convenience, the electronic personal shopping assistant will increasingly support shoppers as they negotiate a bricks store, and we argue below that the development should lead to future benefits for e-retailers and e-shoppers.

Linked to a future shopping trolleymounted touch screen, an EPSA will provide shoppers information on current store merchandise, in-store events, specialized product demonstrations/taste testing and, of course, store specials.The audio visual shopping trolley will act as a two-way shopping data vehicle presenting benefits to customers and retailers. Benefits to customers from using the EPSA-linked shopping trolleys are:

- A quicker shopping trip for those customers who do *not* enjoy the shopping experience.
- Personalization of the product offering and related information.
- Recall of frequently purchased items to reduce the chance of forgetting items.
- Reduced embarrassment in asking for item locations.
- Reduced delays by transmitting special orders to specific departments before arriving at those sections, e.g. special cuts of meat from the meat department.
- Suggested recipes for a grocery item on special or in bulk.

Management equally receives benefits from EPSA-linked shopping trolleys through greater control over their operations resulting from improved knowledge and awareness of stock issues. Advantages to the future e-retailer will be:

- Real time inventory levels.
- Better understanding of customer shopping habits and profiling.
- Promotion of specialized or seasonal merchandise direct to the customers with the greater likelihood of making a purchase.
- Shelving that recommends cross-sells and up-sells to increase sales volumes.
- Improved feedback to suppliers on what sells and daily traffic patterns for demonstrations and gondola-end displays.
- Alerts for corrective action being needed in dramatic

situations, e.g. staffing issues with long queues of customers at checkouts or other sections of the store.

The future of e-retailing is, as is the case for most estimates of the future, encouraging, but the format is uncertain. What can be said with certainty is that success and profitability will revolve around an historical truism: when the retailer knows the customer, the customer will continue to know the retailer and that translates into repeat sales and profits. The solution is in adopting the appropriate technology to meet the needs of customers.

Index

P

Q

R

S

T

U

V

W

P

Q

R

S

T

U

V

W